Nebraska Symposium on Motivation

Volume 71

Series Editor

Lisa Crockett, Department of Psychology, University of Nebraska–Lincoln
Lincoln, USA

The Nebraska Symposium on Motivation has been sponsored by the Department of Psychology at the University of Nebraska-Lincoln since 1953. Each year the Symposium invites leading scholars from around the world on a topic of current interest in psychology for a conference at the University followed by publication of an edited volume.

2019 2-year Impact Factor: 1.643   2019 5-year Impact Factor: 1.464

Richard L. Wiener • David J. Hansen
Editors

Legal Judgment and the Motivation for Justice

Springer

Editors
Richard L. Wiener
Department of Psychology
University of Nebraska-Lincoln
Lincoln, NE, USA

David J. Hansen
Department of Psychology
University of Nebraska-Lincoln
Lincoln, NE, USA

ISSN 0146-7875 ISSN 2947-9479 (electronic)
Nebraska Symposium on Motivation
ISBN 978-3-031-98811-0 ISBN 978-3-031-98812-7 (eBook)
https://doi.org/10.1007/978-3-031-98812-7

This Springer imprint is published by the registered company Springer Nature Switzerland AG
The registered company address is: Gewerbestrasse 11, 6330 Cham, Switzerland

This work is dedicated to the pursuit of democracy and social justice.

Acknowledgments

The editors would like to thank Pamela Waldvogel, Jamie Longwell, and Melody Scholl-Miller for their tireless support in coordinating the annual Symposium on Motivation event, on which this volume is based.

About the Book/Conference

This symposium examined the antecedents of the motivation for justice, described how that motivation activates and manifests in various legal institutions (i.e., elections, legislatures, courts, and executive offices), and traced its successes and failures to influence legal decision making. The presentations at the conference and the chapters in this volume reviewed research and commentary describing (a) where the motivation for justice comes from when people make legal judgments and decisions, (b) how the motivation for justice influences legal judgments and decisions, and (c) how legal judgments and decisions influence the motivation for justice in positive and negative ways. This topic is paramount at the current time in our history in view of the apparent breakdown of society's beliefs in our institutions and trust in the democratic process, which has contributed to a system that has increasingly operated from tribalistic impulse rather than from a richer motivation for authentic justice.

Contents

Legal Judgment and the Motivation for Justice 1
Richard L. Wiener, Daniella Cluver, Kitra Monnier, and David J. Hansen

Toward a Community Model in the Motivations for Justice and Legal Judgment 17
Christian H. Bijoux

Police Discretion as a Vulnerability Factor for Disparate Treatment 25
Jack Glaser

Zeal, Motivation, and the Adversarial Bias 41
Dan Simon

Sentencing for Multiple Offenses: When Seeking Justice Is Too Cruel and Cognitively Demanding 63
Mandeep K. Dhami and Charis Bechan

Does Ideology Undermine Procedure-Based Legitimacy? 87
Tom R. Tyler

Motives for Civil Justice 123
Jennifer K. Robbennolt

Why Do People Use ADR? 143
Donna Shestowsky

Justice and Culture 183
Kees van den Bos

Legal Judgment and the Motivation for Justice: What Have We Learned? 199
Richard L. Wiener, Kitra Monnier, Daniella Cluver, and David J. Hansen

Index 213

About the Editors

Richard L. Wiener received his Ph.D. in Psychology from the University of Houston and studied law at the University of Nebraska/Lincoln (UNL) College of Law, where he earned a Master's degree in Legal Studies. He is currently the Charles Bessey Professor of Psychology and Law at UNL, where he served as the director of the Law and Psychology Program from 2002 until 2015. Dr. Wiener is the past editor of *Law and Human Behavior*, the official journal of the American Psychology/Law Society (Division 41 of the American Psychological Association). Professor Wiener studies the application of social and cognitive psychology to problems of legal decision-making with a focus on juvenile and criminal justice. He is the recipient of funding from the National Science Foundation, National Institute of Justice and the Substance Abuse and Mental Health Services Administration (SAMHSA). Dr. Wiener has published numerous research articles, edited volumes, book chapters, and law review articles. Professor Wiener teaches courses at the graduate level and in the Law College at UNL. Dr. Wiener is best known and cited for his work in legal decision making including judgments about sexual harassment, jury decision making in capital murder, and emotion in the law. He has published numerous articles in the *Journal of Applied Psychology*, *Law and Human Behavior*, *Sex Roles*, *Psychology Public Policy and the Law*, and *the Journal of Experimental Psychology—Applied*. In addition, he was the editor, co-editor, and major contributor to several books in the University of Nebraska Law and Psychology book series, which include *Problem Solving Courts (2012) and Justice, Conflict and Wellbeing (2014).*

David J. Hansen is a Professor of Psychology at the University of Nebraska-Lincoln (UNL). He received his Ph.D. in Clinical Psychology from the University of Mississippi in 1985. Prior to coming to UNL in 1992, he was a faculty member in the Department of Psychology at West Virginia University. Dr. Hansen has served as director of the interdisciplinary Law-Psychology Program since 2017 and has previously served as Department Chair, Director of the Clinical Psychology Training Program, and Director of the Center for Brain, Biology and Behavior. His primary research area is child maltreatment (sexual abuse, physical abuse, and neglect), including development of assessments and interventions for victims and families, maltreatment prevention, and understanding the correlates and consequences of maltreatment. Much of his research activity occurs in conjunction with clinical services and training provided in collaboration with community agencies. Dr. Hansen has co-authored more than 130 publications, including peer-reviewed journal articles and book chapters, as well as one co-authored book and two co-edited volumes. Dr. Hansen is a licensed psychologist in the state of Nebraska. Within the UNL Psychological Consultation Center, Dr. Hansen is the Director of Project SAFE, a clinical treatment program for sexually abused children and their families. Dr. Hansen serves on the Editorial Boards of *Aggression and Violent Behavior*, *Clinical Case Studies*, and *Education and Treatment of Children*.

Legal Judgment and the Motivation for Justice

Richard L. Wiener, Daniella Cluver, Kitra Monnier, and David J. Hansen

The Motivation for Justice

Is there motivation for seeking justice? Coming up with a working definition of justice as a psychological construct is a formidable assignment but one that is necessary in order to make progress toward understanding the motivation that underlies our efforts to seek justice. We adopt a psychological perspective defining justice after the work of Decety and colleagues (Decety & Wheatley, 2015; Decety & Yoder, 2017; Yoder & Decety, 2020) who describe it as a normative process that members of a society accept for the purpose of distributing rights, responsibilities, and resources in a fair and equitable manner. Furthermore, seeking justice is fundamental to moral judgment, decision-making, and behavior that is the bedrock of all human cultures (Yoder & Decety, 2020). At the heart of the psychology of justice lies the subjective perception of what people perceive as fair, distinguishable from a philosophic understanding that seeks to understand objectively what is and is not equitable (Gollwitzer & van Prooijen, 2016). Thus, while philosophers are concerned with an objective definition of justice, psychologists study the cognitions, emotions, and behaviors that determine how we think about justice as well as what motivates us to seek it out. People who perceive that they, themselves, or those with whom they closely identify, are the victims of injustice react with strong moral emotions (i.e., contempt, anger, and disgust—CAD emotions) (Rozin et al., 1999) usually, but not always, accompanied by the equally potent motivation to try and set things right.

R. L. Wiener (✉) · D. J. Hansen
Department of Psychology, University of Nebraska-Lincoln, Lincoln, NE, USA
e-mail: rwiener2@unl.edu

D. Cluver · K. Monnier
University of Nebraska-Lincoln, Lincoln, NE, USA

R. L. Wiener, D. J. Hansen (eds.), *Legal Judgment and the Motivation for Justice*, Nebraska Symposium on Motivation 71,
https://doi.org/10.1007/978-3-031-98812-7_1

Types of Justice

From a psychological point of view, there are at least four different ways in which people think about justice. First, distributive justice refers to the fairness that we attribute to the exchange and distribution of resources, opportunities, and burdens (Gollwitzer & van Prooijen, 2016). People who perceive a lack of fairness in the allocation of material outcomes (i.e., rewards and punishments) or even intangible outcomes (i.e., opportunities for influence and control) experience strong CAD feelings, which often produce motivation to alter the outcomes. Here, the perception of balance in the distribution depends upon an equity principle in which people compare the "inputs" that they provide and the "outputs" that they obtain as a result of their efforts. People compare the ratio of outputs to inputs that they observe for themselves to the ratios that they observe for their peers in similar situations (Walster et al., 1978). For example, a person of color who experiences the justice system cracking down on Black law violators, while it sanctions more leniently white people who commit the same offenses will likely interpret the differences in equity as an injustice accompanied by strong negative moral feelings (i.e., CAD emotions).

Distributive justice is a function of self-interest and balance, while wprocedural justice is less concerned with comparing output-to-input ratios and more concerned with the decision-making process that determines how those in charge distribute resources, opportunities, and burdens. People are sensitive not only to the outcome of the authorities' judgments but also with the quality of the process of making those judgments (Thibaut & Walker, 1975). Tyler (2006; and Chap. 6, "*Does Ideology Undermine Procedure-Based Legitimacy?*" in this volume) has shown in legal contexts, as well as in other domains (i.e., in the political arena), that people stop voluntarily following agreed-upon social norms when they perceive that the decision-makers failed to provide them the opportunity to voice their concerns or if the decision-makers act in ways that lack impartiality (i.e., arbitrarily side with one side of a confrontation). Accordingly, we all regularly assess both distributive and procedural justice in our social environments, so that when the distribution of material inputs and outputs violate principles of equity (Smith et al., 2012) or the manner in which authorities allocate those tangible outcomes lacks respect, voice, or impartiality (Blader & Tyler, 2003, 2009; Tyler & Lind, 1992), we perceive a fundamental injustice.

Retributive justice is similar to distributive justice but applies only to transgressions and sanctions. Again, according to equity theory (Walster et al., 1978), people hold a strong belief that those who violate social norms should receive punishments that are in direct proportion to the seriousness and harm that the violators caused. It follows that people punish wrongdoers that violate legal and social norms to restore a sense of balance and equity. In fact, Gollwitzer and Keller (2010) showed that people punish norm violators from their in-groups more severally than those from their out-groups in order to restore the balance of justice that prevailed between the groups before the transgression took place (i.e., the Black Sheep Effect). Furthermore, several social psychological investigations have documented that people punish others for violations of criminal law out of a motivation for retribution or just deserts rather than for the utilitarian motivation to deter future crime or to incapacitate (i.e., incarceration) and therefore prevent future transgressions (Carlsmith et al., 2002; Carlsmith & Darley, 2008; Vardsveen & Wiener, 2021).

Finally, a fourth type of justice that is fundamental to civil law and that plays a significant, if not central, role in the criminal system is restorative justice. The focus of restorative justice is making victims whole by compensating them for their losses. Restorative justice goes further, however, by seeking reconciliation between the transgressor and the victim. Restorative justice re-establishes balance in a damaged relationship by compensating the victim, requiring a formal or informal apology from the transgressor (Robbennolt, 2003, 2006, 2008, 2013, and Chap. 7, *"Motives for Civil Justice"* in this volume), and requesting reconciliatory actions on the part of the transgressor. In the end, the goal of restorative justice is to repair the relationship between the transgressor and the victim, in part, by helping the victim forgive the transgressor and helping the transgressor to atone for their wrongful and harmful behavior (McCullough et al., 2003). People seek distributive, procedural, retributive, and restorative justice in many different ways depending upon the nature of the threat that disrupted the balance in the first place. That tendency to seek equitable balance in social relationships gives rise to the motivation for justice.

Motivation to Seek Balance and Justice

Just World and Moral Disengagement Lerner (1977) argued convincingly that underlying the motivation to seek justice is the fundamental belief that the world is and ought to be a just place (Lerner, 1977, 1980). Lerner and colleagues (Lerner et al., 1976; Lerner & Clayton, 2011; Lerner & Miller, 1978) theorized that a belief in justice is at the center of how people live their lives allowing them to engage in social behavior to achieve their goals. If people did not believe that the world was ultimately just, then they would always act to achieve immediate gratification. It is only the belief that justice will prevail in the end that enables us to delay gratification and plan actions that will eventually result in the attainment of our long-term aims (Lerner, 1980). In fact, people who violate their own justice norms to obtain their objectives are likely to experience a drop in their self-esteem. Because people believe that the world is fundamentally just, when they behave immorally, the knowledge that they engaged in wrongful conduct creates a conflict between their fundamental belief in a just world and the knowledge of their own immoral behavior. The resulting cognitive dissonance, if unresolved, will ultimately lead to a loss of self-esteem. One way to resolve this dissonance is to morally disengage in order to protect one's own self-worth (Bandura, 1991, 2002). In other words, the stronger the belief in a just world, the stronger is the motivation to morally disengage when confronted with one's own wrongdoing or the wrongdoing of others with whom we empathize. This extends to judging morally questionable policies of legal actors in the civil or criminal justice systems (Kirshenbaum et al., 2020).

According to Bandura (2002), people morally disengage through several actions designed to lower the cognitive dissonance of acting immorally in a just world. These include (1) moral justification—thinking about a transgression as producing a positive outcome for the greater community, (2) euphemistic labeling —speaking of the transgression using positive and misrepresentative language, (3) advantageous comparisons—identifying individuals who behave in even more immoral ways than did the transgressor, (4) displacement of responsibility—blaming immoral conduct on those who are in charge, (5) diffusion of responsibility—justifying immoral actions by the fact that others have engaged in the same behaviors, (6) minimization of consequences—claiming that the harms caused by moral misbehavior are neither serious nor long-lasting, (7) attribution of blame—claiming that the victims of wrongdoing are partly to blame for the actions, and (8) dehumanization—considering victims of transgressions as less than human and therefore deserving of harsh treatment.

Examples of the use of these moral disengagement strategies are not difficult to find in the domain of legal decision-making. For example, prior research has shown that people who scored high on a moral disengagement scale were more likely to support the torture of suspected terrorists (McDermott & Miller, 2016) and more likely to endorse the use of capital punishment in death penalty cases (Osofsky et al., 2005). In both examples, observers who believe in a just world were able to reduce the dissonance created by confronting potentially immoral conduct, the use of torture in the first instance and executing a fellow human being in the second instance, with the use of one or more of Bandura's (2002) strategies to disengage from the resulting moral responsibility. In the first instance, people high in moral disengagement did not see the torture of suspected terrorists as a violation of the just world principle because the end results would bring about the positive outcome of protecting the greater good and because it was easy to dehumanize the suspected terrorists. In the second example, the application of capital punishment was justified and was not seen as a violation of a belief in a just world because those on death row had killed others, so they are to blame for their own fates. Therefore, the responsibility for their deaths is easily displaced onto those in the criminal justice system responsible for delivering retributive justice.

Kirshenbaum et al. (2020) extended this line of argument by developing a 5-factor general scale of moral disengagement in legal settings using items that tapped into Bandura's (2002) moral disengagement strategies. They found that those scoring high in legal moral disengagement also scored high in belief in a just world. Furthermore, high scorers compared to low scorers were more likely to support police using controversial warrant-seeking procedures and endorsing the use of oppressive interrogation procedures. Moreover, these higher scorers were more likely to view pregnant drug users as child abusers, support a Muslim ban against travelers to the United States, hold punitive attitudes toward immigration, and favor the death penalty for capital murder cases. In summary, people with strong beliefs in the just world fallacy were the same ones who scored high on legal moral disengagement and supported controversial legal procedures and unjust governing policies. One interpretation of these findings is that a strong belief in a just world provides the motivation to morally disengage when faced with potentially unjust procedures and policies.

Threat to the Just World Illusion The belief in a just world is a strong illusion that is foundational to how people organize their lives, so that threats to this belief challenge our sense of security and calmness (Lerner & Clayton, 2011). These threats, which can be any real or imagined event that questions the principle that "people get what they deserve and deserve what they get", generate cognitive dissonance and, as a result, motivation to repair one's own just world illusion (Ellard et al., 2016). Such challenges can be any instance when people acknowledge that a victim of harm was not the causal agent that produced the injurious outcome but instead unjustifiably suffered from that harm (Hafer & Bègue, 2005). For example, both an otherwise healthy person contracting a serious disease (Triplet & Sugarman, 1987) and an innocent member of one's in-group suffering a criminal attack would challenge the belief that people get what they deserve and deserve what they get. Going in the other direction, a challenge to the belief in a just world might also occur when people observe someone receiving a positive outcome or collecting an award who did little, if anything, to deserve the reward. Consider these two examples: (1) a fellow worker receives a promotion when that person worked no harder than anyone else in the work group and (2) an out-group member inherits a large sum of money when a distant relative passed away. While most of the research on threats to date have involved undeserved negative outcomes as opposed to undeserved positive outcomes (Hafer & Bègue, 2005), both have the potential of challenging the just world fallacy and triggering efforts to repair the belief.

Attempts to Repair the Broken Illusion Ellard et al. (2016) described a few limited rational strategies and many more abundant irrational strategies that people utilize to re-establish their illusions that the world is fair after experiencing a threat to their just world illusion. A rational strategy for restoring justice after an innocent person suffers an undeserved harm is to assist the victim after the injustice has transpired (Hafer & Gosse, 2011). One might assist and perhaps offer rehabilitative services to the innocent in-group crime victim described above, and one might search out information to learn that the out-group person who inherited a large sum of money spent several prior years supporting and caring for their distant relatives' children. Of course, the resources to assist victims of undeserved negative outcomes are limited as is the ability to gain information to establish the deservedness of a recipient of unexpected good fortune. At the same time, the ability to irrationally distort one's views to re-establish the just world fallacy requires little more than the willingness to accept a compromised view of reality.

Derogating and Blaming the Victim The most well-known irrational strategy for re-establishing the just world fallacy is to derogate and blame the victim who experienced undeserved harm, which ultimately reaffirms the belief that good things only happen to good people and, most importantly, bad things only happen to bad people (Hafer & Bègue, 2005). In the original study demonstrating this effect,

Lerner and Simmons (1966) had participants watch a video of an individual experiencing electric shocks as punishment for failing to learn in an associate learning task. They found that the participants devalued the victim, especially if they believed that the victim would continue to suffer in the future, as compared to when they were led to believe the victim's suffering was over. According to Lerner and Simmons, by devaluing the victim, people protected themselves with the knowledge that bad things (i.e., continued electric shock) only happen to bad people. If the shocking was over, then there was no need to devalue the victim to bolster the just world fallacy or to protect themselves against future harm.

Work since that time has found a number of other factors that moderate the derogation effect (Ellard et al., 2016; Hafer & Bègue, 2005). For example, in a recent study, Mikani and Rafiee (2022) had Iranian participants read about an assault in which a respectable professor or unrespectable car dealer was the victim of a stabbing and suffered severe internal injuries during an attack, which was the result of a cell phone robbery that had gone bad. Results showed that the stronger the participants' Beliefs in a Just World (BJW) were, as measured by the general BJW scale (Dalbert et al., 1987), the more they derogated the innocent car dealer victim of the attack. However, the effect was nullified when the victim was the highly respected professor who commanded empathy from the observers, which blocked their ability to devalue him in order to re-establish their just world fallacy. However, it was not difficult to devalue the lower-status car salesman who did not trigger an empathetic response. Mikani and Rafiee's (2022) results echo the work of Aderman et al. (1974) who used the Lerner and Simmons (1966) paradigm but manipulated whether people watched the video from an empathy-inducing perspective (i.e., imagine yourself in the place of the victim) or an empathy-inhibiting perspective (i.e., watch the victim to see exactly what they do). Aderman et al. replicated the Lerner and Simmons derogation effect in the empathy inhibition condition, but the effect disappeared in the empathy-inducing condition.

The Role of Empathy in the Perception of Injustice Empathy may indeed play a central role in offsetting just world derogation, so much so, as to suggest its use as an intervention for victim blaming. People who approach just world threat situations and take the perspective of a victim are more likely to perceive the injustice in the situation and lose the motivation to derogate the victim in order to repair their just world illusions. Urbanska et al. (2019) (study 2) had two groups of participants observe a dictator game in which round 1 began with Person A (the dictator) deciding how much money they would provide to Person B to play the round. For half of the participants, Person A shared 50% of their money to Person B (equal condition), and for the other half, Person A only shared 20% of their money (unequal condition). The experimenters gave half of each group of participants an empathy instruction, i.e., play the game by trying to imagine how Player B felt, and the other half an objective perspective instruction, i.e., play the game by being detached from Player B.

At the conclusion of round 2, participant observers completed emotion and perceived fairness measures. The results of a moderated mediation analysis showed that those in the empathy instruction condition felt more anger in the unequal offer condition as compared to the equality offer condition, and the increased anger predicted higher rates of perceived unfairness for Person B. However, the path from the dictator offer (unequal vs. equal) through experienced anger to perceived unfairness was not significant in the objective instruction condition. Participants in the objective instruction condition devalued Player B in order to repair their view of the world as fair, by re-establishing that bad things (i.e., unequal distribution of money) only happened to people who deserved the loss. As a result, those in the objective instruction condition did not see the unfairness that those in the empathy condition saw. However, when participants who took on the emotional experience of Player B as their own, the resulting empathy that they experienced short-circuited the just world derogation of the victim and replaced it with an attribution of unfairness for negative outcomes that befall innocent people.

Other Irrational Forms of Just World Repair According to Ellard et al. (2016), the process of repairing the belief in a just world after a threat has occurred has the property of equifinality, so that reinstating the illusion of fairness can be reached by a number of different strategies. Cognitive repair of the illusion also has the property of substitutability, meaning that the strategies used to achieve a new balance are somewhat interchangeable (Kruglanski, 1996). Regardless of the strategy, the motivation to maintain the belief in a just world is that once the belief is reinstated, people are once again able to benefit from the calm and orderliness that result. Other attempts to maintain the belief in a just world after a threat include denying and withdrawing from the situation or ignoring the injustice (Lerner, 1980), reinterpreting the outcome as positive (i.e., believing that poor people are happier than rich people (Kay & Jost, 2003)), engaging in ultimate justice reasoning by embracing the illusion that "justice will be done in the end" (Ellard et al., 2016, p. 135), and locating the cause of a person's misfortune in the person's prior misdeeds (Callan et al., 2013). All these largely irrational strategies allow the perceiver to repair their belief in the just world after a threat to the belief has occurred. More recent research has begun to take on the challenge of finding moderators that determine when each strategy is likely to come in to play (e.g., Mikani & Rafiee, 2022).

In-Group Victim Blaming Research has established that participants are more likely to blame and derogate victims of injustice that are most similar to themselves because similar others suffering undeserved harm is a violation of the just world fallacy which threatens the well-being of the self (van den Bos & Bal, 2016; and Chap. 9, *"Justice and Culture"* in this volume). People reason, if it happened to him or her, it could happen to me. For example, Aguiar et al. (2008, study 1) presented to Portuguese participants a video about an innocent boy who grabbed an electrical cable to avoid falling when he went after a ball, and as a result of a massive shock, lost both of his arms. The video described the boy either as part of a Portuguese family (in-group), a Gypsy family (out-group), or made no reference to the victim's social group (noncategorized). The results of an emotional Stroop test after participants viewed the video showed that those who watched in-group victim showed more just world derogation, as evidenced through interference on the Stroop test, than did those who watched the video of the out-group child.

In study 2, Aguiar et al. (2008) added a nonvictim video in both the in-group and out-group conditions. They observed greater threat, again as measured through Stroop test interference, for the in-group victim compared to the in-group nonvictim but no differences for the out-group victim and nonvictim. Furthermore, the same pattern was found for implicit derogation of the victim and nonvictim measured through reaction times to positive and negative traits accompanied by the subliminally presented word "Portuguese" in the in-group condition and "Gypsie" in the out-group condition. These results supported similar findings showing that in-group victims pose greater threat and result in greater derogation than do out-group victims (Correia et al., 2007; Lodewijkx et al., 2005).

The Psychological Processes Underlying In-Group Victim Blaming The question remains that if in-group derogation occurs in order to restore one's belief in a just world, what underlying psychological process might explain the effect. Van den Bos et al. (2009; 2016) proposed a two-stage model to explain victim blame as a reaction to just world threat. In the first stage, people respond to the victim through self-interested responses that are largely the result of experiential processing, i.e., relying mostly on emotional reactions to the victim and implicit attitudes about the victim. It occurs nearly automatically. A second stage requires more deliberative processing that consciously recognizes the threat to the just world fallacy due to the suffering of an in-group member, which then may produce a victim derogation and blaming response to maintain the belief in a just world to counter the in-group threat.

Van den Bos and Maas (2009) tested the model by first measuring participants' General Belief in a just world (GBJW) using Dalbert et al.'s (1987) scale. Next, in an ostensibly different experiment, the researchers induced either an experiential mindset or a rational mindset through instructions to process information in one of those two ways (Pacini & Epstein, 1999). The experiential instructions explained to the participants that they should rely on their associative thoughts, their own experiences, and their gut feelings to make expressive judgments. This is akin to the first stage in the Van den Bos model where people make judgments through emotional reactions, heuristics, and implicit attitudes. In the rational condition, the instructions explained that the participants should carefully read all the material presented and carefully weigh the pros and cons in a logical and analytic way to reach their judgments. This represents the second stage in the Van den Bos model where people think more deliberatively and as a result recognize a threat to their just world belief, if one exists. After practicing their mindsets on a moral transgression borrowed from Haidt (2001), participants read two victim-based scenarios, one in which a thief robbed a girl traveling alone on her way home from a party and a second one in which a different girl was sexually assaulted when she was alone in a park.

Participants rated the blame that they attributed to the girls for their own victimization.

The results supported the two-stage model by showing no differences in victim blaming in the experiential condition between the low and high GBJW participants, but in the rationalistic condition, only those with high GBJW showed high blame reactions. Thus, when processing the just world threat experientially, GBJW was not relevant to assigning blame (the first stage), but when processing rationally (the second stage), only those with strong just world beliefs blamed the girls for their own victimization, in order to repair their just world fallacy. These results suggest that victim derogation as a result of just world thinking is a deliberative process for those who hold strong just world beliefs.

Individual Differences and Belief in a Just World While a good amount of research has manipulated threat to a just world and measured how people react to that threat, another large body of research treats measured belief in a just world as an individual difference factor. In the early efforts, Rubin and Peplau (1975) developed the self-report Just World Scale (JWS) that included scales to measure agreement with items tied to the prevalence of justice in some specific domains such as law and health, along with some general statements, which purported the world to be a safe place. Rubin and Peplau's (1973) early research showed that men who scored high on the JWS and who were eligible for the draft lottery in the U.S. were more likely to derogate their peers who received low draft numbers, as compared to those with high draft numbers (Rubin & Peplau, 1973). This was not true for those who scored low on the JWS.

Later, Dalbert and colleagues (Dalbert et al., 1987) separated belief in a just world into two separate constructs, Belief in a Just World for the self (BJWS) and Belief in a Just World generally (BJWG). BJWS measures the belief that the world is just for one's self, that is, the world that the respondent lives in is a fair one. On the other hand, BJWG measures the view that the world is fair for everyone. According to the theory, BJWS motivates people to use moral means to obtain their personal goals (Bartholomaeus & Strelan, 2019), and studies do indeed show that people high in BJWS conduct their lives in a more prosocial manner (Bartholomaeus & Strelan, 2016; Bègue et al., 2015; Sutton et al., 2017). People high in BJWS are confident that they will reap long-term benefits of acting in a prosocial manner (Bartholomaeus & Strelan, 2019; Sutton & Winnard, 2007). Most interestingly, people with higher levels of BJWS but not those with higher BJWG levels possess a stronger sense of psychological well-being (Hafer & Sutton, 2016), show more positive emotion (Hafer & Sutton, 2016), experience lower signs of depression (Kamble & Dalbert, 2012), and are generally more satisfied with their lives (Sutton & Douglas, 2005).

At the same time, BJWG is implicated in the way in which people judge others in their social environments resulting in diminished prosocial activity because people who believe that the world is just for everyone feel less pressure to act to make the world a better place. For example, people high in BJSG as compared to their lower scoring peers are less sensitive to discrimination against minorities (Hafer &

Choma, 2009), more likely to support the political status quo (Jost & Hunyady, 2002), less likely to be active in politics (Furnham, 2003), and less likely to support affirmative action policies (Wilkins & Wenger, 2014). Apparently, people who are high in general BJWG lack the motivational drive to right moral wrongs, in part, because they see the world as fair enough as it exists. Indeed, Bartholomaeus et al. (2024) completed a latent profile analysis and follow-up multilevel multinomial logistic regression with data from the European Social Survey ($n = 43{,}209$ across 29 countries) to find that those who scored high on BJWG were mostly young men with higher incomes and with better education. They were, in fact, politically conservative individuals who had not experienced discrimination and were very unlikely to have been crime victims.

These findings could blur the distinction between Belief in a Just World—General and some forms of political ideology because both may lead to a stronger sense of well-being and lower the motivation to engage in justice-seeking behavior. Jost et al. (2015) wrote about the palliative function of ideology in which seeing the status quo as legitimate and fair was a kind of motivation inhibitor, for people who occupy higher levels of social status (i.e., the world is fair enough for them) but not for those with lower status (i.e., the world is fair for some but not for me). This fundamental proposition in system justification theory (Jost et al., 2019; Jost & Banaji, 1994; Jost & Hunyady, 2002) states that the relationship between system justification ideology and psychological well-being ought to be negative for those lower in social status because while they believe that the system is just, their lower social status is affiliated with a lower well-being. This proposition suggests that a strong sense of system justification ideology and not BJWG might be the active ingredient in bolstering well-being and as a result reduces the motivation to seek justice but only for high-status individuals. Furthermore, there are a number of other ideologies which overlap somewhat with system justification but are different enough to correlate only moderately with the construct, indicating that they are separate measures of ideology. These include "conservatism, system justification, economic system justification, fair market ideology, gender system justification, belief in a just world, protestant work ethic, descriptive meritocracy, prescriptive meritocracy, SDO [Social Dominance Orientation], RWA [Right Wing Authoritarianism], sexism, benevolent sexism, hostile sexism, modern sexism, racism, and modern racism" (Vargas Salfate et al., 2024).

Vargas Salfate et al. (2024) examined these issues in a large meta-analysis that tested the association between all of the above justification ideologies (including BJW) and psychological well-being and whether that association varied as a function of social status as the system justification theory would suggest. They examined the relationship using 1627 studies from 121 countries involving over 1.8 million respondents and found a weak ($r = 0.069$) but significant ($p < 0.001$) relationship between the endorsement of a justice ideology and well-being. Most importantly, the interaction between the social status and ideology on well-being was not significant, and, in fact, in both the higher and lower social status groups, the relationship was positive—a contraction to system justification theory. It was not negative, as the system justification theory would predict, for the lower status group. Furthermore, the relationship between ideology and well-being was the strongest for ideologies that communicated fairness and legitimacy, such as BJW, which demonstrated a significant association with well-being ($r = 0.19$), the strongest observed among the measures investigated. The authors concluded: "Adding all these arguments together provides support for the just world theory, which also proposes that believing that the world is fair is associated with subjective psychological wellbeing, but without assuming that system justification is a distinct motivation" (Vargas Salfate et al., 2024, p. 61).

Motivation for Justice and Legal Decision-Making

What Is the Motivation for Justice? Perhaps the best way to think about the motivation for justice is by alluding to the ancient Buddhist parable of the four unsighted men who come across an elephant and each tries to describe what he has come across. Each man details a part of the elephant that he has discovered including the animal's trunk, its leg, its tail, or its side. Each understands the animal in a very different way. Similarly, each of the authors of the chapters in the 2024 Nebraska Symposium on Motivation understand the motivation for justice in a somewhat different way. Nonetheless, the remaining nine chapters explicitly or implicitly rely on the basic justice concepts described above. That is, the motivation for justice comes in several related but different forms, including distributive, procedural, retributive, and restorative justice, all of which are based on the belief that the world is fair and just. When the belief is violated, some morally disengage to protect their own self-esteem from the cognitive dissonance that results from believing the world is just but being cognizant of times when it is not. Others face a threat to their belief in a just world through rational strategies to repair the illusion (e.g., help those who are harmed) or through irrational belief repair (e.g., blaming or derogating the victim). The chapters have implications for one or more of these fundamental concepts to describe what the motivation for justice is and how it is expressed in a variety of political, legal, and social institutions in Western democracies.

Chapters 2 Through 10: Describing the Elephant In Chap. 2, "*Toward a Community Model in the Motivations for Justice and Legal Judgment*", Christian Bijoux examines the history of racism in the United States, discussing its implications for the just world illusion. Jack Glaser takes on a similar topic in Chap. 3, "*Police Discretion as a Vulnerability Factor for Disparate Treatment*" in which he considers elements of distributive, procedural, and retributive justice through a decision-making lens applied to officers interacting with people of color in the U.S. The chapter says a lot indirectly about the belief in a just world. In Chap. 4, "*Zeal, Motivation, and the Adversarial Bias*", Dan Simon looks at the adversarial justice system as a compromised effort to achieve morally meaningful outcomes but as a result of the compromise may require attorneys to engage in some form of moral disengagement. Dan's analysis relies on social cognitive psychology to gain insights into havoc that the adversarial system plays upon the Western belief in a just and fair world. Next, in Chap. 5, "*Sentencing for Multiple Offenses: When Seeking Justice is too Cruel and Cognitively Demanding*", Mandeep Dhami and Charis Bechan take a deep dive into the cognitive complexities and motivations that drive the sentencing of offenders who have committed simultaneous crimes. This work, partly theoretical and partly empirical, explores the problem in the context of law in the United Kingdom and as a result has a lot to say about retributive and distributive justice. It also speaks quite directly to the equity principal as it shapes the perceptions of procedural justice.

Tom Tyler switches our focus away from the criminal justice system to the changing nature of politics in the Western democracies in Chap. 6, "*Does Ideology Undermine Procedure-Based Legitimacy*?" Tom tests his well-known theory of procedural justice with several sets of survey data applied to current problems in the rise of authoritarianism and the polarization of political ideology in the U.S. and other Western democracies. He concludes that both, but especially increasing polarization in ideology, represent threats to political legitimacy. Another switch of focus takes us away from both criminal law and politics to examine the underlying justice issues in civil law in Jennifer Robbennolt's Chap. 7, "*Motives for Civil Justice*". Jennifer's work focuses on why people bring civil law suits and the many ways in which the search for restorative justice can be fulfilled after the injured party suffers a threat to a belief in a just world that results from a civil harm. The chapter has a lot to say about procedural justice as well. In Chap. 8, "*Why Do People Use ADR?*", Donna Shewtowsky takes a detailed look at one of the many ways in which people who suffer a civil harm can seek restorative justice. She explicates the motivation to make us of ADR using processes that seek to repair the just world breach resulting from civil injuries. The results explain much about the procedural justice demands for voice and trust.

Chapter 9, "*Justice and Culture*" examines in some detail the invariance hypothesis that is central to procedural justice theory as Kees van den Bos critically evaluates existing cross-cultural justice research. He argues that there is a reciprocal connection between culture and justice that has not been fully explored to the limits of cross-cultural methodology. Kees describes his and his colleagues' use of the *counterculture* design to probe the causal connection between some aspects of culture and procedural justice. Finally, in Chap. 10, "*Legal Judgment and the Motivation for Justice: What Have We Learned*?" Wiener, Cluver, Monnier, and Hansen do just what the chapter title states; they review what we have learned from the 2024 Nebraska Symposium. They frame their discussion in terms of the review provided in this first chapter, "*Legal Judgment and the Motivation for Justice*." Chap. 10 summarizes how each of the chapters in the book addresses one or more of the issues of distributive, procedural, retributive, and restorative justice and how they directly or indirectly make use of Lerner's (1977) just world illusion to integrate a specific analysis of legal decision-making with efforts to seek justice.

References

Aderman, D., Brehm, S. S., & Katz, L. B. (1974). Empathic observation of an innocent victim: The just world revisited. *Journal of Personality and Social Psychology, 29*(3), 342–347. https://doi.org/10.1037/h0036001

Aguiar, P., Vala, J., Correia, I., & Pereira, C. (2008). Justice in our world and in that of others: Belief in a just world and reactions to victims. *Social Justice Research, 21*, 50–68. https://doi.org/10.1007/s11211-007-0059-3

Bandura, A. (1991). Social cognitive theory of self-regulation. *Organizational Behavior and Human Decision Processes, 50*(2), 248–287. https://doi.org/10.1016/0749-5978(91)90022-L

Bandura, A. (2002). Social cognitive theory in cultural context. *Applied Psychology: An International Review, 51*, 269–290. https://doi.org/10.1111/1464-0597.00092

Bartholomaeus, J., & Strelan, P. (2016). Just world beliefs and forgiveness: The mediating role of implicit theories of relationships. *Personality and Individual Differences, 96*, 106–110. https://doi.org/10.1016/j.paid.2016.02.081

Bartholomaeus, J., & Strelan, P. (2019). The adaptive, approach-oriented correlates of belief in a just world for the self: A review of the research. *Personality and Individual Differences, 151*, 109485. https://doi.org/10.1016/j.paid.2019.06.028

Bartholomaeus, J., Strelan, P., & Burns, N. (2024). Does the empowering function of the belief in a just world generalize? Broad-base cross-sectional and longitudinal evidence. *Social Justice Research, 37*, 57–75. https://doi.org/10.1007/s11211-023-00412-y

Bègue, L., Beauvois, J.-L., Courbet, D., Oberlé, D., Lepage, J., & Duke, A. A. (2015). Personality predicts obedience in a Milgram paradigm. *Journal of Personality, 83*(3), 299–306. https://doi.org/10.1111/jopy.12104

Blader, S. L., & Tyler, T. R. (2003). A four-component model of procedural justice: Defining the meaning of a "fair" process. *Personality and Social Psychology Bulletin, 29*(6), 747–758. https://doi.org/10.1177/0146167203029006007

Blader, S. L., & Tyler, T. R. (2009). Testing and extending the group engagement model: Linkages between social identity, procedural justice, economic outcomes, and extrarole behavior. *Journal of Applied Psychology, 94*(2), 445–464. https://doi.org/10.1037/a0013935

Callan, M. J., Harvey, A. J., Dawtry, R. J., & Sutton, R. M. (2013). Through the looking glass: Focusing on long-term goals increases immanent justice reasoning. *British Journal of Social Psychology, 52*(2), 377–385. https://doi.org/10.1111/bjso.12022

Carlsmith, K. M., & Darley, J. M. (2008). Psychological aspects of retributive justice. In M. P. Zanna (Ed.), *Advances in experimental social psychology* (pp. 193–236). Elsevier Academic Press. https://doi.org/10.1016/S0065-2601(07)00004-4

Carlsmith, K. M., Darley, J. M., & Robinson, P. H. (2002). Why do we punish? Deterrence and just deserts as motives for punishment. *Journal of Personality and Social Psychology, 83*(2), 284–299. https://doi.org/10.1037/0022-3514.83.2.284

Correia, I., Vala, J., & Aguiar, P. (2007). Victim's innocence, social categorization, and the threat to the belief in a just world. *Journal of Experimental Social Psychology, 43*(1), 31–38. https://doi.org/10.1016/j.jesp.2005.12.010

Dalbert, C., Montada, L., & Schmitt, M. (1987). Belief in a just world as motive: Validity correlates of two scales. *Psychologische Beitrage, 29*, 596–615.

Decety, J., & Wheatley, T. (2015). *The moral brain: A multidisciplinary perspective*. The MIT Press. https://doi.org/10.7551/mitpress/9988.001.0001

Decety, J., & Yoder, K. J. (2017). The emerging social neuroscience of justice motivation. *Trends in Cognitive Sciences, 21*(1), 6–14. https://doi.org/10.1016/j.tics.2016.10.008

Ellard, J., Harvey, A. J., & Callan, M. J. (2016). The justice motive: History, theory, and research. In C. Sabbagh & M. Schmitt (Eds.), *Handbook of social justice theory and research* (pp. 127–143). Springer. https://doi.org/10.1007/978-1-4939-3216-0_7

Furnham, A. (2003). Belief in a just world: Research progress over the past decade. *Personality and Individual Differences, 34*(5), 795–817. https://doi.org/10.1016/S0191-8869(02)00072-7

Gollwitzer, M., & Keller, L. (2010). What you did only matters if you are one of us: Offenders' group membership moderates the effect of criminal history on punishment severity. *Social Psychology, 41*(1), 20–26. https://doi.org/10.1027/1864-9335/a000004

Gollwitzer, M., & van Prooijen, J. W. (2016). Psychology of justice. In C. Sabbagh & M. Schmitt (Eds.), *Handbook of social justice theory and research* (pp. 61–82). Springer. https://doi.org/10.1007/978-1-4939-3216-0_4

Hafer, C. L., & Bègue, L. (2005). Experimental research on just-world theory: Problems, developments, and future challenges. *Psychological Bulletin, 131*(1), 128–167. https://doi.org/10.1037/0033-2909.131.1.128

Hafer, C. L., & Choma, B. L. (2009). Belief in a just world, perceived fairness, and justification of the status quo. In J. T. Jost, A. C. Kay, & H. Thorisdottir (Eds.), *Social and psychological bases of ideology and system justification* (pp. 107–125). Oxford University Press. https://doi.org/10.1093/acprof:oso/9780195320916.003.005

Hafer, C. L., & Gosse, L. (2011). Predicting alternative strategies for preserving a belief in a just world: The case of repressive coping style. *European Journal of Social Psychology, 41*(6), 730–739. https://doi.org/10.1002/ejsp.807

Hafer, C. L., & Sutton, R. (2016). Belief in a just world. In C. Sabbagh & M. Schmitt (Eds.), *Handbook of social justice theory and research*. Springer. https://doi.org/10.1007/978-1-4939-3216-0_8

Haidt, J. (2001). The emotional dog and its rational tail: A social intuitionist approach to moral judgment. *Psychological Review, 108*(4), 814–834. https://doi.org/10.1037/0033-295X.108.4.814

Jost, J. T., Badaan, V., Goudarzi, S., Hoffarth, M., & Mogami, M. (2019). The future of system justification theory. *British Journal of Social Psychology, 58*(2), 382–392. https://doi.org/10.1111/bjso.12309

Jost, J. T., & Banaji, M. R. (1994). The role of stereotyping in system-justification and the production of false consciousness. *British Journal of Social Psychology, 33*(1), 1–27. https://doi.org/10.1111/j.2044-8309.1994.tb01008.x

Jost, J. T., Gaucher, D., & Stern, C. (2015). "The world isn't fair": A system justification perspective on social stratification and inequality. In M. Mikulincer, P. R. Shaver, J. F. Dovidio, & J. A. Simpson (Eds.), *APA handbook of personality and social psychology* (pp. 317–340). American Psychological Association. https://doi.org/10.1037/14342-012

Jost, J. T., & Hunyady, O. (2002). The psychology of system justification and the palliative function of ideology. *European Review of Social Psychology, 13*(1), 111–153. https://doi.org/10.1080/10463280240000046

Kamble, S. V., & Dalbert, C. (2012). Belief in a just world and wellbeing in Indian schools. *International Journal of Psychology, 47*(4), 269–278. https://doi.org/10.1080/00207594.2011.626047

Kay, A. C., & Jost, J. T. (2003). Complementary justice: Effects of "poor but happy" and "poor but honest" stereotype exemplars on system justification and implicit activation of the justice motive. *Journal of Personality and Social Psychology, 85*(5), 823–837. https://doi.org/10.1037/0022-3514.85.5.823

Kirshenbaum, J. M., Kaplan, T., Miller, M. K., & Cramer, R. J. (2020). Development and validation of a general legal moral disengagement scale. *Psychology, Crime & Law, 27*(2), 1–28. https://doi.org/10.1080/1068316X.2020.1850722

Kruglanski, A. W. (1996). Motivated social cognition: Principles of the interface. In E. T. Higgins & A. W. Kruglanski (Eds.), *Social psychology: Handbook of basic principles* (pp. 493–520). The Guilford Press.

Lerner, M. J. (1977). The justice motive: Some hypotheses as to its origins and forms. *Journal of Personality, 45*(1), 1–52. https://doi.org/10.1111/j.1467-6494.1977.tb00591.x

Lerner, M. (1980). *The belief in a just world: A fundamental delusion*. Plenum. https://doi.org/10.1007/978-1-4899-0448-5

Lerner, M. J., & Clayton, S. (2011). *Justice and self-interest: Two fundamental motives*. Cambridge University Press. https://doi.org/10.1017/CBO9780511976698

Lerner, M. J., & Miller, D. T. (1978). Just world research and the attribution process: Looking back and ahead. *Psychological Bulletin, 85*(5), 1030–1051. https://doi.org/10.1037/0033-2909.85.5.1030

Lerner, M. J., Miller, D. T., & Holmes, J. G. (1976). Deserving and the emergence of forms of justice. *Advances in Experimental Social Psychology, 9*, 133–162. https://doi.org/10.1016/S0065-2601(08)60060-X

Lerner, M. J., & Simmons, C. H. (1966). Observer's reaction to the "innocent victim": Compassion or rejection? *Journal of Personality and Social Psychology, 4*(2), 203–210. https://doi.org/10.1037/h0023562

Lodewijkx, H. F. M., de Kwaadsteniet, E. W., & Nijstad, B. A. (2005). That could be me (or not): Senseless violence and the role of deservingness, victim ethnicity, person identification, and position identification. *Journal of Applied Social Psychology, 35*(7), 1361–1383. https://doi.org/10.1111/j.1559-1816.2005.tb02174.x

McCullough, M. E., Fincham, F. D., & Tsang, J.-A. (2003). Forgiveness, forbearance, and time: The temporal unfolding of transgression-related interpersonal motivations. *Journal of Personality and Social Psychology, 84*(3), 540–557. https://doi.org/10.1037/0022-3514.84.3.540

McDermott, C., & Miller, M. (2016). Individual differences impact support for vigilante justice. *Journal of Aggression, Conflict and Peace Research, 8*(3), 186–196. https://doi.org/10.1108/JACPR-09-2015-0186

Mikani, M., & Rafiee, P. (2022). Why we derogate victims and demonize perpetrators: The influence of just-world beliefs and the characteristics of victims and perpetrators. *Social Justice Research, 36*, 1–18. https://doi.org/10.1007/s11211-022-00404-4

Osofsky, M. J., Bandura, A., & Zimbardo, P. G. (2005). The role of moral disengagement in the execution process. *Law and Human Behavior, 29*(4), 371–393. https://doi.org/10.1007/s10979-005-4930-1

Pacini, R., & Epstein, S. (1999). The relation of rational and experiential information processing styles to personality, basic beliefs, and the ratio-bias phenomenon. *Journal of Personality and Social Psychology, 76*(6), 972–987. https://doi.org/10.1037/0022-3514.76.6.972

Robbennolt, J. K. (2003). Apologies and legal settlement: An empirical examination. *Michigan Law Review, 102*(3), 460. Available at https://repository.law.umich.edu/mlr/vol102/iss3/3

Robbennolt, J. K. (2006). Apologies and settlement levers. *Journal of Empirical Legal Studies, 3*(2), 333–373. https://doi.org/10.1111/j.1740-1461.2006.00072.x

Robbennolt, J. K. (2008). Apologies and civil justice. In B. H. Bornstein, R. L. Wiener, R. Schopp, & S. L. Willborn (Eds.), *Civil juries and civil justice: Psychological and legal perspectives* (pp. 195–231). Springer Science & Business Media. https://doi.org/10.1007/978-0-387-74490-2_11

Robbennolt, J. K. (2013). The effects of negotiated and delegated apologies in settlement negotiation. *Law and Human Behavior, 37*(2), 128–135. https://doi.org/10.1037/lhb0000020

Rozin, P., Lowery, L., Imada, S., & Haidt, J. (1999). The CAD triad hypothesis: A mapping between three moral emotions (contempt, anger, disgust) and three moral codes (community, autonomy, divinity). *Journal of Personality and Social Psychology, 76*(4), 574–586. https://doi.org/10.1037/0022-3514.76.4.574

Rubin, Z., & Peplau, A. (1973). Belief in a just world and reactions to another's lot: A study of participants in the national draft lottery 1. *Journal of Social Issues, 29*(4), 73–93. https://doi.org/10.1111/j.1540-4560.1973.tb00104.x

Rubin, Z., & Peplau, L. A. (1975). Who believes in a just world? *Journal of Social Issues, 31*(3), 65–89. https://doi.org/10.1111/j.1540-4560.1975.tb00997.x

Smith, H. J., Pettigrew, T. F., Pippin, G. M., & Bialosiewicz, S. (2012). Relative deprivation: A theoretical and meta-analytic review. *Personality and Social Psychology Review, 16*(3), 203–232. https://doi.org/10.1177/1088868311430825

Sutton, R. M., & Douglas, K. M. (2005). Justice for all, or just for me? More evidence of the importance of the self-other distinction in just-world beliefs. *Personality and Individual Differences, 39*(3), 637–645. https://doi.org/10.1016/j.paid.2005.02.010

Sutton, R. M., Stoeber, J., & Kamble, S. V. (2017). Belief in a just world for oneself versus others, social goals, and subjective well-being. *Personality and Individual Differences, 113*, 115–119. https://doi.org/10.1016/j.paid.2017.03.026

Sutton, R. M., & Winnard, E. J. (2007). Looking ahead through lenses of justice: The relevance of just-world beliefs to intentions and confidence in the future. *British Journal of Social Psychology, 46*(3), 649–666. https://doi.org/10.1348/014466606X166220

Thibaut, J. W., & Walker, L. (1975). Procedural justice: A psychological analysis. L. Erlbaum Associates, Hillsdale.

Triplet, R. G., & Sugarman, D. B. (1987). Reactions of AIDS victims: Ambiguity breeds contempt. *Personality and Social Psychology Bulletin, 13*(2), 265–274. https://doi.org/10.1177/0146167287132011

Tyler, T. R. (2006). Psychological perspectives on legitimacy and legitimation. *Annual Review of Psychology, 57*, 375–400. https://doi.org/10.1146/annurev.psych.57.102904.190038

Tyler, T. R., & Lind, E. A. (1992). A relational model of authority in groups. In M. P. Zanna (Ed.), *Advances in experimental social psychology* (pp. 115–191). Academic Press. https://doi.org/10.1016/S0065-2601(08)60283-X

Urbanska, K., McKeown, S., & Taylor, L. K. (2019). From injustice to action: The role of empathy and perceived fairness to address inequality via victim compensation. *Journal of Experimental Social Psychology, 82*, 129–140. https://doi.org/10.1016/j.jesp.2019.01.010

Van den Bos, K., & Bal, M. (2016). Social-cognitive and motivational processes underlying the justice motive. In C. Sabbagh & M. Schmitt (Eds.), *Handbook of social justice theory and research* (pp. 181–198). Springer. https://doi.org/10.1007/978-1-4939-3216-0_10

Van den Bos, K., & Maas, M. (2009). On the psychology of the belief in a just world: Exploring experiential and rationalistic paths to victim blaming. *Personality and Social Psychology Bulletin, 35*(12), 1567–1578. https://doi.org/10.1177/0146167209344628

Van den Bos, W., van Dijk, E., Westenberg, M., Rombouts, S. A. R. B., & Crone, E. A. (2009). What motivates repayment? Neural correlates of reciprocity in the Trust Game. *Social Cognitive and Affective Neuroscience, 4*(3), 294–304. https://doi.org/10.1093/scan/nsp009

Vardsveen, T. C., & Wiener, R. L. (2021). Public support for sentencing reform: A policy-capturing experiment. *Journal of Experimental Psychology: Applied, 27*(2), 430–446. https://doi.org/10.1037/xap0000339

Vargas Salfate, S., Spielmann, J., & Briley, D. A. (2024). Supporting the status quo is weakly associated with subjective well-being: A comparison of the palliative function of ideology across social status groups using a meta-analytic approach. *Psychological Bulletin, 150*(11), 1318–1346. https://doi.org/10.1037/bul0000446

Walster, E., Walster, G. W., & Berscheid, E. (1978). *Equity: Theory and research*. Allyn & Bacon.

Wilkins, V. M., & Wenger, J. B. (2014). Belief in a just world and attitudes toward affirmative action. *Policy Studies Journal, 42*(3), 325–343. https://doi.org/10.1111/psj.12063

Yoder, K. J., & Decety, J. (2020). Me first: Neural representations of fairness during three-party interactions. *Neuropsychologia, 147*, 107576. https://doi.org/10.1016/j.neuropsychologia.2020.107576

Toward a Community Model in the Motivations for Justice and Legal Judgment

Christian H. Bijoux

Racial Disparities Within the Law

Amidst the backdrop of persistent racial disparities within legal systems, this chapter embarks on a journey to unravel the intricate dynamics of contemporary racial injustice in the United States, with a specific focus on the motivations for justice within the Black community. Within the psychology of legal judgment and the motivations for change within legal institutions, it is essential to place contemporary social perceptions of legal justice and accountability in a broader context of historical trauma and systemic racism. The theme of Legal Judgment and Motivation at the 71st Annual Nebraska Symposium for Justice animates this work. Radiating into the dark corners of the symposium's theme are the junctures where individual and group motivations, institutions, and mores collude in generating law, in this case, racial injustice. The symposium then forges a pathway toward the intricate interplay between individual and collective motivations, institutional frameworks, and societal norms shaping legal outcomes.

To address the contemporary harms of racial injustice and the moral push for transformative change, we must reckon with the harsh reality of systemic harms and entrenched inequities across legal systems. For example, Black, Latino, and American Indian people are more likely than their White counterparts to end up in the legal systems in the United States, where our "criminal justice system" is rife with systematic inequities (Manza & Uggen, 2006). The numbers when it comes to race and our criminal legal system are alarming. Consistent data indicate that Black, Latino, and other non-White people are unfairly treated at every different turn of the system. They are disproportionately stopped by police, often for minimal violations

C. H. Bijoux (✉)
Georgetown University, Washington, DC, USA
e-mail: cb1498@georgetown.edu

R. L. Wiener, D. J. Hansen (eds.), *Legal Judgment and the Motivation for Justice*, Nebraska Symposium on Motivation 71,
https://doi.org/10.1007/978-3-031-98812-7_2

or merely because of their race. Suppose they have been initiated into the system in this manner. In that case, they are more often held in pretrial detention, possibly because of discriminatory systemic practices or because of economic disparities and challenges that lead to their failure to post bail. Finally, sentencing disparities bring some of the starkest and most infuriating statistics: Blacks and Latinos are disproportionately punished—much more so than white people—for the same crimes.

Everyone agrees that these "whats" exist. They are well documented. Yet, the "why" continues to be difficult for many to accept. There are various reasons. Legacies of historical racism, racial discrimination, and segregation have left biases in the fabric of our society, including within legal systems. Understanding these background causes is crucial, but it is equally important, and in some cases, more important, to understand how to motivate ourselves and society to change this troubling reality. Therefore, any comprehensive understanding of racial injustice requires an understanding of the lived experiences of communities burdened by chattel slavery, American Apartheid, and the entire history of systemic racism. The impact of centuries of dehumanization and racially subjugated conditions remains deep-seated in the collective consciousness of Black Americans.

In considering motivations to act justly, it is paramount to consider how history and experiences of trauma have shaped racial motivations to seek justice through a variety of initiatives and movements. Historical experiences of slavery and segregation fuel motivations to achieve equity and justice. We feel and often remember collective injustices long after they have occurred. These historical injustices further shape how motivation works within and across Black communities today. We need to consider how the narrative of progress that has been embraced by society as a symptom of post-racialism has distorted the way we have come to think about racial injustice in the modern age of colorblind racism. Although we live in a time when people loudly proclaim that race is no longer a significant factor in our society due to declining racism, the data on the racial disparity that pervades nearly all institutions in the United States suggests otherwise. However, this chapter is not focused on reiterating these data points. For those wishing to acquaint or reacquaint themselves with compelling statistics and analyses, the author highly recommends reading the chapters from his esteemed colleagues, who have brilliantly leveraged data in ways more convincing than he could.

This chapter is instead focused on the motivations and mindsets toward addressing racial injustice. It is essential to shift motivations and mindsets toward racial justice to be grounded in the principles of Community Development (Robinson, 2005). By exploring motivations for justice through Community Development, we can better understand how to inspire meaningful change and transformation and create a more just, equitable, and inclusive society. Understanding the history of racial injustice requires us to examine present-day forms of systemic racism and challenge us to think about how Community Development can bring about change. Exploring why the Black community specifically and non-White communities in general continue to feel motivated by a commitment to justice can help us see avenues toward an equal legal system anchored by ideas about Community Development.

Contextualizing Contemporary Racial Injustice in the United States

Knowing where motivations for justice and resistance are the strongest is essential for understanding the present social and political motivations and developing transformation strategies. In essence, knowing who would like to transform the system and who wants to maintain it illuminates the path to transformation. So, how does contemporary racism manifest? Consider, for example, the vital role that racist nationalism plays in animating negative sentiment toward Black people and Black communities. Considering our nation's history of slavery, segregation, and disenfranchisement, we need to see the reinvention of racist nationalism as the newest technology of ethnic cleansing on the planet. This resurgence can be attributed to a confluence of factors, ranging from economic anxieties to perceptions of cultural homogeneity and power dynamics (Walia, 2021).

A further extension of the narrative about White Americans under threat is that of the culture warrior, where Blacks are often depicted as a corrosive force on traditional or Christian culture; they are dangerous specifically for wanting to change. The worst-case scenario is that the legal system—law enforcement, courts, and policymakers alike—is complicit in and a vehicle of the racist nationalist narratives through its reluctance or inability to confront systemic and institutionalized discrimination and violence, including widespread experiences of physical, psychological, and economic victimization. Also, racist nationalism forms an overlapping part of more extensive conversations about social justice. Black communities face a torrent of long-simmering violence that expresses racialized exclusion built into the advantages of American citizenship. In its official forms, this violence conveys systemic injustices at the very mechanisms of state power.

Critical Race Theory (CRT) helps explain how laws and policies repeatedly fail to end systemic bias and the vicious cycle of oppression and to change lives for the better for Black, Indigenous, and other marginalized communities (Bell, 1995). Although CRT has become a polarizing talking point in mainstream media, it offers a perspective for analyzing the operations of racism as a system and an institution—a creation unavoidably linked to the foundation of the United States. The core principles of CRT are necessary to explain the motivation (or lack thereof) to change legal systems. First, racial disparities in legal systems are not simply the result of individual bias but are the product of structural racism endemic to legal institutions (Bell, 1995; Delgado & Stefancic, 2010). What Bell, Delgado, and Stefancic allege about structural racism, as both the generator and perpetrator of racial disparities, positions their claim as an ambitious motivator of transformative change in the minds of practicing policymakers, practitioners, courts, and other legal system stakeholders. This is because, when understood as mattering morally, the result of systemic issues deeply embedded in legal structures can generate a sense of moral urgency and obligation to effect reforms that correct racial injustices.

Furthering policymakers' cognitive understanding and recognition of how structural racism is a core organizing principle of entrenched disparities in our justice system may indeed be enough to compel them to re-examine existing laws and policies that drive these disparities and to seek out and overturn discriminatory and biased practices. If we can find a way around politics to build consciousness, perhaps it can urge policymakers to focus on initiatives that seek to redress systemic inequalities, like recalibrating sentencing guidelines, ending racial profiling practices, and investing in community-based alternatives to incarceration for nonviolent offenders. For judges, attorneys, and law enforcement officers on the front lines of justice who view or perform a duty to protect, understanding these demands that they examine may counter their own biases through reflexive and ongoing education. It encourages them to exercise more equitable decision-making processes. Courts, which are responsible for adjudicating and administering justice, are encouraged to critically examine how their practices and decisions can either reinforce or dismantle structural racism. It would compel them to adopt and impose procedural fairness and equity principles with respect to their rulings and reconsider laws and procedures that excessively harm marginalized people and communities. It might even inspire creative solutions, such as specialized courts for addressing racial disparities or the establishment of oversight judges to monitor and address the harm caused to those in court by structural racism.

Finally, helping shift how structural racism is perceived in the context of legal systems is more of an agentive ask—it motivates all of us to be collectively accountable in our efforts to build more equitable and just legal systems that accord dignity to all, rather than imagine that addressing structural racism is only the "job" of a few. Nevertheless, reckoning with motivations for transformation in our legal systems will be a hard thing to do since confronting centuries of racial oppression, subjugation, and discrimination is a daunting task. The second barrier to progressive race consciousness is even more insidious than the first—and perhaps more powerful—alleged colorblindness. Alleged colorblindness or race neutrality permeates our legal systems. It sustains what can only be described as a dominant, powerful, and pervasive illusion that our legal systems are already colorblind and race-neutral. The illusory nature of this belief sustains disincentives to transform what, in the minds of some, does not need transforming. This is why reconceiving who we are as a people with relevance to these perpetuated acts of racial injustice is critical.

Differences across attitudes about the law show how differently we consider issues in the United States—such as racial justice. For example, perceptions about racial bias in the law differ across racial demographics. In Kaiser's Survey on Americans on Race, Blacks and Latinos are more likely to perceive systemic discrimination compared to Whites (Kaiser Family Foundation, 2017). These differences show that racism endures and can, in turn, shape our motivations for change. Racially marginalized communities see what discriminatory policing really looks like, for instance, whereas Whites are much more likely to see race-neutral legal systems. The so-called "soft" prejudice across these demographics means that Whites may have less of a reason to advocate for deep reform of the law because they may not believe that it is needed in the first place.

Motivations for legal transformation, Community Development, and individual reckoning must, therefore, all be addressed to compel the multifaceted motivation necessary to make lasting changes to address systemic racism. Acknowledging the intersectionality of these factors and ingrained racial bias enables all groups involved to interrogate systemic racism more effectively by centering the goal of making comprehensive, lasting improvements to our legal and social structures to end the cycle of harm caused by systemic racism. Finally, recognizing the unacknowledged place of bias embedded within law provides the moral motivation for all of us to form a collective will to dismantle systemic racism and replace it with legal reforms committed to the virtue of repair.

Motivation for Justice: Challenges and Opportunities

Identifying the forces contributing to the differential motivations for justice and the underlying racial assumptions, attitudes, and professional motivations driving the current iterations of legal reforms must be exposed. What seems to be at the root of the current pushbacks is the shift in the paradigm of racism to a paradigm of prejudice as the root explanator of the observed racial disparities. This shift obscures the systemic nature of racism and makes conversations about race more fraught. Individuals may feel vulnerable, ashamed, or afraid of being labeled racist when faced with difficult truths. When confronted with the realities of racial inequities this discomfort can intensify. Yet it is precisely because of these emotional tensions that the legal system must adopt a new paradigm, one in which racism is directly acknowledged and actively addressed through meaningful and sustained action.

Rechanneling Motivations Within Legal Institutions

Legal institutions can be slow to embrace transformative change since powerful, persistent motivations can be driven by deeply embedded paradigms and institutional inertia that do not serve justice. This is not a motivational problem in the sense of a lack of will. However, it is a motivational challenge when motivations within legal institutions propel change away from justice and toward reinforcing entrenched systems of race privilege. The type of motivation change needed to make legal systems more responsive to concerns with racial biases and inequities requires deliberate motivational change involving direct recognition and redress of racial biases beginning with a questioning of the implicit race assumptions and attitudes that drive and shape legal reforms.

To re-channel motivations toward legal systems' intents, purposes, and goals, one must consider transparency, accountability, and responsiveness to community needs. Emphasizing Community Development raises the voices of the "silenced" and holds authorities to account in the face of persistent structural harms. Legal systems can begin to adopt practices that give voice to these calls for change and rebuild social trust by thinking about how to orient institutional motivations toward the demands of the communities they are intended to serve. A comprehensive approach to achieving the motivation for justice can be realized through the Community Development model (Robinson, 2005), which can catalyze change. This model emphasizes a holistic and integrative strategy for community engagement and empowerment. The Community Development Model comprises three primary axes: Community Competence, Community Development, and Community Prevention. These axes are interconnected and hold profound implications. The model operates on the guiding principle that communities are intricate entities that transcend groups and individuals. This complexity is rooted in the profound influence of history, culture, context, and geography on a population's consciousness, collective experience, and social boundaries. By leveraging this model, we can better understand and address the multifaceted challenges communities face, ultimately leading to more equitable and just outcomes.

The Community Development Model: Catalyst for Change

Community Competence Understanding the motivations for justice requires recognizing the vital role that Community Competence plays in inspiring action—one that ties the recognition of group capacity with the aspiration to be agents of meaningful social change—which seems especially important. If people see themselves as inherently capable of bringing about change for the common good, they might be more motivated to fight for justice. This aspiration might then turn into a collective will to challenge injustice. This knowledge is critical to motivating those with traditional power to raise their own levels of consciousness beyond those who typically see themselves as going into the field to save "the helpless." It challenges the mainstream belief that marginalized people and communities passively wait to be saved. In reality, they have been saving themselves for centuries, demonstrating resilience and ingenuity in the face of chronic barriers., including poverty, oppression, racism, and exclusion. Recognizing the inherent skills and capacities within these communities highlights that they are not merely recipients of aid but active participants in creating solutions. Acknowledging and supporting what they bring to the table allow those with more traditional power to perform their own functions in society better.

Community Development Building upon the foundation of Community Competence, the next axis of the Community Development Model is Community Development itself. This axis focuses on further empowering communities by enhancing their capacity and infrastructure and strengthening their social capital. This axis emphasizes the importance of creating a robust structural framework that supports community advancement and encourages collective action. Community Development focuses on two essential pillars: capacity and infrastructure and social capital. Capacity and infrastructure encompass diverse elements crucial for community advancement, including research and researchers, programs and services, leaders, organizations, and networks. These components are fundamental in building the structural foundation for communities to address systemic challenges effectively and sustainably.

Robust capacity and infrastructure in communities can enable them to have more energy for work on large-scale social change. This works because it helps communities recognize and mobilize assets and strengths and builds their agency and shared sense that they can move mountains. Communities see it works when they can claim and advance other goods. When residents feel their surroundings have improved and well-anchored networks and organizations support their work, they can be further encouraged to continue the fight for justice. Recognizing and embracing what those who are usually considered powerless to society bring to the table allow those with more traditional power to do their job better because they can relate to a broader range of people in a more equitable partnership when they work together to improve the systemic problems that burden society and benefit everyone involved—especially those with less societal privilege. Such a change can help stimulate real community building, ensuring that work toward justice and liberation is sustainable and participatory. This allows legislators, judges, law enforcement personnel, and academics, to name a few, to feel invested in and responsible for the work.

Community Prevention While Community Competence promotes individual and community power, and Community Development builds structural support, Community Prevention emphasizes proactive measures in preventing further harm and promoting positive social change. Community Prevention aims to dismantle and reverse cycles of oppression through intentional interventions and efforts at the community level. Through this approach, we can make systemic changes that build capacity, resilience, and equity and justice, so that oppressive histories are not simply reproduced. That is, framing justice in preventative terms helps us think about what motivates people to act in the name of collective justice first and then how to keep that energy going. Leveraging this momentum often occurs because social problems stem from distinctive structural constraints that are acknowledged and partly assuaged when justice is delivered. In other words, framing justice this way is not merely about easing current symptoms but building our capacity to address—and rectify—systemic injustices. This leads to a more sustainable form of justice. While no one approach to justice is entirely adequate, all justice is not created equal.

Conclusion

While no single justice strategy is adequately comprehensive, the truth that all justice is not created equal clearly delineates why justice requires layered approaches like those of the Community Development Model. The model increases the sense of social identity, self-efficacy, and empowerment, leading to community resiliency and the capacity to take action and make change endure. Community Competence focuses on the strengths and capacities of marginalized people; Community Development develops the structural supports of the community to enable that same agency; and Community Prevention goes to the core—the root causes that bring about systemic injustices. Interventions are responsive, culturally attuned, and relevant to community needs and challenges.

Working toward justice means working together to confront the conditions for injustice—individually and as a collective. Justice is context-specific. It is applied according to the experiences, organizations, and notions of righteousness embedded within each context. Acknowledging the variety of the model's axes and the plurality of each axis helps to keep the collective will alive. All communities have multiple routes to justice. Recognizing the multiplicity of the motivations for justice and the reality that there are different ways of imagining justice will encourage and sustain the collective will to realize a just world.

In other words, it takes understanding what drives justice to see that even if you cannot "have it all," community competence, development, and prevention can all be components of reweaving that "fierce and tangled cloth" of a more just world. When justice is perceived as a journey with multiple pathways rather than a destination reached through a singular practice or a systemic approach versus an individual cure, it becomes possible to see the profound connections among the diverse branches of justice. On the other hand, if justice remains an isolated beacon, it cannot become widely accessible and meaningful for those living in the darkness.

References

Bell, D. A. (1995). Who's afraid of critical race theory. *University of Illinois Law Review, 4*(3), 823–846.

Delgado, R., & Stefancic, J. (2010). *Critical race theory: An introduction* (Vol. 87). NYU press.

Kaiser Family Foundation. (2017). Survey of Americans on race. Retrieved from https://www.kff.org/other/report/survey-of-americans-on-race/

Manza, J., & Uggen, C. (2006). *Locked out: Felon disenfranchisement and American democracy*. Oxford University Press.

Robinson, R. G. (2005). Community development model for public health applications: Overview of a model to eliminate population disparities. *Health Promotion Practice, 6*(3), 338–346.

Walia, H. (2021). *Border and rule: Global migration, capitalism, and the rise of racist nationalism*. Haymarket Books.

Police Discretion as a Vulnerability Factor for Disparate Treatment

Jack Glaser

Introduction

The police killings of unarmed Black people that have sparked protest in America are just the visible tip of the proverbial iceberg of a much broader problem—the thousands of daily indignities of superfluous pedestrian and vehicle stops, detentions, searches, use of force, citations, and arrests for low-level offenses that are disproportionately borne by people of color, primarily young, Black men. Public awakening to the direness of the problem has no doubt been spurred largely by the unprecedented availability of video evidence, facilitated by the fact that virtually everyone is carrying an easily activated, high-resolution recording device at all times. But the phenomenon of excessive enforcement and force by police has long been known to Black and Brown Americans. In fact, policing emerged from inherently racially oppressive institutions like slave patrols and rangers enforcing ethnic boundaries (Brucato, 2023; Graybill, 2007; Reichel, 1988), which then was used through the post-reconstruction and Jim Crow eras to suppress the emergence of minority rights and opportunities (Alexander, 2011).

The kinds of police–civilian encounters that tend to be racially disproportionate, primarily pretextual stops aimed at drug and weapon offenses, are overwhelmingly fruitless (i.e., only rarely lead to discovery of evidence of crime; Charbonneau & Glaser, 2020). Even considering encounters justified ex post by a serious drug or weapon discovery and/or arrest, the disproportionate policing of some groups will lead to rates of punishment that are disproportionate to the rates of offending

J. Glaser (✉)
UC Berkeley, Berkeley, CA, USA
e-mail: jackglaser@berkeley.edu

R. L. Wiener, D. J. Hansen (eds.), *Legal Judgment and the Motivation for Justice*, Nebraska Symposium on Motivation 71,
https://doi.org/10.1007/978-3-031-98812-7_3

(Glaser, 2006; Harcourt, 2000). The direct harms of unnecessary police contact—disruption, stress, stigma, not to mention the monetary and opportunity costs of citations or warnings—are substantial, but there are also profound collateral consequences of disproportionate sanctions. In 2003, the Bureau of Justice Statistics projected that of men in the U.S. born that year, while 5.9% of Whites would be incarcerated at some point in their lives, the rates for Hispanics and Blacks would be 17.2% and 32.2%, respectively (Bonczar, 2003). These disparities are stark, but more devastating is the simple notion that nearly one-third of the males in a group or community would experience imprisonment. When one considers the collateral consequences of incarceration to those individuals, and to their families and communities (e.g., disruption of family systems, legal expenses, voter disenfranchisement, loss of wages, and barriers to future employment), it is all the more troubling. Even prison disease prevalence can spread to broader communities (Johnson & Raphael, 2009).

Incarceration trends and the racial disparities in them have declined since 2003 (Sabol et al., 2020), due at least in part to decriminalization of marijuana and substantial decarceration efforts. The rates of police contact for racial and ethnic minorities, however, remain high and untenable, and the evidence is overwhelming that racially disparate treatment is contributing to racially disparate outcomes (Glaser, 2015; Pierson et al., 2020). These persistent and harmful disparities result in part from biases held, implicitly or not, by individual actors in many domains—police, prosecutors (and even defense attorneys), judges, jurors, probation and parole officers, but also school teachers and administrators, and civilians who report crimes. Here, I will focus solely on one, albeit an objectively central and important subset of these actors, the police. This should not be taken to imply that it is sufficient to focus solely on police to solve the larger problem. To the contrary, I believe that the individual and systemic contributors to the problem of inequitable criminalization are mutually reinforcing and will require broad-based change to break the cycle. At the same time, because racially and ethnically disparate policing undermines minority communities' opportunities while feeding negative stereotypes by distorting crime statistics, broader systemic efforts to improve equity may be in vain without changing how police use their discretion.

In what follows, I will first describe the highly discretionary nature of policing that results from a number of causes, including the vagueness of the relevant laws and the permissiveness of their application, the variability and arbitrariness in training, and the very nature of a job, like many others, that requires the application of rules and procedures by individuals in a complex environment. Then I will turn to a discussion of the causes of racial disparities in policing, focusing in particular on discretion. In turn, I will consider how discretion functions as a cause of disparities before considering promising avenues for reducing racial disparities, emphasizing strategies for effectually reducing discretion.

Discretion in Policing

Policing experts have long understood that police in America have wide discretion in how they carry out their duties (Goldstein, 1960). A major factor in the high discretion that police officers have in how and when they act is the vagueness of the relevant laws and standards, particularly the *reasonable suspicion* standard. Charbonneau and Glaser (2020) and others (e.g., Friedman, 2017) have covered the evolution of the reasonable suspicion standard and its application as the standard for whom officers can detain and conduct limited searches on. The relatively higher standard of *probable cause*, generally required for more intrusive searches as well as arrests, is also similarly vague. By way of illustrating the inherent vagueness of these standards, consider that U.S. courts have studiously avoided providing formal definitions, let alone calculable guidelines of the probabilities of criminal offense they should reflect. Reasonable suspicion is merely defined as more than an *inarticulable hunch* and less than a probable cause. Probable cause, accordingly, is defined as more than reasonable suspicion but less than the *preponderance of evidence*, which is the standard for civil suits and has the advantage of being quantifiable as "more likely than not" (i.e., greater than 50% chance). To make matters worse, reasonable suspicion is sometimes defined, tautologically, as what a reasonable officer would deem suspicious. Even the most consequential and authoritative stakeholders report widely varying beliefs about what reasonable suspicion is. A survey of American federal judges asking them what the chances should be that a determination of reasonable suspicion reflects actual criminal behavior yielded a wide range of responses, from 0 to 100%, with the modal (49 out of 164 respondents) response being 30% (McCauliff, 1982).

While, unlike *preponderance of evidence* or *beyond a reasonable doubt*, reasonable suspicion is not used as a standard for judges or juries in deciding court cases, it is the standard that judges consider as justifying a detention or search by police, and if that standard is deemed to not have been met, evidence resulting would be excluded. Instances where detentions or searches occur in the absence (by some theoretical, future judges' reckoning) of reasonable suspicion, and no evidence is found and/or no arrest is made, become instantaneously moot (they will not be subject to judicial review).[1] Instances in which a detention or search results in a finding of evidence of crime (e.g., possession of an illicit substance, weapon, or stolen property) will have the hindsight advantage of proof. In the absence of documentary evidence of the lack of basis for reasonable suspicion (something potentially more demonstrable in the era of body-worn cameras, if they are reliably activated), these instances, which are the ones that really matter to police officers, their supervisors,

[1] An important but exceedingly rare exception is when civil action is taken and the court is persuaded that there is a persistent pattern of unconstitutional practices (e.g., Floyd, et al. v. City of New York, et al., 959 F. Supp. 2d 540 (S.D.N.Y. 2013).

and prosecutors, will be difficult to deem unjustified.[2] It stands to reason that police officers would know that this is the implication of the reasonable suspicion standard—the calibration is vague and subject to interpretation, and the stakes for violating it are relatively low.

Compounding (and possibly also resulting from) the inherent problem of the vagueness of the reasonable suspicion standard, police departments vary widely in the specificity of their policies on stops and searches, the rigor of their training, and the incentives and priorities they set with respect to avoiding unreasonable searches and seizures. Policing in the U.S. is highly decentralized, with the roughly 18,000 departments each having its own set of rules and training regimens, although there is some standardization resulting from shared resources departments can opt into, such as those coming from California's Commission on Peace Officer Standards and Training. In our reviews of the duty manuals of multiple metropolitan police departments around the U.S. for the Center for Policing Equity, my colleagues and I found substantial variation in the substance and extent of policy language related to reasonable suspicion (see six city reports by Broadus et al., 2019, as cited in Charbonneau & Glaser, 2020). As an example, one department stated simply that "An officer may conduct field interviews or stops when he reasonably believes that some investigative inquiry is warranted," while another provided a more fulsome explanation, explicitly affirming the importance of equitable treatment:

> A. The [department] is committed to unbiased policing and to reinforcing procedures that ensure that police service and law enforcement is provided in a fair and equitable manner to all. B. No person shall be singled out or treated differently as a consequence of his/her race, ethnicity, national origin, gender, sexual orientation or religion. C. Except as provided below, officers shall not consider race, ethnicity, national origin, gender, sexual orientation or religion in establishing either reasonable suspicion or probable cause…

The considerable variability in the content and emphases in departmental guidance on a critical standard in policing, reasonable suspicion, both reveal and promote the high degree of discretion that officers have in their daily activities on the job.

Structural- and Individual-Level Causes of Disparities

Although the primary focus of this chapter is on how individual-level biases, particularly stereotypes associating minorities with crime, in the minds of officers give rise to disparities in law enforcement, it is important to recognize that these disparities result from both individual-level and structural factors, which can be mutually reinforcing. The structural factors include long-standing historical inequities, not

[2] There is, of course, an extensive literature and famous case law on the "exclusionary rule," and many examples of discovered evidence that was deemed inadmissible because the search, seizure, and/or arrest was judged to be unconstitutional (e.g., Mapp v. Ohio, 367 U.S. 643 (1961)), but these instances are likely the exceptions that arise under relatively glaring circumstances and when rigorous legal defense is available.

the least of which being the legacies of slavery, Jim Crow, redlining, and the exploitation of migrant workers, that have been profoundly detrimental to the economic and educational aspirations of non-Whites. With respect to policing, beyond its historical origins in the inherently racially oppressive purpose of slave patrols, contemporary policing imposes structural inequities by, for example, prioritizing certain crime categories (e.g., open air drug dealing and use) and disproportionately deploying personnel to areas with large minority populations.

Compounding these structural factors are individual-level processes that cause disparate treatment in discrete events. These include the biases that individuals, including police officers, possess as a result of living in a cultural environment that is rife with stereotypes associating minorities, particularly Black men, with crime and violence. While these biases are widespread, their strength and salience vary from person to person. In addition to these attitudinal factors, police no doubt vary in terms of their personality types in ways that affect their performance (e.g., Swencionis et al., 2021), and there is evidence that they differ systematically from the general population on some relevant personality dimensions, such as being lower in openness to experience (TenEyck, 2024).

The importance of these individual differences above and beyond the structural inequities that put people of color at a disadvantage with respect to police lies in the many "opportunities" for bias to influence police judgment and behavior. On a continuous basis, officers on patrol face decision points, including where to patrol, who to surveil, who to stop, whether to question those stopped for investigative purposes, how long to question, whether to pat down, search, or order travelers out of a vehicle, whether to use force, and how much, and whether to cite or arrest. Each of these decision points offers an opportunity for bias to be influential. Is that neighborhood problematic? Is that person suspicious? Does he belong here? Is he hiding something? Is he on probation or parole (an automatic basis for search)? Is he a physical threat to me? Is he being disrespectful to me? Will he do this again if I don't cite/arrest him? Each of these questions and the judgments and actions they eventuate have the potential to be influenced by group-based bias. While a general tendency of an officer to avoid bias should attenuate the risk of discrimination at each point and therefore cumulatively, a tendency toward bias (compounded by confirmation bias) will tend to have a cumulative effect—"He looks like he doesn't belong here, and he's suspicious, and I think he's hiding something…".

It is important to note at this juncture that patrol officers on duty are often responding to calls for service (or conducting "radio runs") in response to specific reported incidents of crime or other threats to public safety. These activities are less vulnerable to the effects of intergroup bias, except to the extent that the complainant and/or dispatcher imposes a bias. Calls for service are inherently less discretionary (although there are ample opportunities for discretion in *how* to respond) than traffic and pedestrian stops. Furthermore, within traffic and (to a lesser extent) pedestrian stops, there are those that primarily serve the purpose of promoting public safety (e.g., for excessive speeding in a school zone, running a red light, or reckless driving) and, in contrast, those that appear to primarily serve an ulterior, investigative purpose. These latter, "pretext" stops may target minor infractions like equipment violations (e.g., the classic broken tail light or non-illuminated license plate stop) or minor moving violations relating to marginally unsafe behavior (e.g., rolling stops, lane drifting, and jaywalking)—the kinds of things that a few minutes of observation would reveal in most drivers or pedestrians. The minor equipment violation pretext provides an illustration of the nexus of structural- and individual-level biases, where the economic deprivation legacy of centuries of de facto and de jure discrimination makes owning and maintaining a reasonably new vehicle less feasible for the average minority American, rendering them more susceptible to bias-based decisions at the discretion of individual officers.

It is further useful to distinguish pretext stops, which are, by definition, stops predicated on a code violation that are actually for the purpose of investigating other crime, from stops and detentions associated with reported crime. The pretext (i.e., the violation the stop is legally attributed to) is just an excuse to open the door (sometimes literally) for questioning, a look inside a vehicle and/or a pat down, a supervision (probation or parole) status check, and even possibly a detention until a drug-sniffing canine can be brought on site. In contrast, officers may stop someone because they and/or their vehicle matches a description associated with a specific, reported crime. In this case, a pretext is not necessary to justify the stop or detention. Furthermore, in the latter case, race or ethnicity may be used as a basis, to the extent that *other characteristics* help to identify the suspect. In contrast, race being used as a basis for suspicion in the absence of a suspect description is racial profiling. That said, while most constitutional scholars believe this to be unconstitutional, the U.S. Supreme Court has been decidedly indifferent (see, specifically, Whren v. United States, 517 U.S. 806 (1996), and, generally, Glaser, 2015, for further discussion).

What Is Discretion?

The pretext stop is the ultimate discretionary stop. By virtue of being based on a *pretext*, it is a stop that would not happen but for the ulterior, investigatory purpose it ultimately serves, to lead to a search in the hopes of finding evidence of more serious crime (e.g., possession of drugs, weapons, or stolen property). In our analyses, Charbonneau and Glaser (2020) have found, across a range of large and disparate law enforcement agencies, that the more discretion officers have to stop and search, the greater the racial disparities in the outcomes of those searches. For example, in California, where all police departments are now required to report standardized data on stops to the State, relatively high-discretion searches (e.g., consent searches) show considerably higher rates of contraband discovery among Whites searched than Blacks and Latinos, while low-discretion searches (e.g., those conducted upon arrest) show comparable rates. Search discovery rates are a compelling indicator of bias—higher rates indicating that those searched tend to require exhibiting a higher level of suspiciousness. We see a similar pattern in the results of U.S. Customs searches when comparing contraband discovery rates before and after a policy change that dramatically reduced the number and increased the quality of search criteria (see, originally, Ramirez et al., 2003). Furthermore, there was also an equalization of search discovery rates for Blacks and Whites in New York City after pedestrian stops under the Stop, Question, and Frisk program plummeted.

The stark evidence of racial bias in high-discretion stops and searches raises an important question: Why does discretion give rise to disparate treatment? Before we answer this, we should ask, what is discretion? Oxford Languages online dictionary (2023) defines discretion as "The freedom to decide what should be done in a particular situation." It is a confusing term, with another, almost contradictory definition: "the quality of behaving or speaking in such a way as to avoid causing offense or revealing private information" (Oxford Languages, 2023), as in "being discreet." These definitions are not unrelated; if you use your discretion carefully, you will probably be discreet. But it is the former definition that is of interest here with respect to policing. Merriam-Webster's Online dictionary (2023) offers a somewhat different set of definitions: "individual choice or judgment" and "power of free decision or latitude of choice within certain legal bounds." Interestingly, Webster's references "legal bounds," perhaps reflecting a natural conceptual connection between discretion and the legitimate exercise of authority.

Discretion is not a well-studied psychological phenomenon, but considerable consideration has been given to it in Law and Public Administration. Some criminal legal scholars have traced the application of the concept of discretion to policing to an obscure 1954 progress report on an American Bar Foundation survey (Sherry, 1954), but surely the link is as old as the profession. Underlying the notion of discretion generally is the understanding that in the exercise of any kind of human agency, there is room for judgment. Evans and Peter (2020) trace philosophical notions of discretion back many centuries: "Montaigne, writing in the late sixteenth century, draws on the classical idea of discretion as judgement and anticipates the predominant modern idea of discretion as the freedom to act on judgement." (p. 3). To the extent that someone is vested with authority to carry out acts that require some degree of judgment, discretion is unavoidable. In policing in particular, given that there are a vast number of laws that can be enforced, police must choose which to prioritize and how to enforce them (J. Goldstein, 1960). In patrol policing alone, which is the intended focus of this discussion, officers have numerous laws to enforce, including the many vehicle and traffic codes, low-level offenses like loitering, public nuisance, or littering, as well as investigatory actions like identifying drug traders or thieves. *Full enforcement* (i.e., enforcing all laws all the time) would be impossible, irrespective of the size of the police force, and so it is a matter of officers, often with the guidance of their superiors, deciding which to prioritize (H. Goldstein, 1963). This necessitates making choices and, in fact, knowingly ignoring some offenses. To be more concrete, police often observe minor traffic infractions like speeding or jaywalking without taking enforcement action. But officers also have considerable discretion, even for high-priority crimes, in where they enforce and whom they surveil, stop, question, search, and arrest, including the discretion to issue a citation or make an arrest, or not, even when legally justified.

How Does Discretion Promote Disparate Treatment?

While Psychology may not have much to offer yet specifically on the topic of discretion, it has produced many decades of theory, research, and fundamental insights on relevant constructs and phenomena. Perhaps most relevant is the process of decision-making under uncertainty. This is, in fact, one of Psychology's most celebrated topics. Tversky and Kahneman's (1974) extraordinarily influential paper spawned a field of research that spanned disciplines and turned the field of Economics on its head, identifying a host of biases and heuristics, from confirmation bias to hindsight bias, that plague the economic "rational actor." Fundamental to the issue of decision-making under uncertainty is the emphasis on uncertainty. When decision criteria and evidence are unambiguous, most people make reasonably unbiased (i.e., rational and accurate) decisions. But much of the time, because of incomplete information, people use mental shortcuts to fill in the gaps. In the case of policing, if an officer directly observes someone in possession of an illicit object like a weapon (depending on the jurisdiction), the officer can detain the individual and get more information about the circumstances. On the other hand, if an officer is hoping to find people in possession of illicit weapons, the officer may not wish to wait for direct observation to occur. If taking weapons off the streets is a departmental or unit (or, for that matter, personal) priority, the officer may resort to exercising his or her discretion to conduct pretext stops and find reasons to search (or ask for consent to search, if there is no arguable reasonable suspicion or probable cause basis). In these cases, the objects of judgment are necessarily more ambiguous—the putative weapon is not visible, and an implicit probabilistic estimate is being made by the officer of the likelihood that the individual is in possession of something illicit. This is merely an inference, which involves some informal mental calculus and, probably, an internal subjective (and no doubt variable) threshold that the estimated likelihood of possession has to exceed to make the officer inclined to stop or search. We know from large and diverse sets of police stops that most of these searches (let alone the stops that necessarily precede them) prove fruitless (Pierson et al., 2020), indicating that the evidence is indeed ambiguous and generally non-probative. Furthermore, we know that among these searches, those conducted using higher discretion (e.g., consent searches) are more likely to have racially disparate discovery rates (Charbonneau & Glaser, 2020), indicating that they are indeed skewed by biases and heuristics.

High discretion stops and searches (i.e., those that are least clearly necessitated by the observed behavior and applicable laws) are more likely to occur under ambiguous circumstances—when the subject's appearance and behavior only *suggest* criminal offending. This reveals a reciprocal relationship between discretion and ambiguity: The more ambiguous the situation, the wider the discretion that needs to be asserted if the officer wishes to search; and the more discretion an officer (or any decision-maker) has to investigate, the greater the number of relatively ambiguous events that will fall within their set of activities. All else being equal, if officers are including more stops with ambiguous cues in their searches, the modal search will be more ambiguous (not to mention less fruitful). Perhaps more important than the modal event are the events in the right tail of the distribution of stops and searches, the ones that would not occur at all under low discretion. At this point, it is important to pause and reflect on the fact that most (if not all) of the fruitless searches reflect unnecessary intrusions on civilian's liberties.[3]

As my colleagues and I have argued elsewhere (Spencer et al., 2016), biases like stereotypes are more influential under uncertain and ambiguous conditions. In the absence of certainty, people will, mostly without conscious awareness or intent, apply cognitive schemas like racial and gender stereotypes to disambiguate what they observe. Studies of stereotype application show, for example, that when an actor's behavior is ambiguous with respect to whether it is playful or aggressive, race of the actor will cause observers to rate the identical behavior differently (e.g., Duncan, 1976; Sagar & Schofield, 1980). Stereotypes linking minorities, particularly young, Black men, with crime are persistent and pervasive (Devine & Elliot, 1995). Several important social psychological studies have demonstrated quite directly how race–crime stereotypes cause people, including, in some of these studies, police officers, to be faster and more likely to perceive ambiguous objects as weapons or otherwise crime-related when in the context of Black men relative to White men (Correll et al., 2007; Eberhardt et al., 2004; Plant & Peruche, 2005). In fact, Knowles and I (Glaser & Knowles, 2008) found that "shooter bias" (i.e., the tendency in a simulation to issue a "shoot" response relative to a "don't shoot" response for Black relative to White male targets) demonstrated by Correll et al. (2002, 2007) was associated with an implicit race–weapons stereotype.

Surveys and experiments like those referenced above reveal that police officers, like most Americans, hold and are affected by race–crime stereotypes. Administrative data reveals that, not coincidentally, police officers also tend to disproportionately stop and search Black people even though those searches tend to have very low rates of contraband discovery. This indicates that the officers are exercising considerable discretion (stopping and searching people who, overwhelmingly, are not offending) under conditions of ambiguity. We also know that searches of Black people tend to be *less* likely than searches of Whites to yield evidence of crime and that this is especially true when stops and searches are more discretionary (as opposed to that necessitated by policy). The evidence is clear that police in many locales are using considerable discretion in a racially disproportionate manner that is almost certain to cause racial disparities in criminal justice outcomes, probably compounded as people move through the system.

[3] Some might argue that there is deterrent value to fruitless searches, and this is a debatable assertion, but with respect to discretion causing disparities, deterrence is most likely an orthogonal consideration. For that matter, Gerstein and Prescott (2014) point out that there are "process costs" (i.e., low level offenses nonetheless resulting in detention, plea deals, etc.) of high discretion policing.

What Can Be Done About Disparities Resulting from Excess Discretion?

The disparate treatment that results from the influence of racial bias when conditions are ambiguous and discretion is high surely explains only a part of a systemic problem stemming from a history of centuries of racial oppression and a government that continues to fail to be representative of the population it governs. Profound systemic change may be necessary to fully address the larger problem. Nevertheless, the clarity of the evidence with respect to the confluence of individual-level bias and discretion in causing pronounced, immediate racial disparities in criminal justice implicates an imperative to reduce these harms while more systemic change is considered.

One important dimension of the challenge of overcoming individual-level bias is that one does not need to endorse (i.e., believe) a stereotype in order for it to influence one's judgments. This was an early lesson of Devine's (1989) influential thesis, and it has been borne out in recent research on bias in police decision-making, where Correll et al. (2002) found that shooter bias was correlated with research participants' knowledge of the cultural "Black-aggression" stereotype but not their self-reported belief in the stereotype (see also Devine & Elliot, 1995, for consideration of the split between knowledge and endorsement). As a consequence, merely *lacking the intent* to discriminate will not be sufficient to impede the activation and application of stereotypes. Rather, an *affirmative intent to control* those biases (or at least disrupt their impact) may be necessary, although not likely sufficient. Following her early recognition of the automaticity of stereotyping and prejudice and the subsequent explosion of research demonstrating that biases operate, for the most part, outside of conscious awareness and control (Banaji & Greenwald, 2016), Devine has been a leader in the pursuit of understanding the *motivation to control prejudice* (Devine et al., 2002; Plant & Devine, 1998; see also Dunton & Fazio, 1997; Fazio et al., 1995).

Devine et al. (2002) have found that questionnaire-measured motivation to control prejudice, particularly intrinsic motivation, is associated with weaker implicit bias, and Fazio et al. (1995) have similarly found that motivation to respond without prejudice moderates the relation between implicit bias and explicit bias. Recognizing that, because they operate largely outside of our conscious awareness or control, the effects of implicit biases will typically elude conscious efforts to control them, my colleagues and I have explored the possibility of *implicit* motivation to control prejudice (IMCP) (Glaser & Knowles, 2008; Park et al., 2008; see also Moskowitz et al., 1999), finding that those relatively high in IMCP exhibited a weaker relationship between an implicit Black–weapons association and shooter bias. This, of course, suggests that even the most well-meaning and good-intentioned efforts at conscious bias control will not be sufficient to limit the effects of implicit bias in judgments under uncertainty.

Nonetheless, recognizing that unwarranted racial disparities persist in policing, and perhaps especially motivated by public outcry over police killings of unarmed

Black people, policing leaders have sought strategies to address the problem and have largely turned to trainings, in particular, "implicit bias trainings." Evidence to date, supported by the science on implicit bias, indicates that such lecture-based, short-term trainings are not effective in reducing disparate treatment by police in the field (Lai & Lisnek, 2023; Worden et al., 2020; see Glaser, 2024), as is generally the case for trainings across industries (Paluck et al., 2021).

Building toward his work on motivation to control prejudice, Fazio (1990) had put forward the MODE model of attitude–behavior consistency, arguing that Motivation and Opportunity serve as Determinants of whether our behaviors match our attitudes (assuming that we want them to). To reconcile that many of our implicit stereotypes are at odds with our values (e.g., of nondiscrimination), Fazio and colleagues, like Devine and her colleagues, worked to specifically address the motivation to control prejudiced responses. As Fazio's earlier work on automatic attitude activation (Fazio et al., 1986), building on the work of cognitive psychologists in regard to implicit and automatic memory (e.g., Neely, 1977), had shown, people can override the influence of mental constructs, such as attitudes, but only if they have enough time to do so. In the absence of opportunity and motivation, implicit attitudes will influence behavior.

In the domain of the effect of implicit biases on discriminatory behavior, we might add *strategy* as a determinant, meaning that even if one is motivated and has the time and cognitive bandwidth to try to override the effect of an implicit bias on a judgment or action, without having a way to correct the judgment or action, the bias will still be influential. Furthermore, the motivation will need to be chronic, meaning that it will have to be active at all times (Moskowitz et al., 1999). We may be able to increase motivation to control prejudice by telling people about its pervasiveness and harms, but, even if we assume that motivation lasts more than a few days after training, without opportunity and strategy, the motivation is not sufficient. In policing, this would require that, while officers are on patrol and interacting with civilians, they are consistently motivated to make judgments (about suspicion) in an unbiased manner, and that they possess effective strategies for doing that, and have sufficient time without distraction, to override the biases. This is, in theory, not impossible, but it is a tall order. Robust, systematic tests of strategies to temporarily mute or override implicit bias have shown only some of the strategies to only partially work and for the control to be fleeting (Lai et al., 2014, 2016).

Given the high degree of discretion that officers have, and that it engenders decision-making under ambiguity and uncertainty, which is vulnerable to bias, effective remediation is imperative. Until scalable training methods can be developed that meaningfully, consistently, and lastingly reduce the impact of bias on policing decisions, structural reforms to reduce discretion are necessary to at least reduce the pervasive harms, from disparate stops and searches to lethal force. As discussed above, when discretion is constrained in policing, racial disparities markedly decline (Charbonneau & Glaser, 2020). One obvious approach, therefore, is to simply restrict high discretion activities. This is, in fact, happening at the policy level as cities, including Los Angeles, place limits on officers' powers to make pretext stops (Jany & Poston, 2022). Because U.S. Supreme Court precedent effectively allows pretextual stops (Whren v. US, 1996), these rule changes have generally been designed to, rather than fully prohibit pretext stops, constrain them through administrative (e.g., reporting) requirements, what Eberhardt and colleagues call "friction" (e.g., Hetey et al., 2024).

Another method to reduce discretion is to displace it with specific, probative information. In studies of employment discrimination, economists have found that employers who conduct criminal background checks are more likely to hire Black applicants than are those who do not (Holzer et al., 2006), suggesting that, in the absence of the specific information, the employers use their discretion to make stereotype-based assumptions about criminality (or, perhaps, trustworthiness, more nebulously). Similarly, Wozniak (2015) found that the passage of legislation facilitating employee drug testing was followed by higher rates of Black employment and wages. Again, in the absence of specific information, people are more likely to rely on stereotypes.

Related to the notion of increasing information is to provide formality and structure to the decision-making process. This can take the form of checklists, as has proven highly effective in reducing medical errors, for example (Gawande, 2011). The implementation of a short, simple checklist routine for officers prior to making a stop or search, including items such as "Can I identify a specific behavior that is related to crime?" and "Would I suspect this person if s/he were White?" could move officers away from a reliance on vague hunches toward concrete criteria.

Similarly, providing officers with a smaller number of more reliable indicators of criminality would reduce the number of unnecessary stops. This is what was evidenced in the U.S. Customs case, where a reduction in search criteria from 43 to 6 reduced the search rate roughly 75% while quadrupling the search discovery rate and nearly eliminating a large ethnic disparity in search yield rates. Goel et al. (2016) have shown that NYPD stops for suspected criminal possession of a weapon are largely unfruitful but that stops based on a small subset of criteria could be far more efficient.

Short of reducing discretion, changing incentives to move officers away from high discretion actions could have an indirect effect. For example, rather than encouraging officers to make a lot of stops to demonstrate productivity, department commanders could focus on downstream effects such as crime rates and community relations. However, one of the unintended consequences of police stop data collection requirements is that the stop reports can become the measure of productivity at least as much as the measure of fairness. To the extent that officers and/or their supervisors are operating under the assumption that high rates of stops serve a deterrent effect on criminal offending, prioritizing crime reduction may not be an effective way to dissuade high discretion stops and searches.

Because in some departments officers are, even if only tacitly, rewarded for making (and reporting) a lot of stops as a measure of productivity, emphasis on quality over quantity could reduce the number of high-discretion stops and searches. Operationally, this would involve supervisors monitoring the *rate* at which contraband is discovered *among* stops, rather than the number of stops or even the total number of discoveries (which can be made high through a large number of stops even if the discovery rate is low). Great care would need to be taken to ensure that officers were reliably reporting all stops, given that a high discovery rate could be presented by deceptively lowering the denominator—the total number of stops.

These are all relatively near-term strategies to reduce harm. I would be remiss not to include that long-term strategies are still necessary, not the least of which would be to leverage the vast empirical knowledge base on the bias-reducing effects of intergroup contact (Pettigrew & Tropp, 2006) to optimize diversification and meaningful integration of police departments to lastingly reduce bias. This is a major undertaking that may need to unfold over multiple generations but holds great promise for real, lasting change.

Conclusion

The focus of this chapter has been on discretion in policing, and the causal theory most heavily relied upon is a social cognitive one—that decision-making under uncertainty is vulnerable to biases such as racial stereotypes. Surely, this only explains a slice of the large disparities we see in criminal justice as in so many other domains of modern society. It should not be taken to imply that this is the largest, let alone the sole cause of the problem. Given the markedly racist history of policing in America, from slave patrols to Jim Crow, the war on drugs, and present-day racial profiling, it is important to acknowledge the likelihood that a persistent culture of racism is still operative and must be confronted and dismantled in order to approach (if not achieve) truly just criminal justice. In the meantime, and perhaps in an effort to soften the structural barriers to lasting change, a harm reduction approach—reducing disparities and their downstream effects by constraining discretion—holds promise for progress.

References

Alexander, M. (2011). *The new Jim Crow: Mass incarceration in the age of colorblindness*. The New Press.

Banaji, M. R., & Greenwald, A. G. (2016). *Blindspot: Hidden biases of good people*. Bantam Books.

Bonczar, T. P. (2003). *Prevalence of imprisonment in the U.S. population, 1974–2001 (NCJ 197976)*. Bureau of Justice Statistics, U.S. Department of Justice.

Brucato, B. (2023). *Race and police: The origin of our peculiar institutions*. Rutgers University Press.

Charbonneau, A., & Glaser, J. (2020). Suspicion and discretion in policing: How laws and policies contribute to inequity. *UC Irvine Law Review, 11*(5), 1327–1349. Retrieved from https://escholarship.org/uc/item/63m1s5h6

Correll, J., Park, B., Judd, C. M., & Wittenbrink, B. (2002). The police officer's dilemma: Using ethnicity to disambiguate potentially threatening individuals. *Journal of Personality and Social Psychology, 83*(6), 1314–1329. https://doi.org/10.1037/0022-3514.83.6.1314

Correll, J., Park, B., Judd, C. M., Wittenbrink, B., Sadler, M. S., & Keesee, T. (2007). Across the thin blue line: Police officers and racial bias in the decision to shoot. *Journal of Personality and Social Psychology, 92*(6), 1006–1023. https://doi.org/10.1037/0022-3514.92.6.1006
Devine, P. G. (1989). Stereotypes and prejudice: Their automatic and controlled components. *Journal of Personality and Social Psychology, 56*(1), 5–18. https://doi.org/10.1037/0022-3514.56.1.5
Devine, P. G., & Elliot, A. J. (1995). Are racial stereotypes really fading? The Princeton trilogy revisited. *Personality and Social Psychology Bulletin, 21*(11), 1139–1150. https://doi.org/10.1177/01461672952111002
Devine, P. G., Plant, E. A., Amodio, D. M., Harmon-Jones, E., & Vance, S. L. (2002). The regulation of explicit and implicit race bias: The role of motivations to respond without prejudice. *Journal of Personality and Social Psychology, 82*(5), 835–848. https://doi.org/10.1037/0022-3514.82.5.835
Duncan, B. L. (1976). Differential social perception and attribution of intergroup violence: Testing the lower limits of stereotyping of blacks. *Journal of Personality and Social Psychology, 34*(4), 590–598. https://doi.org/10.1037/0022-3514.34.4.590
Dunton, B. C., & Fazio, R. H. (1997). An individual difference measure of motivation to control prejudiced reactions. *Personality and Social Psychology Bulletin, 23*(3), 316–326. https://doi.org/10.1177/0146167297233009
Eberhardt, J. L., Goff, P. A., Purdie, V. J., & Davies, P. G. (2004). Seeing black: Race, crime, and visual processing. *Journal of Personality and Social Psychology, 87*(6), 876–893. https://doi.org/10.1037/0022-3514.87.6.876
Evans, T., & Peter, H. (Eds.). (2020). *Discretion and the quest for controlled freedom* (1st ed.). Palgrave. https://doi.org/10.1007/978-3-030-19566-3
Fazio, R. H. (1990). Multiple processes by which attitudes guide behavior: The MODE model as an integrative framework. *Advances in Experimental Social Psychology, 23*, 75–109. https://doi.org/10.1016/S0065-2601(08)60318-4
Fazio, R. H., Jackson, J. R., Dunton, B. C., & Williams, C. J. (1995). Variability in automatic activation as an unobtrusive measure of racial attitudes: A bona fide pipeline? *Journal of Personality and Social Psychology, 69*(6), 1013–1037. https://doi.org/10.1037/0022-3514.69.6.1013
Fazio, R. H., Sanbonmatsu, D. M., Powell, M. C., & Kardes, F. R. (1986). On the automatic activation of attitudes. *Journal of Personality and Social Psychology, 50*(2), 229–238. https://doi.org/10.1037/0022-3514.50.2.229
Floyd v. City of N.Y., 959 F. Supp. 2d 540 (2013).
Friedman, B. (2017). *Unwarranted: Policing without permission*. Macmillan Publishers.
Gawande, A. (2011). *The checklist manifesto*. Profile Books.
Gerstein, C., & Prescott, J. J. (2014). Process costs and police discretion. *Harvard Law Review Forum, 128*, 268–288. Retrieved from https://repository.law.umich.edu/articles/1561/
Glaser, J. (2006). The efficacy and effect of racial profiling: A mathematical simulation approach. *Journal of Policy Analysis and Management, 25*(2), 395–416. https://doi.org/10.1002/pam.20178
Glaser, J. (2015). *Suspect race: Causes and consequences of racial profiling*. Oxford University Press.
Glaser, J. (2024). Disrupting the effects of implicit bias: The case of discretion & policing. *Daedalus, 153*(1), 151–173. https://doi.org/10.1162/daed_a_02053
Glaser, J., & Knowles, E. D. (2008). Implicit motivation to control prejudice. *Journal of Experimental Social Psychology, 44*(1), 164–172. https://doi.org/10.1016/j.jesp.2007.01.002
Goel, S., Rao, J. M., & Shroff, R. (2016). Personalized risk assessments in the criminal justice system. *American Economic Review, 106*(5), 119–123. https://doi.org/10.1257/aer.p20161028
Goldstein, J. (1960). Police discretion not to invoke the criminal process; low-visibility decisions in the administration of justice. *Yale Law Journal, 69*(4), 543–594. Retrieved from http://hdl.handle.net/20.500.13051/1741
Goldstein, H. (1963). Police discretion: The ideal versus the real. *Public Administration Review, 23*(3), 140–148. https://doi.org/10.2307/973838

Graybill, A. R. (2007). *Policing the Great Plains: Rangers, mounties, and the north American frontier, 1875–1910*. University of Nebraska Press.
Harcourt, B. (2000). *Against prediction*. University of Chicago Press.
Hetey, R. C., Hamedani, M. G., Markus, H. R., & Eberhardt, J. L. (2024). "When the cruiser lights come on": Using the science of bias & culture to combat racial disparities in policing. *Daedalus, 153*(1), 123–150. https://doi.org/10.1162/daed_a_02052
Holzer, H. J., Raphael, S., & Stoll, M. A. (2006). Perceived criminality, criminal background checks, and the racial hiring practices of employers. *The Journal of Law and Economics, 49*(2), 451–480. https://doi.org/10.1086/501089
Jany, L., & Poston, B. (2022, November 14). Minor police encounters plummet after LAPD put limits on stopping drivers and pedestrians. *Los Angeles Times*. Retrieved from https://www.latimes.com/world-nation/newsletter/2022-11-14/2022-11-13-los-angeles-police-fewer-stops-todays-headlines
Johnson, R. C., & Raphael, S. (2009). The effects of male incarceration dynamics on acquired immune deficiency syndrome infection rates among African American women and men. *The Journal of Law and Economics, 52*(2), 251–293. https://doi.org/10.1086/597102
Lai, C. K., & Lisnek, J. A. (2023). The impact of implicit-bias-oriented diversity training on police officers' beliefs, motivations, and actions. *Psychological Science, 34*(4), 424–434. https://doi.org/10.1177/09567976221150617
Lai, C. K., Marini, M., Lehr, S. A., Cerruti, C., Shin, J. E. L., Joy-Gaba, J. A., et al. (2014). Reducing implicit racial preferences: I. A comparative investigation of 17 interventions. *Journal of Experimental Psychology: General, 143*(4), 1765–1785. https://doi.org/10.1037/a0036260
Lai, C. K., Skinner, A. L., Cooley, E., Murrar, S., Brauer, M., Devos, T., et al. (2016). Reducing implicit racial preferences: II. Intervention effectiveness across time. *Journal of Experimental Psychology: General, 145*(8), 1001–1016. https://doi.org/10.1037/xge0000179
Mapp v. Ohio, 367 U.S. 643 (1961).
McCauliff, C. M. (1982). Burdens of proof: Degrees of belief, quanta of evidence, or constitutional guarantees. *Vanderbilt Law Review, 35*(6), 1293–1335. Retrieved from https://scholarship.law.vanderbilt.edu/vlr/vol35/iss6/1
Merriam-Webster. (2023). Discretion. In *Merriam-Webster.com dictionary*. Retrieved June 1, 2024, from https://www.merriam-webster.com/dictionary/discretion
Moskowitz, G. B., Gollwitzer, P. M., Wasel, W., & Schaal, B. (1999). Preconscious control of stereotype activation through chronic egalitarian goals. *Journal of Personality and Social Psychology, 77*(1), 167–184. https://doi.org/10.1037/0022-3514.77.1.167
Neely, J. H. (1977). Semantic priming and retrieval from lexical memory: Roles of inhibitionless spreading activation and limited-capacity attention. *Journal of Experimental Psychology: General, 106*(3), 226–254. https://doi.org/10.1037/0096-3445.106.3.226
Oxford Languages. (2023). Discretion. In *Oxford languages online dictionary*. Retrieved June 1, 2024, from https://www.oxfordlanguages.com
Paluck, E. L., Porat, R., Clark, C. S., & Green, D. P. (2021). Prejudice reduction: Progress and challenges. *Annual Review of Psychology, 72*(1), 533–560. https://doi.org/10.1146/annurev-psych-071620-030619
Park, S. H., Glaser, J., & Knowles, E. D. (2008). Implicit motivation to control prejudice moderates the effect of cognitive depletion on unintended discrimination. *Social Cognition, 26*(4), 401–419. https://doi.org/10.1521/soco.2008.26.4.401
Pettigrew, T. F., & Tropp, L. R. (2006). A meta-analytic test of intergroup contact theory. *Journal of Personality and Social Psychology, 90*(5), 751–783. https://doi.org/10.1037/0022-3514.90.5.751
Pierson, E., Simoiu, C., Overgoor, J., Corbett-Davies, S., Jenson, D., Shoemaker, A., Ramachandrun, V., Barghouty, P., Phillips, C., Shroff, R., & Goel, S. (2020). A large-scale analysis of racial disparities in police stops across the United States. *Nature Human Behaviour, 4*(7), 736–745. https://doi.org/10.1038/s41562-020-0858-1

Plant, E. A., & Devine, P. G. (1998). Internal and external motivation to respond without prejudice. *Journal of Personality and Social Psychology, 75*(3), 811–832. https://doi.org/10.1037/0022-3514.75.3.811

Plant, E. A., & Peruche, B. M. (2005). The consequences of race for police officers' responses to criminal suspects. *Psychological Science, 16*(3), 180–183. https://doi.org/10.1111/j.0956-7976.2005.00800.x

Ramirez, D. A., Hoopes, J., & Quinlan, T. L. (2003). Defining racial profiling in a post-September 11 world. *American Criminal Law Review, 40*(3), 1195–1233. https://doi.org/10.1177/0887403408327403

Reichel, P. L. (1988). Southern slave patrols as a transitional police type. *American Journal of Police, 7*(2), 51–77.

Sabol, W., Johnson, T., & Caccavale, A. (2020). Trends in correctional control by race and sex. *Federal Sentencing Reporter, 32*(3), 157–177. https://doi.org/10.1525/fsr.2020.32.3.157

Sagar, H. A., & Schofield, J. W. (1980). Racial and behavioral cues in black and white children's perceptions of ambiguously aggressive acts. *Journal of Personality and Social Psychology, 39*(4), 590–598. https://doi.org/10.1037/0022-3514.39.4.590

Sherry, A. H. (1954). Progress report: The American Bar Foundation's survey of the administration of criminal justice. *American Bar Association Journal, 40*(4), 296–298.

Spencer, K. B., Charbonneau, A. K., & Glaser, J. (2016). Implicit bias and policing. *Social and Personality Psychology Compass, 10*(1), 50–63. https://doi.org/10.1111/spc3.12210

Swencionis, J. K., Pouget, E. R., & Goff, P. A. (2021). Supporting social hierarchy is associated with White police officers' use of force. *Proceedings of the National Academy of Sciences, 118*(18), e2007693118. https://doi.org/10.1073/pnas.2007693118

TenEyck, M. F. (2024). The "police personality": Is it real? *Police Quarterly, 27*(3), 271–291. https://doi.org/10.1177/10986111231193032

Tversky, A., & Kahneman, D. (1974). Judgment under uncertainty: Heuristics and biases: Biases in judgments reveal some heuristics of thinking under uncertainty. *Science, 185*(4157), 1124–1131. https://doi.org/10.1126/science.185.4157.1124

Whren v. United States, 517 U.S. 806 (1996).

Worden, R. E., McLean, S. J., Engel, R. S., et al. (2020). *The impacts of implicit bias awareness training in the NYPD*. The John F. Finn Institute for Public Safety, Inc. and The Center for Police Research and Policy at the University of Cincinnati. Retrieved from https://www.theiacp.org/research

Wozniak, A. (2015). Discrimination and the effects of drug testing on black employment. *Review of Economics and Statistics, 97*(3), 548–566. https://doi.org/10.1162/REST_a_00482

Zeal, Motivation, and the Adversarial Bias

Dan Simon

Introduction

It is a profound honor to be included in the Nebraska Symposium on Motivation. My reverence for this tradition goes back many years (actually, decades) to my first encounter with Fritz Heider's contribution to this very symposium 65 years ago. Heider's (1960) contribution, *The Gestalt Theory of Motivation*, interweaves motivation, Gestalt psychology, and Balance Theory (1946, 1958), the very same topics that reverberate through my chapter. The intellectual lineage is not hard to trace. The psychological framework that underlies this chapter, *coherence-based reasoning* and the cognitive architecture that undergirds it—connectionism and parallel constraint satisfaction—are the progeny of Gestalt psychology, as reincarnated through cognitive consistency theories (Abelson et al., 1968). It must not be overlooked that the venerable cognitive consistency theorists—Solomon Asch (1946), Robert Abelson (1968), William McGuire (1968), Leon Festinger (1957), Milton Rosenberg (1968), and others—stood squarely on the shoulders of Fritz Heider and his foundational Balance Theory (Heider, 1946, 1958). Heider's influence on generations of scholars, this humble one included, is immeasurable.

D. Simon (✉)
Gould School of Law and Department of Psychology, University of Southern California, Los Angeles, CA, USA
e-mail: dsimon@law.usc.edu

R. L. Wiener, D. J. Hansen (eds.), *Legal Judgment and the Motivation for Justice*, Nebraska Symposium on Motivation 71,
https://doi.org/10.1007/978-3-031-98812-7_4

Legal Procedure and Advocacy

This chapter is concerned with the psychological impact of legal procedure on legal actors, focusing on the adversarial form of procedure. While the adversarial procedure is one of the defining characteristics of Anglo-American law (Damaska, 1986; Fuller, 1961; Langbein, 2003), it belies a uniform description. The process is typically characterized by its reliance on lay jurors as ultimate decision-makers, conducting proceedings in open court, presentation of evidence by means of oral testimony, judicial detachment, party autonomy over the cases and, crucially, vigorous and partisan advocacy (Damaska, 1986; Feely, 1987; Fuller, 1961; Kagan, 2019; Landsman, 1984; Sklansky, 2008). Adversarialism is habitually contradistinguished from European civil-law procedural regimes, also known as "inquisitorial" systems, which are known for their reliance on decisions made by professional judges, presentation of evidence by means of written testimony, high degrees of judicial involvement, and tempered advocacy by lawyers (Damaska, 1986; Feely, 1987; Fuller, 1961; Kagan, 2019; Landman, 1984; Langer, 2016; Sklansky, 2008).

The specific focus of this chapter will be on the procedure's pronounced reliance on vigorous advocacy. Vigorous advocacy is heralded for upholding democratic values, by way of shielding individuals against governmental overreach and affording them the autonomy to build the case that best serves their interests (Fuller, 1961, citing John Stuart Mill; Crawford v. Washington, 2004). More prominently, vigorous advocacy is revered for promoting the reaching of correct outcomes and the finding of truth. As Lon Fuller (1961, p. 35) famously explained, "before a judge can gauge the full force of an argument, it must be presented to him with partisan zeal." Stephen Landman (1984, p. 2) explained that a correct decision is most likely to emanate from a "sharp clash of proofs presented by adversaries." This discovery of truth is said to provide the decision-maker with evidence that is both voluminous (Freedman, 1998; Landman, 1984) and reliable (Crawford v. Washington, 2004). Notably, the vigorous cross-examination of witnesses—a core feature of the adversarial process—is widely viewed as the "greatest legal engine ever invented for the discovery of truth" (Wigmore, 1974, p. 32. See also Lilly v. Virginia, 1999; Watkins v. Sowders, 1981). The Supreme Court routinely lauds the discovery of truth by means of "powerful statements on both sides of a question." (United States v. Cronic, 1984. see also Herring v. New York, 1975; United States v. Nobles, 1975; Portuondo v. Agard, 2000; James v. Illinois, 1990; United States v. Agurs, 1976).

Lon Fuller's (1961) conception of partisan zeal has become the modus operandi of American lawyering and the cornerstone of the profession's ethical responsibility (Landman, 1984, p. 5). Indeed, the preamble to the ABA's Model Rules of Professional Conduct instructs lawyers to "zealously assert the client's position under the rules of the adversary system," and the Commentary to the Rules commands lawyers to act "with zeal in advocacy upon the client's behalf." (comment, Rule 3.1.).

This chapter sets out to explore the nature of adversarial zeal. One could imagine that zeal is a tactic purposefully deployed by advocates to advance their case, a tool not unlike a carpenter's hammer, a surgeon's scalpel, or a school teacher's blackboard. The chapter proposes instead that zeal is largely a genuine reflection of how lawyers actually view the dispute, a cognitive bias rather than an instrumental tool. Concretely, the research reviewed below suggests that zeal is best understood as a product of the *adversarial bias* (Aviram, 2019; Simon, 2025), a mindset that impacts how legal actors experience and react to their cases in adversarial settings. After describing the bias, the chapter will explore its underlying psychological mechanisms, with a special focus on motivation and coherence-based reasoning. The chapter will conclude with a discussion of some of the bias's implications.

The Adversarial Bias

A large body of psychological literature demonstrates that slight changes in the structure of a task can impact the way people think and act (Beersma & De Dreu, 2002; Carnevale & Probst, 1998; De Dreu & McCusker, 1997; Polzer et al., 1998; Pruitt, 1967). Famously, labeling a prisoners' dilemma game as a "Community Game" increases the cooperation rate significantly relative to when it is labeled a "Wall Street Game" (Liberman et al., 2004; see also Engel & Rand, 2014). One line of research that falls within this body of literature is *role-induced bias*, according to which the role that an actor plays in a given situation can alter their mindset toward greater congruence with the respective role. This line of research can be traced back to a study by Janis and King (1954) that assigned participants to argue for a position in a debate. The study found that the debaters' opinions became more aligned with their (randomly) assigned positions and were held with greater confidence as compared to participants who only observed the debate (Janis & King, 1954).

A sizable body of research has been devoted to role effects in legal adversarial settings, much of it focusing on lawyers. An early study by Lind et al. (1973) set out to test the prediction that adversarial procedures would produce more correct outcomes than inquisitorial procedures. This advantage would be attributed to adversarial lawyers being more diligent in searching for evidence and advocating more strenuously for their clients. Contrary to predictions, the study did not find a main effect for diligence, in that participants assigned to adversarial roles did not search any harder for evidence and did not submit more evidence favoring their clients than did those assigned to non-adversarial roles. Nor did the study find an overall increase in the strength of presentation of evidence, though it did reveal invigorated presentation when adversarial lawyers faced a legal situation that was unfavorable to their clients. This admittedly unpredicted observation led the authors to suggest that the adversarial procedure can offer protection to the "underdog," deeming it to be of "great social and humanitarian concern" (p. 1143). The study also found that participants assigned to adversarial roles reported being more acrimonious, namely, less cooperative, less fair, less peaceful, less likeable, and more biased. Oddly, Lind and colleagues deemed these self-conceptions to be beneficial for the legal process. Summarizing this and other studies, Thibaut and Walker (1975) struck an upbeat note, asserting that the adversarial procedure is "clearly superior" to its rivals (p. 118).

Subsequent research has been considerably less sanguine, revealing little in the way of humanitarian benefits and much in the way of biased processing. In a study by Simon et al. (2004, Study 4), lay participants were asked to simulate the role of a legal intern working for an arbitrator in a labor dispute. The study found that participants' judgments of the case were skewed toward the role expected of them by the arbitrator. Notably, the effect of the role assignment went beyond the guilt determinations, as it skewed participants' interpretation of the entire factual pattern. Participants assigned to a guilty condition viewed the case facts as more incriminating, while those assigned to the innocence condition viewed them as more exculpating.

A study by Eigen and Listokin (2012) observed the role-induced bias among law students participating in moot court contests. The study found that these students came to view the side to which they were (randomly) assigned as having both greater legal merit and being morally superior to the opposing side. Notably, the preference for one's position was associated with poorer performance in advocating one's position, in that those with the most inflated opinion of their cases' legal merits did significantly worse in the competitions than those who viewed the strength of their cases as more debatable (Eigen & Listokin, 2012). An important study by Engel and Glöckner (2013) assigned participants to play the role of a legal intern working either for the prosecution or the defense in a criminal case. The study found that the former judged the defendant's guilt and the probability that he committed the act to be higher than the latter (Engel & Glöckner, 2013. See also Egli-Anthonioz et al., 2019). Holger Spamann (2020) introduced law students to a mock Supreme Court oral argument, assigning them to represent the petitioner, the respondent, or a neutral judge. The study found that over 50 percent of those assigned to the role of the petitioner's counsel expected the petitioner to prevail, while that judgment was reached by fewer than 20 percent of those assigned to the role of the respondent's counsel. Students assigned to the neutral role reported positions that were in between the adversarial conditions (Spamann, 2020).

David Melnikoff and Nina Strohminger (2020) presented participants with overwhelming evidence of a defendant's guilt and assigned them to the role of defense attorney or prosecutor in that defendant's trial. Despite forewarning the participants about the bias and incentivizing them to judge the case accurately, and notwithstanding the unambiguous evidence of guilt, over half of those playing the role of defense attorney concluded that the defendant was innocent of the crime. Mihael Jeklic (2023) assigned law students to the roles of claimants and defendants in a civil monetary suit and found that the former expected the awarded damages to be almost 70 percent higher than the latter. Each party also found the arguments supporting their side to be considerably stronger than those in favor of their opponent (Jeklic, 2023).

Two studies by Simon et al. (2020) took a deeper dive into the role-induced bias in legal adversarial settings. These studies presented participants with quasi-legal adversarial proceedings. Study 1 concerned a labor arbitration dispute wherein a company sought to fire an employee, Jason Wells, for allegedly stealing money from its safe. Study 2 concerned an academic disciplinary hearing wherein a university charged a student, Debbie Miller, for cheating on an exam. The participants were asked to act as a "representative" (akin to a lawyer) in study 1 and an "investigator" in study 2. They were randomly assigned to one of three role assignments: acting in the service of the individual (Jason, Debbie), in the service of the institution (the company, the university), or a non-adversarial assignment serving accurate outcomes. Participants received a flat fee for their participation, but no incentives were offered in relation to their performance or responses.

Consistent with the abovementioned research, Simon et al. (2020) found that participants judged the appropriate verdict as more in line with their assigned role. Importantly, the impacts of adversarialism extended well beyond that judgment, as participants came to view the entire case as strongly aligned with their assigned roles. Signs of bias were observed in the inferences drawn from the rich and ambiguous factual pattern, estimations of the likelihood that Jason and Debbie committed the transgressions, positive and negative emotions toward the protagonists, liking of the protagonists, affective reactions to the assigned side winning or losing the case, and more. As will be discussed in greater depth below, the adversarial assignment also had a strong impact on participants' motivation to see their assigned side prevail. Crucially, in both studies, responses given by participants assigned to the non-adversarial role were close to the midpoint between the responses offered in the two adversarial conditions.

The Simon et al. (2020) studies also found that adversarialism impacted participants' views of their (fictitious) adversarial counterparts. For one, participants expected that their counterparts' views—proposed verdicts, likelihoods that Jason and Debbie committed the respective transgressions, and motivation to win the case—would be starkly different from their own. The judgments imputed to the counterparts were more extreme than the responses that were actually provided by participants assigned to those opposing conditions. These distortions are consistent with the phenomenon known as *imagined extremism*, by which members of groups in conflict tend to exaggerate their opponents' extremism and intensity of conflict (Keltner & Robinson, 1996; Kenyon, 2014; Monin & Norton, 2003). Adversarialism was also found to impact how participants evaluated themselves and their fictitious counterparts. Specifically, participants assessed their own objectivity fairly highly but judged their counterparts as being biased and expected to be evaluated unfavorably by their counterparts in return. The fact that both sets of objectivity judgments were unfavorable suggests that participants envisioned a state of mutual distrust between themselves and their counterparts.

In all, the psychological effects borne by adversarial setting have proven to be robust. Across studies, adversarialism has been shown to alter a wide array of beliefs and judgments including the interpretation of facts (Engel & Glöckner, 2013; Schwardmann et al., 2022; Simon et al., 2004, 2020), judgments of strength of arguments (Eigen & Listokin, 2009; Jeklic, 2023; Schwardmann et al., 2022), judgments of the moral soundness of arguments (Eigen & Listokin, 2009), judgments of the probability that a defendant committed the crime (Engel & Glöckner, 2013; Simon et al., 2004, 2020; O'Brien, 2009), predictions of judicial judgments (Engel & Glöckner, 2013, Simon et al., 2020; Spamann, 2020), predictions of judicial receptivity of the arguments (Eigen & Listokin, 2012), prediction of damage payouts (Jeklic, 2023), judgments of the appropriate verdict (Simon et al., 2004, 2020), judgment of the appropriate prison sentence (Melnikoff & Strohminger, 2020), judgment of the appropriate damage payout (Melnikoff & Strohminger, 2020), plea bargaining offers (Engel & Glöckner, 2013), judgments of the defendant's character (Melnikoff & Strohminger, 2020), and confidence in one's judgments (Schwardmann et al., 2022; Spamann, 2020; Simon et al., 2004, 2020).

In all, the findings have been observed using a variety of stimuli, tasks, and different laboratories, as well as in naturalistic settings (Eigen & Listokin, 2009; Schwardmann et al., 2022). The studies have simulated a range of different roles, including legal interns (Engel & Glöckner, 2013; Simon et al., 2004), investigators (Simon et al., 2020), debaters (Eigen & Listokin, 2009; Melnikoff & Strohminger, 2020; Schwardmann, 2022), and lawyers (Spamman, 2020; Melnikoff & Strohminger, 2020; Jeklic, 2023). The findings have been made using different sample populations, including lay people (Engel & Glöckner, 2013; Simon et al., 2004, 2020), law students (Eigen & Listokin, 2009; Jeklic, 2023; Spamann, 2020), experienced debaters (Schwardmann et al., 2022), and trained lawyers (Melnikoff & Strohminger, 2020). The bias has also been shown to spill over beyond the confines of the specific role assignment, such as in persisting after the person has exited the role (Engel & Glöckner, 2013; Spamann, 2020), and in punishing a counterpart in subsequent unrelated tasks (Melnikoff & Strohminger, 2020).

The paradigm's robustness is manifested by its sensitivity to the minimalistic treatment employed in the experimental designs (Engel & Glöckner, 2013; Jeklic, 2023; Simon et al., 2004, 2020; Spamann, 2020), and it is bound to be considerably stronger when the role assignment is accompanied by tangible incentives. Linda Babcock and colleagues have shown that assigning people to roles of disputants in an incentivized simulated civil dispute triggers a self-serving bias that hinders the prospect of settlement and thus ends up harming the participants' own interests (Babcock & Loewenstein, 1997; Loewenstein et al., 1993). The paradigm is also noteworthy for its resilience to debiasing efforts. Biases were observed even when participants were warned about the bias and implored to resist it (Melnikoff & Strohminger, 2020, study 3), urged to be fair and objective (Simon et al., 2020), admonished to offer opinions from the vantage point of "a neutral, sober observer" (Spamann, 2020), and exposed to arguments from the opposing side (Spamann, 2020; Jeklic, 2023). Strikingly, the bias has persisted even in the face of significant monetary incentives for accurate judgments that offered a chance to win as much as 100 Euros (Engel & Glöckner, 2013) and $200 (Melnikoff & Strohminger, 2020). The bias was reduced somewhat—but not eliminated—by Jeklic's (2023) use of "dialectical bootstrapping" (Herzog & Hertwig, 2014, pp. 84–85), whereby participants were asked to assume their judgments were wrong and to generate reasons for those errors (see also Babcock & Loewenstein, 1997).

In all, the breadth and depth of research findings support the conceptualization of an *adversarial bias*, a term that appears to have first been coined by Aviram (2019;

see also Simon, 2025). This bias suggests that assignment to an adversarial role leads the actor to perceive, experience, and behave toward the case in a manner that is skewed toward congruence with that role. The adversarial bias encompasses distortions of just about every type of judgment, assessment, and prediction relating to the task, as well as one's motivation, affective reactions, emotional arousal, and more.

Underlying Psychological Mechanisms

A convenient starting point for exploring the psychological mechanisms that underlie the adversarial bias is the abovementioned study by Engel and Glöckner (2013) that examines two alternative mechanisms. First, the authors posit that the bias could be driven by motivation. Legal actors are deemed to feel motivated to see their assigned party prevail in accordance with their professional role. This conception of the adversarial bias fits the familiar mold of motivated reasoning, by which the activation of directional goals—say, a "wish, desire, or preference that concerns the outcome of a given reasoning task" (Kunda, 1990, p. 480)—can skew the reasoning process toward those respective goals (Kunda, 1990; Dunning, 2015; Ditto et al., 2003; Munro et al., 2002; Wyer & Frey, 1983. For an application to law, see Sood, 2013). Indeed, motivation was deemed to underly biases borne by adversarialism in early studies by Neil Vidmar and colleagues (Sheppard & Vidmar, 1980; Vidmar & Laird, 1983).

Alternatively, Engel and Glöckner (2013) posit that the bias could be the product of *coherence-based reasoning*. Coherence-based reasoning is a general model of cognition that is credited for transforming the complexity that pervades our lives into comprehensible and sensible conclusions, thus enabling people to engage successfully with their environment (Thagard, 1989; Holyoak & Thagard, 1989; Holyoak & Simon, 1999; Read et al., 1997; Simon, 2004; Simon & Holyoak, 2002; Glöckner et al., 2010; Engel et al., 2020; for a comprehensive review, see Simon & Read, 2023). By this account, complex judgment tasks are understood to be represented in connectionist networks (Eliasmith, 2013; Holyoak, 1991; Hummel & Holyoak, 2003; Smolensky, 1989; Thagard, 2019), wherein the elements of the task are all connected to other elements via relational links. As articulated by Heider (1946), links can be positive when they connect elements that are deemed to "go together" and negative when they are deemed incongruous or contradictory. The framework posits that the cognitive task is processed through a neurally inspired cross-activation, governed by mechanisms of parallel constraint satisfaction (Hopfield, 1982, 1984; Rumelhart et al., 1986). These processes are driven by structural forces that transform conflict-laden representations into states of equilibrium or *coherence*. Coherence is defined as the state wherein positively linked elements are similarly activated and negatively linked elements have dissimilar activations. The imposition of coherence is attained through an alteration of the nodes—whether by way of strengthening, weakening, or morphing—to bring them into line with the emerging conclusion (see Heider, 1946, 1958; Abelson et al., 1968; McGuire, 1968; Asch, 1946). As a result, the winning conclusion ends up being supported by highly activated attributes and the rejected conclusion by poorly activated attributes, a disparity that yields confident resolution. Coherence-based reasoning is a ubiquitous, essential, and overwhelmingly adaptive cognitive apparatus (Thagard, 1989, 2019; Read et al., 1997; Simon & Holyoak, 2002).

As conceived by Engel and Glöckner (2013), the core difference between the vying mechanisms lies in the consciousness of the process. They deem motivation as a deliberate process that can be switched on and off at will. Accordingly, they expect the bias to dissipate as soon as the actor's motivational goals change, such as when the original adversarial role has been replaced with a non-adversarial assignment, and especially when participants are offered a hefty monetary bonus for accurate responses. Conversely, Engel and Glöckner (2013) point out that the coherence-based processing occurs automatically and that once coherent representations emerge, they become stable and resistant to change (citing Read et al., 1997). As a consequence, the newly formed judgments and interpretations of evidence—which have been distorted to cohere with the adversarial borne outcome—are expected to outlast the duration of the assignment to the respective role. Thus, Engel and Glöckner (2013) predict that even when the assigned role changes or when the person is assigned an accuracy goal, the distorted judgments are bound to remain unchanged. The authors' study (Engel & Glöckner, 2013) found that participants adhered to the biased judgments even when no longer acting in the adversarial role and even when faced with a role that encourages accuracy. Their findings also show by way of a mediation analysis that the adversarial bias is explained by coherence-based reasoning and parallel constraint satisfaction processes. Thus, the authors conclude that coherence-based reasoning is the preferred explanation for the adversarial bias (Engel & Glöckner, 2013).

Motivated Coherence

There seems little reason to question Engel and Glöckner's (2013) propositions that the adversarial bias operates mostly in an automatic fashion beneath the level of conscious awareness (see Simon & Read, 2023) and that the bias is readily explainable as an instantiation of coherence-based reasoning. There is, however, good reason to question their presumed zero-sum nature of the two explanations and the pursuant exclusion of motivation as a contributory factor. For one, as Engel and Glöckner (2013, note 2) concede, motivation is not confined to deliberate processing, and it can readily affect the reasoning process automatically, without conscious awareness. Indeed, the prospect of automatic activation of motivational goals is well established in the literature (see Forgas et al., 2005; Kihlstrom, 2019). It is also questionable whether biases borne by motivated reasoning will necessarily dissipate once the motivational goal is removed or replaced. There is ample research that speaks to the surprising staying power of judgments and conclusions that are derived from even the flimsiest and most fleeting bases (e.g., Anderson et al., 1980; Markman & Hirt, 2002; Tversky & Kahneman, 1974). There seems to be no obvious reason why the same would not apply to motivated reasoning.

Importantly, there are good theoretical reasons that cut against the juxtaposition of motivation with coherence-based reasoning as competitive explanations. A connectionist representation of a complex cognitive task will naturally include the full gamut of elements that pertain to that task, such as perceptions, preferences, factual propositions, beliefs, and evaluations, all of which are classically classified as "cold cognitions" (see Abelson, 1963; Sorrentino & Higgins, 1986). But it must be acknowledged that complex judgments are frequently suffused also with elements such as motivation and emotion. These "hot cognitions" (Abelson, 1963; Sorrentino & Higgins, 1986) are known to be capable of influencing, even dominating, cognitive processing (see Loewenstein & Lerner, 2003; Kunda, 1990; Simon & Read, 2023). In the terminology of parallel constraint satisfaction, such factors are said to constitute "attractors," in that they attract a great deal of activation and can possibly drag the entire network in their direction (Churchland & Sejnowski, 1992; Hopfield, 1982; Read et al., 1997).

To explore the plausibility of the interconnectivity of motivation with coherence-based reasoning, Simon et al. (2015) report on four experiments that explored the intuition that cold and hot cognitions will blend with one another through the connectionist process of coherence maximization. Study 1 was concerned with a romantic couple, Jenny and Mark, whose relationship was strained by Jenny's uncertain commitment and incomplete honesty toward Mark. The study found that participants who doubted Jenny were more inclined to report negative valence toward the continuation of the relationship, less liking of Jenny, greater anger toward her, and greater sympathy and sadness toward Mark. Notably, these participants also reported a stronger motivation to see the relationship end with a breakup. Thus, we see that motivation gets pulled along with all other cold and hot cognitions toward coherence with the emerging conclusion. Study 2 found that strengthening one piece of inculpatory evidence in the criminal case against Jason Wells led to higher estimations of his guilt and elevated conviction rates. This manipulation also drove concordant interpretations of the other pieces of evidence toward a stronger indication of guilt. The novelty of this study lies in the manipulation's effect on participants' hot cognitions. Altering the strength of the evidence against Jason swept through all the measured hot cognitions: more positive valence toward the prospect of a conviction, stronger anger and less sympathy toward him, and greater disliking of him. Notably, the manipulation also resulted in a stronger motivation to see Jason get convicted.

Employing an opposite treatment, Studies 3 and 4 examined the effect of manipulating hot cognitions on all other features of the task, both cold and hot. Study 3 employed an emotional manipulation to influence judgments of whether Debbie Miller cheated on a college exam. Informing participants that her brother had been killed by a drunken driver months earlier was found to lower the judgments of her guilt and result in more exculpatory inferences drawn from the ambiguous evidence. Importantly, the manipulation also spilled over into the other hot cognitions, resulting not just in elevated levels of sympathy toward her but also in lower anger toward her, greater liking of her, more negative valence toward the prospect of seeing her disciplined, and, importantly, stronger motivation to see her win the case. Study 4 replicated these findings by manipulating participants' motivation toward the eventual outcome of the case. In one treatment, participants were informed that students who previously cheated on exams had benefited at the expense of honest students (the "Cheaters Prosper" manipulation). As planned, this manipulation increased participants' motivation to see the university win the case, and, as predicted, it resulted in concordant judgments throughout the case. These included higher estimations of the likelihood that Debbie cheated, higher guilty findings, more inculpatory interpretations of the ambiguous evidence, as well as more positive valence toward the prospect of seeing Debbie get disciplined and greater anger toward her (though the prediction of less sympathy was not borne out).

To compliment these empirical findings with a theoretical backing, Simon et al. (2015) constructed a constraint satisfaction neural network that mimicked the abovementioned Study 4. The simulation was built from the "CS" (constraint satisfaction) module in O'Reilly et al. (2012) emergent neural-network-modeling system. The network comprised of all the important independent and dependent variables that were contained in the experimental studies. As seen in Fig. 1, at the center of the model were the two decision choices: Cheated (Debbie did indeed cheat on the exam) and Did Not Cheat (Debbie was innocent of the alleged cheating). As these two nodes are in opposition to one another, they were connected via an inhibitory link (dashed line). The "Cheated" node was connected via excitatory links (solid lines) to three dummy facts that connoted guilt (GuiltFacts), as well as to four nodes representing hot cognitions: Anger (toward Debbie), Disliking (of Debbie), Valence (four measures collapsed in feeling good about Debbie

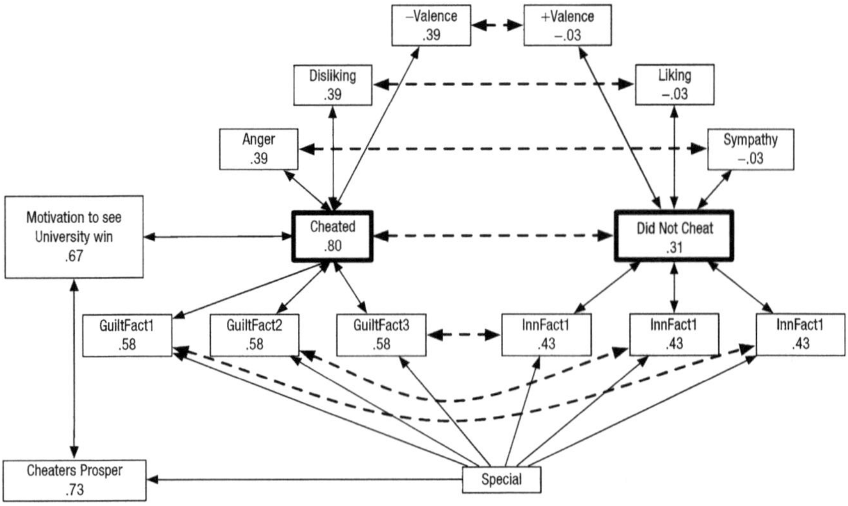

Fig. 1 Computer simulation of the Cheaters Prosper manipulation (Simon et al., 2015), Study 4

prevailing), and Motivation (to see the university win). The opposing "Did Not Cheat" node was connected to a mirror set of nodes positively related to the conclusion of Debbie's innocence, including the exculpatory facts (InnFacts) and the four opposing hot cognitions. The "Special" node provides starting activations for the facts of the case and for the treatment (Cheaters Prosper).

Figure 1 represents the network once it had settled or reached maximal coherence, where the values of the nodes represent their level of activation at that final state. For the sake of brevity, we present only the simulation of the Cheaters Prosper treatment. We see that the manipulation succeeded in that it had a strong and direct effect on the node representing the motivation to see the university win which, in turn, impacted the entire network, both cold and hot cognitions. The model settled with a high activation of the central node Cheated (v. Did Not Cheat), which was accompanied by strong activation of the inculpating facts (GuiltFacts, as compared to InnFacts), greater anger toward Debbie, disliking her, and positive valence over the prospect of the university prevailing. The relevance of the simulation findings is punctuated by the fact that the activation values of its nodes corresponded closely to the mean ratings of the behavioral data, yielding an overall correlation of 0.81.

The interconnectivity of motivation with the rest of the network was observed in both studies reported by Simon et al. (2020). For one, the studies found strong evidence for the impact of the assignment on participants' motivation to see their assigned party prevail. Table 1 presents the effect of assignment on the hot cognitions across the three treatment conditions in Study 2. Consistent with coherence-based reasoning, participants assigned to Debbie's side reported positive feelings toward her (high liking, low negative emotions, and high positive emotions) and low liking of the proctor. Participants assigned to the university reported opposite feelings, and participants in the neutral assignment were close to the midpoint in between. Importantly, the motivation measure was more responsive to the adversarial assignment than any of the other hot cognitions, as manifested by its heightened effect size (with the motivation value aligned so that positive values represented motivation to see the university prevail).

Table 1 Hot cognitions by condition (Simon et al., 2020), Study 2

	Debbie assign.	Neutral assign.	Univ. assign.			
Measure	*M*	*M*	*M*	$F(2,292)$	p	h^2
Liking of Debbie	64.63^{a}	59.91^{a,b}	55.99^{b}	5.32	<0.01	0.035
Negative emotions toward Debbie	3.06^{a}	3.50^{a,b}	3.99^{b}	3.88	<0.05	0.026
Positive emotions toward Debbie	6.78^{a}	6.03^{b}	5.43^{b}	6.90	<0.001	0.045
Liking of the proctor	46.05	50.21	53.21	4.33	<0.05	0.029
Motivation*	3.72^{a}	4.58^{b}	5.67^{c}	11.34	<0.001	0.072

Abbreviations: assign. (assignment); Univ. (University)

Note: Means that do not share a common subscript (a, b, c) are significantly different at p 0.05

*This method of reporting is commonly used when comparing more than 2 conditions. We report the difference by noting which columns are different from each of the other columns

That study shows not only that motivation is highly sensitive to the role assignment but also that it is strongly interconnected with the rest of the adversarial mindset. The motivation measure was found to correlate strongly with the factual inferences ($r(189) = 0.724^{**}$), the likelihood that Debbie cheated ($r(188) = 0.773^{**}$), and to how participants would have decided the case ($r(189) = 0.761^{**}$). Motivation was also intertwined with the other hot cognitions, namely, negative emotions toward Debbie ($r(188) = 0.497^{**}$), positive emotions toward her ($r(188) = -0.598^{*}$), and liking of her ($r(188) = -0.608^{***}$). That study found also that participants' motivation predicted their tendency to impute extreme judgments to their counterparts (coefficients ranging from 0.04** to 0.21**), thus exacerbating the tendency to engage in imagined extremism (see Keltner & Robinson, 1996; Kenyon, 2014; Monin & Norton, 2003).

In sum, the motivation to win the case is readily influenced by the role assignment, and, thanks to coherence-based reasoning, it has the potency to spread throughout the network and thus impact the outcome of the task. It follows that motivation and coherence-based reasoning should not be viewed as alternative explanations for the adversarial bias. On the contrary, they combine to bias reasoning processes toward directional goals. This powerful combination could be labeled "motivated coherence"—a term first used by Braman et al. (2005). It feels safe to say that this combined construct provides the best available explanation for the adversarial bias.

Conclusion

This chapter set out to explore the psychological implications of legal procedure on the behavior of legal actors. Our starting point was the proposition that accurate adjudication is said to be best served by zealous advocacy, by way of boosting a lawyer's diligence in both building their case and arguing it forcefully (Fuller, 1961; Landman, 1984). On the face of it, proponents of adversarialism have a point. As observed in the abovementioned research, motivation – a well-known catalyst of behavior (see e.g., Cosmides & Tooby, 2013; Gollwitzer & Bargh, 1996) is indeed boosted by adversarial assignment. Still, there are reasons why heightened motivation might not be an unmitigated good for the legal process.

Recall that motivation is not the only effect borne by acting in an adversarial role. Adversarial actors become engulfed by the wide-ranging and powerful adversarial bias that affects their beliefs, judgments, emotions, affective reactions, and more. It must also be appreciated that while coherence-based reasoning is a highly adaptive process, when the network is dominated by factors that are incorrect, overweighted, or otherwise nonnormative, it will readily lead to biased conclusions. Due to the process' connectionistic nature, activation will tend to spread far and deep (McGuire, 1968; Simon & Read, 2023; Simon & Melnikoff, 2024) and thus sweep through different facets of the task. That means that a feature that is considered beneficial for a particular purpose might have deleterious effects on other aspects of the task

(Simon, 2012). Thus, to appreciate the overall impact of the adversarial procedure, we ought to consider how it might affect the diverse functions that lawyers and other legal actors play in the process. I discuss three examples.

Implications

Legal Analysis

Lawyers are not mere courtroom mouthpieces. In order to build a strong legal case, lawyers must perform a sound evaluation of the factual and legal terrain so as to reach a realistic assessment of the strengths and weaknesses of their position. A sober reading of the situation is essential also for the crucial task of counseling clients about their legal situation and guiding them through the available courses of action. When gripped by the adversarial bias, providing an even-handed assessment might be a difficult feat. The self-serving distortions of the case can readily blind lawyers to the weaknesses of their argument and undermine their sensitivity to the sensibilities of their audience. As mentioned, Eigen and Listokin (2012) found that the stronger the moot court contestants believed in the superiority of their assigned position, the worse they performed. A naturalistic study conducted with practicing American lawyers found evidence of unduly optimistic forecasts: while 24% of lawyers exceeded their minimal expectations, 44% fell short of meeting them (Goodman-Delahunty et al., 2010). Likewise, archival studies indicate that parties negotiating in advance of litigation tend to optimistically misjudge the eventual award of adjudicated cases and thus proceed to engage in costly and misguided litigation (Gross & Syverud, 1991; Kiser et al., 2008; Rachlinski, 1996). In short, the adversarial role could lead lawyers to advocate forcefully for positions that might not be in the best interests of their clients.

The Battle Model

The adversarial bias might also be responsible for the notorious *battle model* of legal procedure. Notwithstanding the widespread lauding of the truth-seeking function of the adversarial process (Portuondo v. Agard, 2000; James v. Illinois, 1990; Freedman, 1998; Landman, 1984; Fuller, 1961), one can hardly ignore the persistent critique of that proposition. Scholars, practitioners, and judges have long contested that the adversarial process is more combative than epistemological in nature and that adversarial actors are driven predominantly by the desire to win, rather than by a quest for truth. This critique can be traced to Jeremy Bentham (1843), who likened the trial to a foxhunt. Back in 1906, Roscoe Pound framed the process in terms of a "sporting theory of justice," according to which:

> The idea that procedure must of necessity be wholly contentious disfigures our judicial administration at every point. … It leads counsel to forget that they are officers of the court and to deal with the rules of law and procedure exactly as the professional football coach with the rules of the sport. … It turns witnesses, and especially expert witnesses, into partisans pure and simple. It leads to sensational cross-examinations "to affect credit," which have made the witness stand "the slaughter house of reputations." It prevents the trial court from restraining the bullying of witnesses and creates a general dislike, if not fear, of the witness function which impairs the administration of justice. (Pound, 1906, 404).

In the words of Jerome Frank (1949), the adversarial process promotes gamesmanship, rather than truth. Justice Brennan (1990) stated that "Our adversary system of criminal justice has invited many comparisons to sporting events, and generally to the more barbarous among them" (p. 16), and Marvin Frankel (1978) lamented that adversarialism is dominated by combativeness that "achieves truth only as a convenience, a byproduct, or an accidental approximation" (p. 1037). Similar critiques have been offered by Lloyd Weinreb (1977), Barbara Babcock (1982), Hadar Aviram (2019), and many others.

There is good reason to believe that this gamesmanship is largely a byproduct the adversarial bias, and, quite likely, zeal has much to do with this. The adversarial role boosts legal actors' motivation to see their side win the case, and it makes them feel good about the prospect of winning and bad about the prospect of losing. Indeed, as mentioned above, the study by Lind et al. (1973) found that participants assigned to adversarial roles reported being less cooperative, less fair, less peaceful, less likeable, and more biased than those assigned to non-adversarial roles. But to take strong partisan positions, legal actors need also to believe in their case, lest they fall into a state of incongruence between their actions and their beliefs. That eventuality is solved by the coherence effect, in that one's view of the case morphs to align with one's role in the process, all distorted by the adversarial bias. By generating a self-serving view of the case, the adversarial bias gives legal actors the epistemological license to battle their way toward their desired goals.

Biased Testimony

There is good evidence to suggest that the adversarial bias is not confined to lawyers. As shown in the abovementioned experiments, people fall under the spell of the bias in response to even the lightest of experimental treatments and social situations. The same could occur to other legal actors who become affiliated in one way or another with an adversarial party. Such affiliation is facilitated by the facile manner by which people form and join social groups (Tajfel, 1982; Tajfel et al., 1979). One concern that follows is that the adversarial bias might skew the testimony of percipient witnesses, that is, witnesses who testify about events that they perceived through their senses. In a pioneering study conducted by Sheppard and Vidmar (1980), witnesses to a simulated event were interviewed by participants role-playing one of the adversarial lawyers and were then asked to testify about the event at a mock trial. The study found that the eventual testimony became skewed in favor of that lawyer's side. These effects were mediated by the manipulativeness of the individuals playing the role of the lawyers. A study by Wells et al. (1981) exposed witnesses to a mock criminal event and asked them to testify about their identification of the culprit in a mock trial. The study found that forewarning the witnesses about an expected hostile cross-examination by the defense attorney resulted in a strengthening of the witness's inculpating testimony, which led in turn to higher conviction rates by a simulated jury. Ironically, the effect was most pronounced for witnesses whose testimony was factually wrong. This concern is particularly acute given that US law (but not UK law, for example) permits lawyers to interact extensively with their witnesses, a practice known as witness preparation and which verges on subornation of perjury (Frankel, 1978). Testimony can be biased even by the mere summoning of a witness by one of the parties. Vidmar and Laird (1983) found that the bystander witnesses testified more favorably to the side that called them for testimony. It is not difficult to imagine that over the course of an unfolding adjudication; such an affiliation can deepen and evolve into a level of camaraderie that bears a strong sense of commitment to the respective side.

Expert witnesses pose another reason for concern. Here too, we face a risk that the expert witnesses will be influenced by the fact that they are retained by or affiliated with one of the parties in an adversarial contest. Indeed, the tendency of expert witnesses to testify in favor of their retaining party has long been a source of lamentation, as expressed in the excerpt by Roscoe Pound (1906) reproduced above (see also Hand, 1901; Wigmore, 1923). This phenomenon, labeled *adversarial allegiance*, has been carefully researched by Murrie and his colleagues (see Murrie & Boccaccini, 2015). For example, archival studies of actual criminal proceedings show that clinical psychologists' testimony on measures of psychopathy and predictions of criminality were biased toward higher scores when they were retained by the prosecution, as compared to the defense (Edens et al., 2015; DeMatteo et al., 2014; Murrie et al., 2009). Similar biases were demonstrated in an ecologically valid experimental setting, wherein clinical psychologists were led to believe that they were testifying in real cases. This study found that the assessments were skewed in favor of whichever side that the experts believed had retained them (Murrie et al., 2013).

One might argue that the effects of a biased expert opinion will be cancelled out by the countervailing testimony presented on behalf of the opposing expert. True, under some conditions, opposing expert testimony may serve to weaken or balance out each other's biases. But that prospect is highly dependent on the parity in skill and resources available to the parties. In reality, one party might not be able to afford an expert, have access to a less qualified or less persuasive expert, or be represented by a lawyer who is less competent and knowledgeable about the subject matter. It follows that fact finders will often be presented with either one skewed expert testimony or with two contradictory and often uneven, expert opinions. There is reason to question whether this adversarial format—which could readily seem cacophonic from the perspective of lay jurors—is the optimal way to determine scientific truth (see MacCoun, 2015; Mnookin, 2008; Thibaut & Walker, 1978).

In sum, in the eyes of this observer, the zeal we so cherish is purchased at too high a cost.

References

Abelson, R. P. (1963). Computer simulation of "hot cognition." In S. Tomkins & S. Messick (Eds.), Computer simulation of personality (pp. 277–298). Wiley.

Abelson, R. P. (1968). Psychological implication. In R. P. Abelson, E. Aronson, W. J. McGuire, T. M. Newcomb, M. J. Rosenberg, & R. H. Tannenbaum (Eds.), *Theories of cognitive consistency: A sourcebook* (pp. 112–139). Rand McNally.

Abelson, R. P., Aronson, E. E., McGuire, W. J., Newcomb, T. M., Rosenberg, M. J., & Tannenbaum, P. H. (1968). *Theories of cognitive consistency: A sourcebook.* Rand McNally.

Anderson, C. A., Lepper, M. R., & Ross, L. (1980). Perseverance of social theories: The role of explanation in the persistence of discredited information. *Journal of Personality and Social Psychology, 39*(6), 1037–1049. https://doi.org/10.1037/h0077720

Asch, S. E. (1946). Forming impressions of personality. *Journal of Abnormal and Social Psychology, 41*, 258–290.

Aviram, H. (2019). Adversarial bias and the criminal process: Infusing the organizational perspective on criminal courts with insights from behavioral science. The Legal Process and the Promise of Justice: Studies Inspired by the Work of Malcolm Feeley. (pp. 19–35).

Babcock, B. A. (1982). Fair play: Evidence favorable to an accused and effective assistance of counsel. *Stanford Law Review, 34*, 1133–1182.

Babcock, L., & Loewenstein, G. (1997). Explaining bargaining impasse: The role of self-serving biases. *Journal of Economic Perspectives, 11*(1), 109–126.

Beersma, B., & De Dreu, C. K. (2002). Integrative and distributive negotiation in small groups: Effects of task structure, decision rule, and social motive. *Organizational Behavior and Human Decision Processes, 87*(2), 227–252. https://doi.org/10.1006/obhd.2001.2964

Bentham, J. (1843). Impropriety of the exclusion put upon Seif-disserving evidence by English Law. In J. Bowring (Ed.), *7 The works of Jeremy Bentham* (p. 454). William Tait.

Braman, D., Kahan, D. M., & Grimmelmann, J. (2005). Modeling facts, culture, and cognition in the gun debate. *Social Justice Research, 18*, 283–304. https://doi.org/10.1007/s11211-005-6826-0

Brennan, W. J., Jr. (1990). The criminal prosecution: Sporting event or quest for truth—a progress report. *Washington University Law Quarterly, 68*, 1–18.

Carnevale, P. J., & Probst, T. M. (1998). Social values and social conflict in creative problem solving and categorization. *Journal of Personality and Social Psychology, 74*(5), 1300–1309. https://doi.org/10.1037/0022-3514.74.5.1300

Churchland, P. S., & Sejnowski, T. J. (1992). *The computational brain.* MIT Press.

Cosmides, L., & Tooby, J. (2013). Evolutionary psychology: New perspectives on cognition and motivation. *Annual Review of Psychology, 64*, 201–229.

Crawford v. Washington. (2004). 541 U.S. 36.

Damaska, M. R. (1986). *The faces of justice and state authority: A comparative approach to the legal process.* Yale University Press.

De Dreu, C. K. W., & McCusker, C. (1997). Gain–loss frames and cooperation in two-person social dilemmas: A transformational analysis. *Journal of Personality and Social Psychology, 72*(5), 1093–1106. https://doi.org/10.1037/0022-3514.72.5.1093

DeMatteo, D., Edens, J. F., Galloway, M., Cox, J., Smith, S. T., et al. (2014). Investigating the role of the psychopathy checklist–revised in United States case law. Psychology, Public Policy, & Law, 20, 96–107. https://doi.org/10.1037/a0035452

Ditto, P. H., Munro, G. D., Apanovitch, A. M., Scepansky, J. A., & Lockhart, L. K. (2003). Spontaneous skepticism: The interplay of motivation and expectation in responses to favorable and unfavorable medical diagnoses. *Personality and Social Psychology Bulletin, 29*(9), 1120–1132. https://doi.org/10.1177/0146167203254536

Dunning, D. (2015). Motivated cognition in self and social thought. In M. Mikulincer, P. R. Shaver, E. Borgida, & J. A. Bargh (Eds.), *APA handbook of personality and social psychology, vol 1. Attitudes and social cognition* (pp. 777–803). American Psychological Association. https://doi.org/10.1037/14341-025

Edens, J. F., Cox, J., Smith, S. T., DeMatteo, D., & Sorman, K. (2015). How reliable are psychopathy checklist revised scores in Canadian criminal trials? A case law review. *Psychological Assessment, 26*, 447–456. https://doi.org/10.1037/pas0000048

Egli-Anthonioz, N., Schweizer, M., Vuille, J., & Kuhn, A. (2019). Role-induced bias in criminal prosecutions. *European Journal of Criminology, 16*(4), 452–465. https://doi.org/10.1177/1477370818772772

Eigen, Z. J., & Listokin, Y. (2012). Do lawyers really believe their own hype, and should they? A natural experiment. *The Journal of Legal Studies, 41*(2), 239–267.

Eliasmith, C. (2013). *How to build a brain: A neural architecture for biological cognition*. Oxford University Press.

Engel, C., & Rand, D. G. (2014). What does "clean" really mean? The implicit framing of decontextualized experiments. *Economics Letters, 122*(3), 386–389.

Engel, C., & Glöckner, A. (2013). Role-induced bias in court: An experimental analysis. *Journal of Behavioral Decision Making, 26*, 272–284. https://doi.org/10.1002/bdm.1761

Engel, C., Timme, S., & Glockner," A. (2020). Coherence-based reasoning and order effects in legal judgments. *Psychology, Public Policy, and Law, 26*(3), 333–352.

Feely, M. (1987). The adversary system. In R. J. Janosik (Ed.), *Encyclopedia of the American Judicial System: Studies of the principal institutions and processes of law* (pp. 753–766). Scribner's.

Festinger, L. (1957). *A theory of cognitive dissonance*. Row, Peterson.

Forgas, J. P., Williams, K. D., & Laham, S. M. (Eds.). (2005). *Social motivation: Conscious and unconscious processes* (Vol. 5). Cambridge University Press.

Frank, J. (1949). *Courts on trial: Myth and reality in American justice*. Princeton University Press.

Frankel, M. E. (1978). *Partisan justice*. Hill & Wang.

Freedman, M. H. (1998). Our constitutionalized adversary system. *Chapman Law Review, 1*, 57–90.

Fuller, L. L. (1961). The adversary system. In H. J. Berman (Ed.), *Talks on American Law: A series of broadcasts to foreign audiences by members of the Harvard Law School Faculty* (pp. 30–43). Vintage Books.

Glöckner, A., Betsch, T., & Schindler, N. (2010). Coherence shifts in probabilistic inference tasks. *Journal of Behavioral Decision Making, 23*(5), 439–462. https://doi.org/10.1002/bdm.668

Gollwitzer, P. M., & Bargh, J. A. (Eds.). (1996). *The psychology of action: Linking cognition and motivation to behavior*. Guilford Press.

Goodman-Delahunty, J., Granhag, P. A., Hartwig, M., & Loftus, E. F. (2010). Insightful or wishful: Lawyers' ability to predict case outcomes. *Psychology, Public Policy, and Law, 16*(2), 133–157. https://doi.org/10.1037/a0019060

Gross, S. R., & Syverud, K. D. (1991). Getting to no: A study of settlement negotiations and the selection of cases for trial. *Michigan Law Review, 90*, 319–393.

Hand, L. (1901). Historical and practical considerations regarding expert testimony. *Harvard Law Review, 15*, 40–58.

Heider, F. (1946). Attitudes and cognitive organization. *Journal of Psychology, 21*, 107–111.

Heider, F. (1958). *The psychology of interpersonal relations*. Wiley.

Heider, F. (1960). The gestalt theory of motivation. In *Nebraska symposium on motivation* (Vol. 8, pp. 145–172). University of Nebraska Press Lincoln.

Herring v. New York. (1975). 422 U.S. 853.

Herzog, S. M., & Hertwig, R. (2014). Think twice and then: Combining or choosing in dialectical bootstrapping? *Journal of Experimental Psychology: Learning, Memory, and Cognition, 40*(1), 218–232. https://doi.org/10.1037/a0034054

Holyoak, K. J. (1991). Symbolic connectionism: Toward third-generation theories of expertise. In K. A. Ericsson & J. Smith (Eds.), *Toward a general theory of expertise: Prospects and limits* (pp. 301–355). Cambridge University Press.

Holyoak, K. J., & Simon, D. (1999). Bidirectional reasoning in decision making by constraint satisfaction. *Journal of Experimental Psychology: General, 128*, 3–31. https://doi.org/10.1037/0096-3445.128.1.3

Holyoak, K. J., & Thagard, P. (1989). Analogical mapping by constraint satisfaction. *Cognitive Science, 13*(3), 295–355. https://doi.org/10.1207/s15516709cog1303_1
Hopfield, J. J. (1982). Neural networks and physical systems with emergent collective computational abilities. *Proceedings of the National Academy of Sciences, 79*(8), 2554–2558.
Hopfield, J. J. (1984). Neurons with graded response have collective computational properties like those of two-state neurons. *Proceedings of the National Academy of Sciences, 81*(10), 3088–3092.
Hummel, J. E., & Holyoak, K. J. (2003). A symbolic-connectionist theory of relational inference and generalization. *Psychological Review, 110*, 220–264. https://doi.org/10.1037/0033-295X.110.2.220
James v. Illinois. (1990). 493 U.S. 307.
Janis, I. L., & King, B. T. (1954). The influence of role playing on opinion change. *The Journal of Abnormal and Social Psychology, 49*(2), 211–218. https://doi.org/10.1037/h0056957
Jeklic, M. A. (2023). Can you trust your lawyer's call? Legal advisers exhibit myside bias resistant to debiasing interventions. *Journal of Empirical Legal Studies, 20*, 409–433. https://doi.org/10.1111/jels.12350
Kagan, R. A. (2019). *Adversarial legalism: The American way of law*. Harvard University Press.
Keltner, D., & Robinson, R. J. (1996). Extremism, power, and the imagined basis of social conflict. *Current Directions in Psychological Science, 5*(4), 101–105. https://doi.org/10.1111/1467-8721.ep11452765
Kenyon, T. (2014). False polarization: Debiasing as applied social epistemology. *Synthese, 191*(11), 2529–2547. https://doi.org/10.1007/s11229-014-0438-x
Kihlstrom, J. F. (2019). The motivational unconscious. *Social and Personality Psychology Compass, 13*(5), e12466. https://doi.org/10.1111/spc3.12466
Kiser, R. L., Asher, M. A., & McShane, B. B. (2008). Let's not make a deal: An empirical study of decision making in unsuccessful settlement negotiations. *Journal of Empirical Legal Studies, 5*(3), 551–591. https://doi.org/10.1111/j.1740-1461.2008.00133.x
Kunda, Z. (1990). The case for motivated reasoning. *Psychological Bulletin, 108*(3), 480–498. https://doi.org/10.1037/0033-2909.108.3.480
Lind, E. A., Thibaut, J., & Walker, L. (1973). Discovery and presentation of evidence in adversary and nonadversary proceedings. *Michigan Law Review, 71*(6), 1129–1144.
Landman, S. (1984). *The adversary system: A description and defense*. The American Enterprise Institute.
Langbein, J. H. (2003). *The origins of adversary criminal trial*. Oxford University Press.
Langer, M. (2016). Strength, weakness, or both? On the endurance of the adversarial-inquisitorial systems in comparative criminal procedure. In *Comparative criminal procedure* (pp. 519–536). Edward Elgar Publishing.
Liberman, V., Samuels, S. M., & Ross, L. (2004). The name of the game: Predictive power of reputations versus situational labels in determining prisoner's dilemma game moves. *Personality and Social Psychology Bulletin, 30*(9), 1175–1185. https://doi.org/10.1177/0146167204264004
Lilly v. Virginia. (1999). 527 U.S. 116.
Loewenstein, G., Issacharoff, S., Camerer, C., & Babcock, L. (1993). Self-serving assessments of fairness and pretrial bargaining. *The Journal of Legal Studies, 22*, 135–159.
Loewenstein, G., & Lerner, J. S. (2003). The role of affect in decision making. In R. J. Davidson, K. R. Scherer, & H. H. Goldsmith (Eds.), *Handbook of affective sciences* (pp. 619–642). Oxford University Press.
Markman, K. D., & Hirt, E. R. (2002). Social prediction and the "allegiance bias". *Social Cognition, 20*, 58–86. https://doi.org/10.1521/soco.20.1.58.20943
MacCoun, R. J. (2015). The epistemic contract: Fostering an appropriate level of public trust in experts. In B. H. Bornstein & A. Tomkins (Eds.), *Motivating cooperation and compliance with authority* (Nebraska symposium on motivation) (pp. 191–214). Springer. https://doi.org/10.1007/978-3-319-16151-8_9

McGuire, W. J. (1968). Theory of the structure of human thought. In Abelson et al. (Eds.), *Theories of cognitive consistency: A sourcebook* (pp. 140–162). Rand McNally.

Melnikoff, D. E., & Strohminger, N. (2020). The automatic influence of advocacy on lawyers and novices. *Nature Human Behaviour, 4*(12), 1258–1264. https://doi.org/10.1038/s41562-020-00943-3

Mnookin, J. L. (2008). Expert evidence, partisanship, and epistemic competence. *Brooklyn Law Review, 73*, 1009–1033.

Monin, B., & Norton, M. I. (2003). Perceptions of a fluid consensus: Uniqueness bias, false consensus, false polarization, and pluralistic ignorance in a water conservation crisis. *Personality and Social Psychology Bulletin, 29*(5), 559–567. https://doi.org/10.1177/0146167203029005001

Munro, G. D., Ditto, P. H., Lockhart, L. K., Fagerlin, A., Gready, M., & Peterson, E. (2002). Biased assimilation of sociopolitical arguments: Evaluating the 1996 US presidential debate. *Basic and Applied Social Psychology, 24*(1), 15–26. https://doi.org/10.1207/S15324834BASP2401_2

Murrie, D. C., & Boccaccini, M. T. (2015). Adversarial allegiance in forensic evaluations. *Annual Review of Law and Social Science, 11*, 37–55. https://doi.org/10.1146/annurev-lawsocsci-120814-121714

Murrie, D. C., Boccaccini, M. T., Guarnera, L. A., & Rufino, K. A. (2013). Are forensic experts biased by the side that retained them? *Psychological Science, 24*, 1889–1897. https://doi.org/10.1177/0956797613481812

Murrie, D. C., Boccaccini, M. T., Turner, D. B., Meeks, M., Woods, C., et al. (2009). Rater (dis) agreement on risk assessment measures in sexually violent predator proceedings: Evidence of adversarial allegiance in forensic evaluation? *Psychology, Public Policy, & Law, 15*(1), 19–53. https://doi.org/10.1037/a0014897

O'Brien, B. (2009). Prime suspect: An examination of factors that aggravate and counteract confirmation bias in criminal investigations. *Psychology, Public Policy, and Law, 15*(4), 315–334. https://doi.org/10.1037/a0017881

O'Reilly, R. C., Munakata, Y., Frank, M. J., & Hazy, T. E. (2012). Computational cognitive neuroscience. Wiki Book. https://github.com/CompCogNeuro/ed4.

Polzer, J. T., Mannix, E. A., & Neale, M. A. (1998). Interest alignment and coalitions in multiparty negotiation. *Academy of Management Journal, 41*(1), 42–54. https://doi.org/10.5465/256896

Portuondo v. Agard. (2000). 529 U.S. 61.

Pound, R. (1906). The causes of popular dissatisfaction with the administration of justice. Presented at the annual convention of the American Bar Association, 1906.

Pruitt, D. G. (1967). Reward structure and cooperation: The decomposed Prisoner's Dilemma game. *Journal of Personality and Social Psychology, 7*(1, Pt.1), 21–27. https://doi.org/10.1037/h0024914

Rachlinski, J. J. (1996). Gains, losses, and the psychology of litigation. *Southern California Law Review, 70*, 113–185.

Read, S. J., Vanman, E. J., & Miller, L. C. (1997). Connectionism, parallel constraint satisfaction processes, and gestalt principles: (Re)introducing cognitive dynamics to social psychology. *Personality and Social Psychology Review, 1*(1), 26–53. https://doi.org/10.1207/s15327957pspr0101_3

Rosenberg, M. J. (1968). Hedonism, inauthenticity, and other goads towards expansion of a consistency theory. In R. P. Abelson, E. Aronson, W. J. McGuire, T. M. Newcomb, M. J. Rosenberg, & P. H. Tannenbaum (Eds.), *Theories of cognitive consistency: A sourcebook* (pp. 73–111). Rand McNally.

Schwardmann, P., Tripodi, E., & Van der Weele, J. J. (2022). Self-persuasion: Evidence from field experiments at international debating competitions. *American Economic Review, 112*(4), 1118–1146. https://doi.org/10.1257/aer.20200372

Sheppard, B. H., & Vidmar, N. (1980). Adversary pretrial procedures and testimonial evidence: Effects of lawyer's role and Machiavellianism. *Journal of Personality and Social Psychology, 39*, 320–332. https://doi.org/10.1037/0022-3514.39.2.320

Simon, D. (2004). A third view of the black box: Cognitive coherence in legal decision making. *University of Chicago Law Review, 71*(2), 511–586.
Simon, D. (2012). *In doubt: The psychology of the criminal justice process*. Harvard University Press.
Simon, D. (2025). The adversarial bias. *Annual Review of Law & Social Science*. 21. Available online: https://doi.org/10.1146/annurev-lawsocsci-121324-110748.
Simon, D., Ahn, M., Stenstrom, D. M., & Read, S. J. (2020). The adversarial mindset. *Psychology, Public Policy, and Law, 26*(3), 353–377.
Simon, D., & Holyoak, K. J. (2002). Structural dynamics of cognition: From consistency theories to constraint satisfaction. *Personality and Social Psychology Review, 6*, 283–294.
Simon, D., & Melnikoff, D. E. (2024). Zeal spillovers: The adversarial bias and pre-trial decision making. *The Journal of Legal Empirical Analysis*, 1(2), 326–342. https://doi.org/10.1037/law0000226
Simon, D., & Read, S. J. (2023). Toward a general framework of biased reasoning: Coherence-based reasoning. *Perspectives on Psychological Science*, 20(3), 421–459. https://doi.org/10.1177/17456916231204579
Simon, D., Snow, C. J., & Read, S. J. (2004). The redux of cognitive consistency theories: Evidence judgments by constraint satisfaction. *Journal of Personality and Social Psychology, 86*, 814–837. https://doi.org/10.1037/0022-3514.86.6.814
Simon, D., Stenstrom, D. M., & Read, S. J. (2015). The coherence effect: Blending cold and hot cognitions. *Journal of Personality and Social Psychology, 109*, 369–394. https://doi.org/10.1037/pspa0000029
Sklansky, D. A. (2008). Anti-inquisitorialism. *Harvard Law Review, 122*, 1634–1704.
Smolensky, P. (1989). Connectionist modeling: Neural computation/mental connections. In L. Nadel, L. A. Cooper, P. Culicover, & R. M. Harnish (Eds.), *Computational models of cognition and perception. Neural connections, mental computation* (pp. 49–67). MIT Press.
Sorrentino, R. M., & Higgins, E. T. (Eds.). (1986). *Handbook of motivation and cognition: Foundations of social behavior*. Guilford Press.
Sood, A. M. (2013). Motivated cognition in legal judgments—An analytic review. *Annual Review of Law and Social Science, 9*(1), 307–325.
Spamann, H. (2020). Extension: Lawyers' role-induced bias arises fast and persists despite intervention. *The Journal of Legal Studies, 49*(2), 467–485.
Tajfel, H. (1982). Social psychology of intergroup relations. *Annual Review of Psychology, 33*(1), 1–39.
Tajfel, H., Turner, J. C., Austin, W. G., & Worchel, S. (1979). An integrative theory of intergroup conflict. *Organizational identity: A reader, 56*(65).
Thagard, P. (1989). Explanatory coherence. *Behavioral and Brain Sciences, 12*(3), 435–467.
Thagard, P. (2019). *Brain-mind: From neurons to consciousness and creativity* (treatise on mind and society). Oxford University Press.
Thibaut, J. W., & Walker, L. (1975). *Procedural justice: A psychological analysis*. Lawrence Erlbaum.
Thibaut, J., & Walker, L. (1978). A theory of procedure. *California Law Review, 66*, 541–566. https://doi.org/10.2307/3480099
Tversky, A., & Kahneman, D. (1974). Judgment under uncertainty: Heuristics and Biases: Biases in judgments reveal some heuristics of thinking under uncertainty. *Science, 185*(4157), 1124–1131. https://doi.org/10.1126/science.185.4157.1124
United States v. Agurs. (1976). 427 U.S. 97.
United States v. Cronic. (1984). 466 U.S. 648.
United States v. Nobles. (1975). 422 U.S. 225.
Vidmar, N., & Laird, N. M. (1983). Adversary social roles: Their effects on witnesses' communication of evidence and the assessments of adjudicators. *Journal of Personality and Social Psychology, 44*, 888–898. https://doi.org/10.1037/0022-3514.44.5.888
Watkins v. Sowders. (1981). 449 U.S. 341.
Weinreb, L. L. (1977). *Denial of justice: Criminal process in the United States*. Free Press.

Wells, G. L., Ferguson, T. J., & Lindsay, R. C. L. (1981). The tractability of eyewitness confidence and its implications for triers of fact. *Journal of Applied Psychology, 66*, 688–696. https://doi.org/10.1037/0021-9010.66.6.688
Wigmore, J. H. (1923). *A treatise on the Anglo-American system of evidence in trials at common law, §563*. Little, Brown and Company.
Wyer, R. S., Jr., & Frey, D. (1983). The effects of feedback about self and others on the recall and judgments of feedback-relevant information. *Journal of Experimental Social Psychology, 19*(6), 540–559. https://doi.org/10.1016/0022-1031(83)90015-X
Wigmore, J. H. (1974). In J. H. Chabourn (Ed.), *Evidence in trials at common law*. Little Brown.

Sentencing for Multiple Offenses: When Seeking Justice Is Too Cruel and Cognitively Demanding

Mandeep K. Dhami and Charis Bechan

Introduction

Criminal sentencing is arguably one of the most visible parts of the criminal justice process. It is at this stage where sentencers demonstrate society's response to those who break the rules, and it is at this stage where *justice* is seen to be done. Indeed, the concept of justice serves as a guiding principle in sentencing, even though, as we note below, this is not the main or sole purpose of sentencing. According to philosophers, psychologists and legal policymakers alike (e.g., Folger, 1977; Lind & Tyler, 1988; Rawls, 1971; Sentencing Council, 2024; United States Sentencing Commission, 2023), justice requires that offenders who have either pled guilty to an offense, or been found guilty of one, should be treated fairly and equitably, with respect for their rights and with dignity, when receiving one or more of several forms of penalty.

Officially, in order of perceived severity, from the least to the most severe (e.g., Sentencing Council, 2024; United States Sentencing Commission, 2023; but also see van Ginneken & Hayes, 2017 for an offender's perspective), these penalties range from payment of fine and/or compensation, through community service/probation, to custody (with interventions or rehabilitation programs potentially available in both the community and in custody). Passing out these penalties in a just manner requires impartiality, objectivity, and avoidance of bias or discrimination.

From a normative standpoint, sentencers are expected to apply relevant legal rules and procedures in a consistent and transparent manner. Sentencers must attend to available, legally relevant information in a case, weight it according to its importance, and integrate it in order to arrive at a penalty that is just and proportionate

M. K. Dhami (✉) · C. Bechan
Middlesex University, London, UK

R. L. Wiener, D. J. Hansen (eds.), *Legal Judgment and the Motivation for Justice*, Nebraska Symposium on Motivation 71,
https://doi.org/10.1007/978-3-031-98812-7_5

(see e.g., Sentencing Council, 2015; United States Sentencing Commission, 2023). However, as Dhami et al. (2015) point out, the search for justice and adherence to the normative model is shaped by a sentencer's ability to perform the cognitive task of sentencing itself. This task, like other legal tasks such as deciding on bail or pre-trial detention, is said to be psychologically implausible for the unaided human mind because people have limited attention, memory, and information processing capacities (e.g., Dhami, 2003; Dhami and Ayton, 2001). In this chapter, we argue that the performance of the task of sentencing is particularly challenging when sentencing offenders who have confessed, pled guilty to, or been convicted of, more than one offense[1]—what we call "multiple-offense" (MO)[2] cases—as opposed to "single-offense" (SO) cases. Our focus is on the task of sentencing an offender in a MO case for all offenses in one hearing (for sentences meted out across different hearings, see Drapul, 2023).

Although official sentencing statistics are mute on the number of MO cases sentenced annually, data from other sources suggest that such cases are equally, if not more, prevalent than SO cases. For example, in the analyses of data collected by the Sentencing Council for England and Wales from Crown Courts,[3] Dhami (2022) found that 48.7% of cases covering 10 broad offense types were MO cases. The proportion of MO and SO cases differed across offense types, with around a third of arson offenses being MO cases to nearly all offenses of possession of indecent photograph of a child being MO cases. Similarly, a US-based analysis of arrest charges by Reaves (2009) revealed that MO cases accounted for 55% of the total, with a range of 47% for public order offenses to 67% for violent offenses. The prevalence of MO cases thus underscores the importance of examining how sentencers search for justice in these cases.

We argue that efforts to develop sentencing policy and guidelines to assist sentencers to perform the cognitive task of sentencing in MO cases may inadvertently undermine the search for justice. In the remaining sections of this chapter, we first describe the sentencing task, emphasizing its cognitive complexity. We next present the approaches that different jurisdictions have adopted to sentencing MO cases, highlighting implications for justice. Following this, we review the small body of past research on the approach taken in England and Wales (as well as several other common law countries), and we present new empirical findings from our analyses of judgments made by the Criminal Court of Appeal in this jurisdiction. Finally, we suggest that sentencing policy and practice in MO cases ought to be based on

[1] We acknowledge the distinction between offenses an offender may have pled guilty to or been convicted of and offenses the offender may have committed, or been charged with.

[2] This is sometimes called 'simultaneous offense' and differs from a single-offense or 'sequential offense'. It may also be referred to as 'multiple offender' or 'multi-count conviction', which differ from a repeat, persistent or serial offender.

[3] This is the higher-tier criminal court in England and Wales which deals with the most serious offenses. Here, sentences are passed by professional judges who have no limits on their sentencing power beyond the maximum penalty associated with an offense.

empirical evidence, pointing to avenues for future research and potential ways in which sentencers can be supported in the search for justice while performing the cognitively complex task of sentencing.

Sentencing as a Complex Cognitive Task

When making a sentencing decision, the sentencer is meant to achieve one, more, or all of the several different goals of sentencing. The purpose may be to *punish offenders*, showing them retribution and giving them their just deserts via imposing a fine or custody proportionate to the seriousness of the offense (including the harm caused and culpability of the offender). Sentencers may wish to *rehabilitate offenders*, thus reducing the likelihood of reoffending via imposing a community- or prison-based intervention such as drug treatment. A sentence could *repair the harm* done and heal victims in order to restore "peace" and facilitate social integration of offenders via imposing a compensation payment or other reparative measures. The goal of sentencing could also be to *protect the public* by incapacitating persistent or dangerous offenders via long-term custody or restricting/supervising their behavior using probation. Finally, sentencers may aim to *reduce crime* via deterring offenders as well as others from committing crimes in the future using penalties that are considered to be both certain and severe (e.g., see Sentencing Act 2020; United States Sentencing Commission, 2023).

Each of the purposes of sentencing typically focuses on either the offender, victim, or society-at-large. However, these goals may be competing (e.g., punishment v. rehabilitation). In addition, there is ambiguity in how to achieve the goals because different sentencing options may be used to achieve the same goal (e.g., payment of compensation may be punishing and reparative), and the same sentencing option may be used to fulfil different, competing goals (e.g., custody may be used to punish offenders, rehabilitate them, protect the public, and/or reduce crime). This competing nature of sentencing goals and ambiguity in how to apply sentencing options to fulfil these goals adds cognitive complexity to the sentencing task.

Indeed, the task is already complex in terms of the number of factors that sentencers are required to consider in order to arrive at a sentence, the varied nature of these factors, and how they are interpreted, assessed, and aggregated. Specifically, in most jurisdictions, sentencers are expected to consider "legal" factors such as offense seriousness, which may be based on preceding judgments of the harm caused and the offender's culpability. In addition, sentencers are expected to consider the offender's criminal history, as well as any relevant aggravating factors (e.g., offense committed on bail and previous convictions) which increase penalty severity, and mitigating factors (e.g., offender pleads guilty, and offender assists authorities) which reduce it. Sentencers may also be obliged to consider victim impact statements, expert assessments about the offender (e.g., psychiatric evaluations and risk of reoffending) as well as recommendations such as those made by a probation officer. The weighting and integration of multiple sentencing-relevant factors arguably require cognitive abilities beyond that of the limited capacity of the unaided human mind.

Finally, sentencers must choose among one or more of the sentencing options available to them. This selection could be constrained by the fact that sentencing options may be differentially applicable to offense types (e.g., more or less serious offenses) as well as offender groups (e.g., adult or youth). Additionally, offenses typically have fixed maximum penalties assigned to them and may also have mandatory minimum penalties. To some extent, such constraints may help in guiding judicial judgment, although the restrictions may sometimes appear somewhat arbitrary.

As mentioned earlier, the sentencer must avoid bias and discrimination in the sentence passed, even though overcoming unconscious bias is extremely difficult, if not impossible (see Calanchini et al., 2020; Fitzgerald et al., 2019; Lai et al., 2014). Further cognitive burden is added by the need to provide individualized justice such that each case is dealt with on its own (de)merits, while simultaneously ensuring there is uniformity or consistency across cases in an effort to reduce disparity. Indeed, critics argue that individualization and uniformity are incompatible in the same decision task (e.g., Dhami et al., 2020; Krasnostein & Freiberg, 2013). Moreover, the sentencing decision needs to be reached in a transparent way and ought to be certain and predictable—so, people have clear expectations and can understand the reasoning process. However, it is arguable whether such conditions can be met, given the difficulties individuals have in accessing and articulating cognitive processing (e.g., Johansson et al., 2006; Johansson et al., 2013; McLaughlin & Somerville, 2013; Nisbett & Wilson, 1977). This requires conscious awareness and accurate recall of the reasoning process, as well as the precise language to unambiguously articulate it.

As a consequence of the aforementioned cognitive complexities of the sentencing task, sentencing behavior is likely to depart from the normative model, and sentencers may (inadvertently) mete out penalties that are perceived as unjust. This is likely both in the absence of any further guidance, as well as in the presence of vague and ill-defined guidance, or guidance that is too complex, too rigid and lacking a reliable and valid evidence base (see Dhami et al., 2015). Appellant courts have therefore found themselves reviewing sentences, some of which they ultimately deem to be unduly excessive or unduly lenient.[4]

Beyond the judgments of appellant courts, there is also a wealth of past research that has documented objectionable sentencing practice and outcomes. For instance, studies have reported inconsistency and bias in sentencing decisions arising from case-related, extra-legal factors such as offender race (see Mitchell, 2005; Spohn, 2015). Research has also shown that sentencers may ignore vast amounts of available and legally relevant information (e.g., Konečni & Ebbesen, 1982). Of particular note is research demonstrating that sentencers are (subconsciously) influenced

[4]Although unduly lenient sentences are uncommon they are nevertheless reviewed by the Appeal Court in England and Wales, which is the subject of the research presented in this paper. In such cases, if the appeal is allowed, the sentence may be substituted or varied.

or biased by irrelevant numerical information which appears as part of the sentencing task (e.g., Englich et al., 2006; Rachlinski et al., 2015) as well as by the continuous nature of numerical sentencing scales (e.g., Dhami et al., 2020; Roberts et al., 2018).

In a series of experiments comprising a combination of German judges, prosecutors, and legal experts, Englich et al. (2006) found that judgments about custodial sentencing lengths were influenced by exposure to irrelevant (high and low) numerical anchors. Even clearly random numbers had an unwanted influence on sentencing, and these findings could not be accounted for by experience/expertise. The numerical anchors affected the processing of case information such that incriminating arguments were categorized faster when participants were exposed to high anchors. Englich et al. state that this is consistent with the idea that the anchors lead to selective accessibility of information in the mind of the sentencer which is then used to produce (high or lower) sentences, depending on the anchor-consistent information processed (for more information on anchoring and adjustment effects, see also Liu, 2023 and Tversky & Kahneman, 1974).

More recently, in the statistical analyses of annual sentencing data from two different jurisdictions (i.e., England and Wales, and New South Wales, Australia), Dhami et al. (2020) revealed that the sentences meted out to around 90% of cases comprised a small number of custodial sentence lengths, community penalty lengths, and amount of fines/compensation. The application of what they call a small number of sentence "doses", or what is essentially a grouping of cases into a small number of "bins", implies that sentences did not reflect (or were proportionate to) the unique characteristics of the offense and offender. Rather, it appears that sentencers were influenced by the continuous nature of the numerical sentencing scales such that they displayed behavior consistent with a predictable pattern of "preferred numbers" (see Albers, 2001; Baird & Noma, 1975), "just noticeable differences," and logarithmic scaling (Algom, 2021). There exist neural bases for this behavior (Dehaene, 2003). It is worth noting that the cross-jurisdictional approach used by Dhami et al. (2020) serves to underscore the psychological, rather than legal, explanation for the observed undesirable sentencing behavior.

Despite the wealth of research on sentencing, our understanding of sentencing MO cases is currently limited. This is because to date, the overwhelming majority of past research on sentencing has either focused solely on SO cases, has conflated MO with SO cases, or controlled for this factor rather than examine its effect. Regardless, given the additional cognitive complexity of dealing with MO cases, it is likely that the normatively divergent patterns of sentencing behavior observed in past research and the apparently unjust sentences meted out will be replicated when studying sentencing in MO cases. In fact, additional concerns may arise when examining sentencing outcomes for "comparable" offenses appearing in SO and MO cases. In the next section, we consider current approaches to sentencing MO cases.

Approaches to Sentencing Multiple-Offense Cases

In MO cases, offenders are sentenced for offenses that are typically linked in some way.[5] For instance, the offenses may be committed in conjunction with one another such as an assault on store staff during theft from a store, or committed contemporaneously such as two residential burglaries on the same day, or against the same victim multiple times, even over a long period of time such as in some cases of fraud and sexual abuse. Thus, MO cases may involve the same or different types of offenses as well as the same or different types of victims, and even the characteristics of offenders themselves may change if these offenses occur over a long period. Consequently, sentencing in MO cases differs from that in SO cases, even though sentencing in the former type of case takes as its starting point sentencing in the latter type of case.

In a SO case, the sentence ought to reflect the output of a consideration of the characteristics of an individual offense and offender (taking account of the goals of sentence along with the other conditions mentioned above). By contrast, the need to consider the characteristics of more than one offense in MO cases adds to the cognitive complexity of the sentencing task. This is especially so when the offenses in a MO case are of different types, making it difficult to assess the overall harm and culpability (seriousness), and when the applicable sentencing options are of different types (i.e., measured in different units), making it difficult to aggregate them.

Indeed, the difficulties associated with sentencing MO cases have been officially acknowledged. Individual sentencers (e.g., Sentencing Council, 2021), courts (e.g., State v. Cloutier, 646 A.2d 358 [1994]) and legal commentators (e.g., Bagaric & Alexander, 2013; Kelly, 2022; Lippke, 2011; Lovegrove, 2000; Manson, 2013; Ryberg, 2005; Thomas, 1970; Wasik, 2012 see also Ryberg et al., 2017) have all long grappled with the problem of how to sentence MO cases. In this chapter, we focus on common law jurisdictions, with a particular emphasis on England and Wales.

When sentencing MO cases, common law jurisdictions have typically rejected a simple cumulative approach whereby sentences for each offense are merely aggregated to produce a final sentence (see also National Judicial College of Australia, 2023). For instance, the United States Sentencing Commission (2023, Chap. 1, Part A, p. 10) states that "The difficulty is that when a defendant engages in conduct that causes several harms, each additional harm, even if it increases the extent to which punishment is warranted, does not necessarily warrant a proportionate increase in punishment." Similarly, the Sentencing Council for England and Wales has stated "It is usually impossible to arrive at a just and proportionate sentence for multiple offending simply by adding together hypothetical single sentences." (Sentencing Council, 2011, p. 4).

[5] There will also be instances where the 'associated' offenses may not be linked, but are simply being sentenced on the same occasion (Wasik, 2012).

Motivations for Rejecting a Cumulative Approach

There are several motivations for rejecting a cumulative approach when sentencing MO cases. One is to avoid meting out disproportionately harsh sentences (e.g., Sentencing Council, 2012b; United States Sentencing Commission, 2023; National Judicial College of Australia, 2023), especially when minor offenses appear in the presence of more serious ones. Relatedly, there is desire to maintain the ordinal proportionality of different offense types in terms of their seriousness so that multiple minor offenses are not sentenced more harshly than one more serious offense (Ashworth, 2015; see also Lovegrove, 2000; Jareborg, 1998). Indeed, there does appear to be some general consensus on crime seriousness across a sample of crimes against the person, crimes against property, and organized and corporate crime (Adriaenssen et al., 2020). A third reason for rejecting a cumulative approach is the wish to avoid crushing prison terms for offenders who would have few prospects after release (Bottoms, 1998).[6] Long prison terms can have negative consequences for offenders' rehabilitation and reintegration into society and their opportunity to lead a meaningful life after release such as having a family and career (e.g., Crawley & Sparks, 2006; Wyse, 2018). Finally, other motivations for rejecting a cumulative approach arguably include the need to minimize the resource and cost burden associated with long-term imprisonment.

As a result of these concerns, by contrast to sentencing in SO cases, there currently exist several general approaches to sentencing MO cases. We propose that these approaches can be categorized into one of three main types.

Simplification, Minimization, and Totality of MO Cases

One approach involves *simplification* of a MO case, another requires *minimization* of some offenses in a MO case, and the third approach deals with a MO case in its *totality*. Specifically, the simplification approach requires the sentencer to simplify the task such that it resembles the task of sentencing a SO case.[7] This is done by

[6] Although, in Australia a crushing prison term may be imposed it is deemed 'effective' (National Judicial College of Australia, 2023).

[7] Another form of simplification involves *disregarding* the other offenses committed by an offender. For instance, in England and Wales and Australia, offenders are allowed to ask the sentencing court for other offenses to be 'taken into consideration' (Sentencing Council, 2012b, pp. 2–4; see also National Judicial College of Australia, 2018). This means that a sentence is passed for the 'conviction offense' only, although the fact that other offenses were taken into consideration serve as an aggravating factor which increases penalty severity. Consequently, those other offenses are treated less severely (more leniently) than if they were in a SO case, while the penalty for the 'conviction offense' would be more severe than if it had appeared in a SO case because the sentence would be aggravated by the presence of the other offenses that were disregarded (i.e., taken into consideration). For (probably most) victims and (at least some of) the public, disregarding (at least some) of the other offenses is likely to be unsatisfactory because it is too lenient and allows offenders to

reconfiguring the offenses in a MO case into one. An illustration of this is provided by the United States Sentencing Commission (2023, Chap. 1, Part A, p. 10; see also Chap. 3, Part D) when it states that "If the offense guidelines…base the offense level primarily on the amount of money or quantity of substance involved (e.g., theft, fraud, drug trafficking, firearms dealing), or otherwise contain provisions dealing with repetitive or ongoing misconduct (e.g., many environmental offenses), add the numerical quantities and apply the pertinent offense guideline, including any specific offense characteristics for the conduct taken as a whole." (United States Sentencing Commission, 2023; Chap. 3, Part D, p. 369). Here, several offenses are reshaped into one for sentencing by essentially aggregating the harm that the totality of the crimes caused.

The minimization approach requires the sentencer to minimize other offenses in a MO case and focus mainly on what is considered to be the most serious offense. According to the United States Sentencing Commission (2023, p. 10; see also Chap. 3, Part D), "When offenses are closely interrelated, group them together for purposes of the multiple-count rules, and use only the offense level for the most serious offense in that group… As to other offenses (e.g., independent instances of assault or robbery), start with the offense level for the most serious count and use the number and severity of additional counts to determine the amount by which to increase that offense level." (United States Sentencing Commission, 2023; Chap. 3, Part D, p. 369–370). The increase is, however, diminishing (i.e., "The amount of the additional punishment declines as the number of additional offenses increases"; see United States Sentencing Commission, 2023, Chap. 3, Part D, p. 369). Thus, the sentence is either based on the most serious offense, or the seriousness of that offense is increased (on a diminishing scale) given the presence of other offenses, and the penalty is meted out on that basis.

Finally, the third approach to sentencing MO cases is to respond to the multiple offenses in their *totality*. What is called the "totality principle" is applied in various forms in England and Wales, Canada, Australia, and New Zealand. In England and Wales, effective from July 2023, a revision to this principle states that "the overall sentence should reflect all of the offending behavior with reference to overall harm and culpability, together with the aggravating and mitigating factors relating to the offenses and those personal to the offender; and be just and proportionate." (Sentencing Council, 2023b, p. 1). Prior to this, effective since June 2012 to July 2023, the totality principle stated that the court "should pass a total sentence which reflects *all* the offending behaviour before it and is just and proportionate….[This consideration of offending behavior should occur] together with the factors personal to the offender as a whole." (Sentencing Council, 2012b, p. 5; emphasis as in original, words in brackets added; see also pp. 6–8). Thus, until very recently, in this jurisdiction, the approach to sentencing MO cases required sentencers to calculate a

'get away with it'. However, for present purposes, we do not consider this as an approach to sentencing MO cases because offenses 'taken into consideration' could occur when sentencing a SO case.

penalty for each offense, aggregate them, and then apply a (downward) adjustment based on personal mitigation. We will consider this approach in more detail later.

Of course, when sentencing a MO case, and especially under the totality approach, the sentencer must also decide if the penalties should run (wholly or partly) concurrently or consecutively (see e.g., National Judicial College of Australia, 2022; Sentencing Council, 2012b, p. 6–8; United States Sentencing Commission, Chap. 5, Part G). This decision may be influenced by the strength of the association between the offenses such that sentences for closely intertwined offenses are likely to be served concurrently. In some jurisdictions such as the State of Victoria, Australia, there is a statutory presumption in favor of passing concurrent sentences (Wasik, 2012). This is also true for some U.S. jurisdictions (see Frase, 2017). Regardless, a consecutive sentence could be passed if concurrency does not reflect the overall criminal conduct, although in doing so, the sentence should be just and proportionate (for forms of "consecutivism" and "concurrentivism" see Lippke, 2011). Again, it is not uncommon for courts to have difficulty in determining whether a sentence should run consecutively or concurrently (e.g., see Lora v. United States, 599, U.S., 2023; see also Sentencing Council, 2021).

Implications for Justice

Each of the approaches to sentencing MO cases attempts to simplify the cognitive task of sentencing MO cases by largely restructuring it so that it more closely resembles the task of sentencing SO cases. Although some question whether this is appropriate (e.g., Wasik, 2012), our concern here is on the implications of these approaches for the pursuit of justice. All result in MO cases receiving less severe penalties than would be so if sentencers followed a simple cumulative approach (i.e., sentencing each case separately and summing the total to arrive at a final sentence).

Legal commentators have debated whether sentences passed in MO cases ought to be more severe than those passed in SO cases (e.g., Bagaric & Alexander, 2013; Frase, 2017; Lippke, 2011). While sentencing is meant to reflect the unique characteristics of an offense and offender, sentencing is also meant to be consistent across similar offenses and offenders (see e.g., Sentencing Council, 2015; United States Sentencing Commission, 2023). As such, sentencing policy typically explicitly dictates that MO cases be treated more punitively than their SO counterparts (see e.g., National Judicial College of Australia, 2023; Sentencing Council, 2012b; United States Sentencing Commission, 2023). It is also suggested that concurrent sentences will be longer than a single sentence for a comparable SO case (e.g., Sentencing Council, 2012b). It is, however, questionable whether offenses appearing in MO cases are sentenced more harshly than comparable offenses appearing in SO cases. This is partly because, as we discuss below, the approaches to sentencing MO cases appear to undermine this dictate.

As Table 1 shows, the different approaches to sentencing MO cases appear to have theoretically different implications for whether an offense in a MO case would receive a penalty that was the same, more severe or less severe than if it appeared alone (i.e., in a SO case). Simplification by *reconfiguring* the offenses in a MO case into one more serious offense would result in a sentence that was more severe than that meted out to an offence in a SO case that was comparable to the original most serious offence in a MO case (before it was reconfigured). However, it is unclear if the penalty for the reconfigured offence would be equal to, more, or less severe than an offense of equivalent seriousness in a SO case.

Under the *minimization* approach, the sentence for the focal (most serious) offense in a MO case is likely to be more severe than that meted out to a comparable offense in a SO because the offense is considered to be more serious given the presence of other offenses. However, again, it remains unclear if the penalty would be equal to, more, or less severe than an equivalently serious offense appearing in a SO case. By contrast, penalties for the other offenses in a MO case that have been minimized would, by default, be less severe (or more lenient) than for comparable offenses in SO cases.

Finally, adjusting the aggregated sentence when viewing a MO case in its *totality* (as per the 2012 "totality" guideline in England and Wales that was in operation until recently) may result in some sort of sentence discount or reduction for all offenses in a MO case because the application of the totality principle allows personal mitigation to be considered (at least) twice. The first opportunity is when a sentence is calculated for each offense separately, and the second opportunity arises when an adjustment is made to these penalties in order to arrive at the final sentence (see also Dhami, 2022). Thus, the sentence for an offense in a MO case may be less severe (more lenient) than for a comparable offense appearing in a SO case.

Therefore, the predicted sentencing outcomes for offenses appearing in MO cases are not always more severe than for comparable offenses appearing in SO cases. Further reinforcing the potential for more lenient outcomes in MO cases are sentencing policies that grant sentencers additional discretion. For example, the United States Sentencing Commission (2023, Chap. 1, Part A, p. 10) states that "The guidelines have been written in order to minimize the possibility that an arbitrary casting of a single transaction into several counts will produce a longer sentence. In addition, the sentencing court will have adequate power to prevent such a result through departures."

Table 1 Predicted penalty severity for offenses appearing in MO and SO cases by the approach to sentencing MO cases

Approach	Relative penalty severity
Simplification—reconfigure into one offense	MO ≥/≤ SO
Minimization	Focal ("most serious") offense: MO > SO Other offenses: MO < SO
Totality	MO ≤ SO

As mentioned, some approaches to sentencing MO cases also require sentencers to consider how the sentence should be served. This "practical" sentence (i.e., the sentence that is actually served) is set apart from the "theoretical" sentence considered here (i.e., the sentence that is imposed). Thus far, we have provided theoretical predictions about sentencing outcomes which need to be empirically tested. Unfortunately, as mentioned earlier, our understanding of sentencing MO cases is hampered by the dearth of past research on this topic and the failure of sentencing statistics and researchers to clearly differentiate between MO and SO cases. There is nevertheless emerging research that tests the predicted sentencing outcomes following the totality approach to sentencing MO cases. In the next section, we review this research and contribute new empirical data on the issue.

Research on the Application of the Totality Principle

Here, we first review a recently published study by Dhami (2022) on the application of the totality principle in England and Wales. Then, we present the method and findings of our study which examine the effect of sentencing guidelines on the application of the totality principle in terms of appeals against sentence and the outcomes of such appeals. Together, these studies provide some support for the theoretical predictions made about sentencing outcomes following the totality approach to sentencing MO cases.

Comparing Sentences for Offenses in Multiple- and Single-Offense Cases

Dhami (2022) examined the application of the totality principle as described by the "totality" guideline which was in operation from June 2012 to 2023 (Sentencing Council, 2012b).[8] The data was originally collected by the Sentencing Council for England and Wales from Crown Courts.[9] Binary logistic regression analyses were used to examine the sentences meted out to offenses in MO cases with those in

[8] The Sentencing Council (2021) conducted a survey of 130 sentencers and brief, follow-up interviews with 10 sentencers in order to understand how the totality guideline was used and to explore sentencers' opinions on the guideline. This revealed that some sentencers may have difficulty in using the guideline, and highlighted some sentencers' concerns about the perceived leniency of sentences meted out following application of the totality principle. Partly in response to these findings, the Sentencing Council embarked upon a revision of the totality guideline.

[9] The Crown Court Sentencing Survey (CCSS) gathers information on factors that the Sentencing Council believes ought to influence sentencing decisions because they reflect the contents of offense-specific guidelines. Courts are asked to complete a form for every sentenced case. The Council conducted the final iteration of the CCSS from 1st January to 31st March 2015 and released the data in 2018. Although only information for the principle offense was provided by the

comparable offenses appearing in SO cases, and these analyses were performed separately for seven broad offense types since they are covered by different offense-specific sentencing guidelines (i.e., actual bodily harm, dangerous driving, domestic burglary, fraud, possession with the intent to supply, robbery, and shoplifting).[10] The analyses also controlled for potential differences between MO and SO cases in terms of extra-legal, offender-related factors[11] (i.e., offender gender and age) and legally relevant (guideline) factors (i.e., offense seriousness in terms of harm caused and culpability of offender, number of aggravating factors which include previous convictions, number of mitigating factors, and percentage guilty plea reduction in sentence[12]). Two sentencing outcomes were considered: one was immediate custody or a noncustodial penalty (including discharge, fine, community order, and suspended sentencing order), and for those cases that received custody, the other sentencing outcome was the length of time in custody, which was dichotomized since it was recorded as categories rather than as a continuous variable.

It was found that for six out of the seven offense types, MO/SO case status was not a significant predictor of sentencing outcome measured in terms of immediate custody (v. non-custodial penalty). This suggests that MO cases were not significantly more likely to receive immediate custody than their SO counterparts. For the exception, i.e., possession with the intent to supply, the odds of a MO case receiving immediate custody were 2.03 times greater than its SO counterpart. For those cases that received immediate custody, it was observed that MO/SO case status was not a significant predictor of custody length for all but one offense type, i.e., robbery. Here, the odds of a MO case receiving over 3 years in custody were 2.49 times greater than its SO counterpart.

Given the lack of difference in the sentencing outcomes of MO and SO cases observed for the majority of offences studied, Dhami (2022, p. 63, word in brackets added) therefore concluded that "application of the totality principle as stated in the [totality] guideline means that some offenders in MO cases (especially those serving their sentences concurrently) may be 'getting off lightly' compared to their SO counterparts." According to Dhami (2022) explanations for this sentencing behavior potentially lie in the totality guideline. One idea is that personal mitigation, which has a penalty reducing effect, is double-counted in MO cases as opposed to SO cases. This is because in MO cases, personal mitigation is first considered when

---

court, there was an indication in the dataset of the MO/SO status of a case which enabled Dhami (2020) to conduct her analyses.

[10] The guidelines apply equally to MO and SO cases and have very low departure rates (Sentencing Council, 2015).

[11] The effect of offender race could not be studied because the Sentencing Council for England and Wales did not collect this data from courts.

[12] In England and Wales, the guilty plea reduction in sentence is not an aspect of mitigation as it is in some other jurisdictions. The reduction is determined by an 'overarching' guideline (see Sentencing Council, 2007) and may be anywhere from 1/3rd (for a guilty plea at the earliest reasonable opportunity) to 1/10th (for a guilty plea during trial), although there is some discretion allowed.

arriving at an initial sentence for each offense as per the offense-specific guidelines and then again when adjusting the overall sentence as per the totality guideline. Relatedly, the weight attached to penalty-reducing personal mitigating factors may be greater than that attached to penalty-enhancing aggravating factors. Indeed, whereas the totality guideline which is applied to MO cases explicitly requires sentencers to consider personal mitigation, the offense-specific guidelines applied to SO cases (and initially also to MO cases) are silent on the relative weight that should be attached to aggravating and mitigating factors. Consistent with this idea, Dhami (2022) found that the number of mitigating factors in a case was a significant predictor of immediate custody (and custody length) in most of the offense types studied, and the weight attached to mitigating factors was greater for those offense types where MO cases were not found to be treated more harshly than SO cases. It is worth noting that the revised totality guideline has now rectified the imbalance in emphasis on mitigating and aggravating factors (see Sentencing Council, 2023a).[13]

The above findings suggest that efforts to aid sentencers in performing the cognitively complex task of sentencing MO cases by introducing the totality guideline may have undermined the search for justice. While Dhami's (2022) study reveals the patterns of sentencing under the totality guideline, it cannot document how introduction of the guideline may have affected sentencing or even perceptions of sentencing. This would require a before-and-after comparison. In the remainder of this chapter, we focus on this comparison.

Effect of Totality Guideline on Sentencing Multiple-Offense Cases

The totality guideline which was introduced by the Sentencing Council for England and Wales came into force in June 2012 (Sentencing Council, 2012b). According to the Council, this guideline did "not set out to bring about any change in sentencing practice but to bring greater clarity and transparency to the sentencing process where a court is sentencing an offender for multiple offences." (Sentencing Council, 2012a; p. 6). The view that the guideline would have no impact on sentencing practice and outcomes is based on the idea that the guideline reflected existing practice. However, this is debatable given the lack of research evidence on sentencing MO cases used to inform the development of the guideline.

The present research therefore had two main aims. The first was to examine the effect of the totality guideline on the focus of appeal (i.e., against sentence only v. against both sentence and conviction)—exploring how offenders in MO cases perceived the fairness of their sentence before and after the introduction of the guideline. The crude assumption here is that defendants who do not appeal against

[13] Dhami's (2022) study was presented as evidence to both the Sentencing Council for England and Wales, and to the UK Parliament's House of Common's Justice Committee Inquiry.

sentence only may perceive their sentence as fair, although it is acknowledged that there are reasons for not appealing which are unrelated to the perceptions of sentence fairness. The second aim was to examine Appeal Court responses to appeals against sentence—exploring whether sentences were considered to be more or less just and proportionate before versus after the guideline was introduced. Finally, we also provide direct quotes from Appeal Court judgments. These serve to reflect the main arguments made in the chapter.

As mentioned, the present research is based on judgments from the Criminal Court of Appeal for England and Wales.[14] In an early analysis of such judgments, Thomas (1970) first identified how lower courts in England and Wales sentenced MO cases. Indeed, it is useful to study appellate court judgments, especially in common law jurisdictions, because these establish legal precedent, clarifying and interpreting laws which help sentencers understand the current state of the law and its application. By scrutinizing the decisions of lower courts, identifying misinterpretations of law and errors in procedure, the Appeal Court represents the main mechanism for quality assurance within the legal system. It can act to rectify matters and so plays a crucial role in promoting fairness and justice.

The data for our analyses were obtained from a sample of Appeal Court judgments held in the British and Irish Legal Information Institute (BAILII) database. This database is public and freely available online.[15] In order to address the first aim of our research, we sampled the first 60 judgments backward from March 2008 (constituting the "before" totality guideline group), and the first 60 judgments onward from July 2013 ("after" totality guideline group). The timeline before March 2008 avoids the impact of the Coroners and Justice Act (2009)[16] on the sentencing framework in England and Wales.[17] The timeline after July 2013 allows time for the courts of first instance to apply the totality guideline which came into force in June 2012. In order to address the second aim of our research, we focused on the subset of judgments that referred to appeals against sentence only. This resulted in 53 judgments before the totality guideline was introduced and 37 judgments afterward.

The inclusion criteria for the Appeal Court judgments in our full sample were that they should be MO cases involving an appeal against sentence or an appeal against both sentence and conviction. Judgments containing at least one of the

[14] Ethics approval for the research was granted by the Department of Psychology Research Ethics Committee at Middlesex University, London, UK.

[15] https://www.bailii.org/ew/cases/EWCA/Crim.

[16] Coroners and Justice Act, 2009 (U.K.)

[17] Amongst other things, the Coroners and Justice Act, 2009 made provisions for a new Sentencing Council to replace the Sentencing Guidelines Council and Sentencing Advisory Panel; provided recommendations on how new or revised guidelines should be developed as well as what they might contain; and proposed the development of a guideline dealing with reduction in sentences for guilty pleas as well as a guideline considering the totality of sentences in cases in which an offender faces sentencing for more than one offense. The 2009 Act retained voluntary application of the guidelines when it stated that the court must "follow" any relevant guidelines "unless the court is satisfied that it would be contrary to the interests of justice to do so."

following keywords were selected: *"multiple offence(s) or offending or crime(s)"*, *'concurrent(ly)"*, *"consecutive(ly)"*, *"totality(principle)"*, *"mercy"*, *"taken into consideration"*, and *"just and proportionate."* Each judgment was read by the second author to determine if the cases were relevant to the aims of the study (e.g., appeals against conviction only were excluded).

A combination of the dates for sampling the Appeal Court Judgments from the BAILII database mentioned earlier and the aforementioned criteria for inclusion of these judgments resulted in the final sample of 60 judgments in the "before" totality guideline group, all being dated 2007, and the final sample of 60 judgments in the "after" group being dated from 2013 to 2014.

A specially designed coding scheme was used to extract information from the full sample of 120 Appeal Court judgments. Briefly, the coding scheme included variables pertaining to the *characteristics of the case* (at the time of appeal) such as whether offenses occurred in single transaction; *appeal case factors* such as whether the appeal was against sentence only or both conviction and sentence; *original trial/sentence factors* including whether the sentence was concurrent or consecutive; and *Appeal Court reactions* including the appeal outcome. Most of the variables were coded into two categories (i.e., yes/no).

We mainly used Chi-square tests of independence, supplemented with effect size measures, as well as binary logistic regression analyses, to examine the association between group (i.e., "before" versus "after" totality guideline) and our main "dependent" variables of interest (i.e., focus of appeal and appeal outcome). In doing so, we also explored the potential for other variables to explain any significant relationships.[18] Before presenting the quantitative findings, we describe the relevant characteristics of the sample of MO cases, noting any statistically significant differences between those in the Appeal Court judgments made before versus after introduction of the totality guideline.

Ninety-two percent ($n = 110$) of the full sample of 120 Appeal Court judgments involved male appellants, and there was no difference in the gender of appellants dealt with in the judgments before and after the totality guideline was introduced. However, judgments made before the guideline was introduced dealt with cases involving significantly younger appellants ($M = 31.51$, $SD = 12.43$) than judgments made afterward ($M = 39.33$, $SD = 15.67$), $t(72) = 2.36$, $p = 0.021$, $d = 0.55$. As described below, we account for this age difference in our later analyses. About a third of judgments (33.6%, $n = 40$ out of 119) referred to cases where multiple offenses occurred in a single transaction, and this did not differ significantly before and after introduction of the guideline, $p > 05$. There was also no significant difference in the number of judgments that dealt with cases involving the same or different offense type before and after the introduction of the guideline, with 43.7% ($n = 52$ out of 119) of judgments referring to cases involving the same offense type,

[18] The use of judgments on real cases means that we are unable to control for all extraneous variables and are unable to account for all variables that might mediate or moderate the effect of the totality guideline on appeals against sentence and appeal outcome. However, many of the variables we have controlled and accounted for are sentencing-relevant.

$p > 0.05$. The appeal was launched by the defense in all of the 120 judgments. A large majority of judgments (85.0%, $n = 102$) dealt with cases where the appeal was made following the first trial/sentence, with no difference before and after the introduction of the guideline, $p > 05$. Similarly, in a large majority of judgments (88.9%, $n = 104$ out of 117), the case was originally tried and sentenced in the Crown Court, with no difference before and after the introduction of the guideline, $p > 0.05$.

In terms of the first aim of our study, namely, to examine the effect of the totality guideline on the focus of appeal, we found that appeals against sentence only (as opposed to both sentence and conviction) were significantly more likely before the guideline was introduced than that afterward, χ^2 (1, $N = 120$) = 11.38, $p < 0.001$, $\phi = 0.31$. Specifically, before the guideline, 88.3% ($n = 53$ out of 60) of judgments referred to appeals against sentence only, whereas after the guideline, only 61.7% ($n = 37$ out of 60) did so. Importantly, this difference cannot be explained by the aforementioned case characteristics because, with the exception of the appellant age, none differed significantly before and after the guideline was introduced. A binary logistic regression analysis revealed that, after controlling for the appellant age, the group remained a significant positive predictor of focus of appeal, $\beta = 2.48$, $p = 0.023$.[19]

The present finding also cannot be explained by how the sentence was to be served. Specifically, the frequency of concurrent, consecutive, and both types of sentence did not differ significantly before and after the totality guideline was introduced (Before: $n = 37$ concurrent, 3 consecutive, and 20 both; After: $n = 43$ concurrent, 3 consecutive, and 14 both), $p > 0.05$. Similarly, the frequency of sentences to be served on top of existing ones did not differ before and after the introduction of the guideline[20]$n = 15$ out of 60; After: $n = 10$ out of 60), $p > 0.05$.

In terms of the second aim of our study, namely, to examine Appeal Court responses to appeals against sentence, we observed that the Appeal Court was significantly more likely to allow an appeal against sentence before the totality guideline was introduced than afterward, χ^2 (1, $N = 90$) = 6.30, $p = 0.012$, $\phi = 0.27$. Specifically, before the guideline, 81.1% ($n = 43$ out of 53) of appeals against sentence were allowed, whereas after the guideline, only 56.8% ($n = 21$ out of 37) were allowed. Crucially, this difference cannot be explained by factors such as whether a guilty plea reduction had been applied because judgments passed before and after the totality guideline referred to cases that did not differ significantly in this respect, with two-thirds having a guilty plea reduction ($n = 60$ out of 90), $p > 0.05$.

There was no significant difference in the number of judgments before and after the totality guideline that regarded the original sentence as "excessive", with 83.3% ($n = 75$ out of 90) being considered so, $p > 0.05$. Very few judgments before and after introduction of the guideline ($n = 5$ out of 90) mentioned misapplication,

---

[19] *A test of the full model against the constant only model was statistically significant, $\chi^2(2) = 10.60$, $p = 0.005$. The Nagelkerke R^2 value was 0.23. Notably, the coefficient for appellant age was not statistically significant, $p = 0.484$.*

[20] The low cell counts for the 'consecutive' category may affect the reliability and validity of the statistical result.

ignorance, and/or dismissal of the totality principle. However, the Appeal Court was more likely to refer to the notion of "adding up" sentences before the totality guideline (i.e., 18.7%, $n = 10$ out of 53) than afterward (2.7%, $n = 1$ out of 37). A binary logistic regression analysis revealed that, after controlling for the Appeal Court's reference to the notion of "adding up", group remained a significant positive predictor of appeal outcome, $\beta = 1.06$, $p = 0.032$.[21]

Therefore, our quantitative analyses of Criminal Court of Appeal judgments in England and Wales reveal that after the original totality guideline was introduced, there were fewer appeals against sentence only and that such appeals were less likely to be successful. In this regard, the present findings do not support the Sentencing Council's (2012a) belief that the totality guideline would have no impact on sentencing practice. Sentencing practice arguably changed to the extent that offenders and the Appeal Court responded differently to the sentences meted out before and after the guideline.

The findings do arguably point to the necessity for the guideline, since appeals against sentence were reduced. It could also be suggested that, to some extent, the guideline resulted in sentences being passed by lower courts which both the Appeal Court and offenders considered to be just and proportionate. Indeed, the idea that offenders in MO cases are satisfied with their sentence may indirectly support Dhami's (2022) earlier observations that offenders in MO cases typically received sentences that were not more severe than those passed on comparable SO cases. However, the question remains as to whether victims and the public would perceive justice as having been served in MO cases since they may expect offenders in such cases to receive a custodial (rather than non-custodial) penalty and/or longer terms in custody.

Future research ought to consider the effect of the revised totality guideline which came into force in July 2023. The rebalancing of mitigating and aggravating factors in application of the totality principle in the more recent version of the guideline could conceivably affect appeals against sentence and appeal outcomes, although the Sentencing Council for England and Wales (2023a, p. 46), again, believes that it is "unlikely to lead to substantive changes to current sentencing practice."

Finally, the quantitative findings, as well as the main issues raised in this chapter are reflected in, and reinforced by, our analyses of quotes from the sample of Appeal Court judgments where there was a specific mention of the totality principle. Specifically, quotes taken from *before* the totality guideline was introduced demonstrate the Appeal Court's rejection of a cumulative approach to sentencing MO cases in favor of applying the totality principle, and the Appeal Court's recognition of the difficulty such cases pose for sentencers. However, the quotes also document the Appeal Court's concerns that the application of the totality principle may result in MO cases receiving less severe penalties than their SO counterparts. The

[21] *A test of the full model against the constant only model was statistically significant, $\chi^2(2) = 7.62$, $p = 0.022$. The Nagelkerke R^2 value was 0.12. Notably, the coefficient for Appeal court mentioning 'adding up' was not statistically significant, $p = 0.300$.*

judgments also provide an indication of appellants' argument for "mercy" and the Appeal Court's acceptance of this argument:

> It was contended by the Appellant that the sentence for the offences of outraging public decency should not have been made consecutive to the sentence on counts 1-9 and the totality of the sentences on counts 1-9 was in any event too long. His career had been ruined and he would have to begin his life again on release... Although we take into account the fact that the [appellant] had not actually distributed any images, we do not consider that a total sentence of three years on the counts of distribution can be said to be manifestly excessive. The sentences of 9 months for the counts of filming up the skirts of the schoolgirl and the women were made consecutive. This made the overall sentence too long. We will therefore make those sentences concurrent to the other sentences...To that extent the appeal on sentence is allowed. (Hamilton, R v [2007] EWCA Crim 2062).

> Finally we emphasise that in this type of sentencing decision a mathematical approach is liable to produce an inappropriate answer, and that the totality principle is fundamental. In this Court, on appeal, focus should reflect all the relevant circumstances, rather than its mathematical computation. (P, R v [2007] EWCA Crim 2290).

> The sentencing exercise confronting the learned judge was a difficult one because there is always the balance to be struck between the public interest on the one hand and the culpability of a defendant on the other. Moreover, the learned judge did not have much guidance in terms of the range of sentences available to him. He had to work them out from basic principles. (Donnelly, R. v [2007] EWCA Crim 2548).

> Each one of those offences we have mentioned, particularly the robberies and the woundings could have led, if they had stood alone, to higher sentences than were imposed on the basis of how the learned judged explained his calculation in respect to them as they stood together. It is plain the learned judge did take account of totality in giving a lesser sentence because he was dealing with them all together than he would had he dealt with them separately...But a court must also guard against any suggestion that someone can have a free go at a further offence because they have already committed others. That is obviously illustrated in this case,... (Crees, R. v [2007] EWCA Crim 2650).

By contrast to the Appeal Court's views on sentencing MO cases before the totality guideline was introduced, *after* introduction of the guideline, the quotes illustrate the Appeal Court's identification of cases where the totality principle was not applied by the original sentencing court. In addition, there is evidence of the Appeal Court's efforts to correct any errors in sentencing of MO cases by applying the totality principle itself. The quotes also show the basis for the Appeal Court's opinion as to whether or not the totality principle was applied by the original sentencing court, namely, through the imposition of concurrent sentences.

> It is said, principally, that the sentence was manifestly excessive because the judge failed to have regard to the principle of totality. Further, though it is accepted that the judge was entitled to place the section 18 offence with category 1 of the relevant sentencing guidelines, nonetheless the sentence on count 2 was too severe because it failed to reflect the mitigation available to him;... and the sentence of 18 months' imprisonment on count 3 failed to reflect the difference between the position of Healey and Kimpton who was older and far more culpable on the facts. (Minchin, R. v [2013] EWCA Crim 2412).

> In our judgment the correct custodial term to reflect the totality of the offending, together with the mitigating features, after credit for the pleas of guilty would be five years. (Burinskas, R v [2014] EWCA Crim 334).

> The judge took full account of totality by ordering that the sentences for the amphetamine offences should be concurrent with one another, and that the sentences for the heroin offences should also be concurrent with one another. (Regina v. Smith, [2014] EWCA Crim 334).

> We are not persuaded by Mr Carville's oral submissions to the effect that all the sentences should have been ordered to run concurrently. On the contrary it would in principle have been open to the judge to impose consecutive sentences in each case, and he plainly had regard to totality when he decided to make only one of the sentences consecutive to the other concurrent terms. (Baybasin & Ors, R v [2013] EWCA Crim 2357).

In sum, although there is a general dearth of research on sentencing in MO cases, there is emerging research on application of the totality principle in England and Wales. This suggests that efforts to aid sentencers in the cognitively complex task of sentencing MO cases may have unintended implications for the pursuit of justice. Such findings are particularly concerning, not simply because of the large volume of MO cases dealt with, but because the approach of sentencing MO cases in their totality is adopted in several common law jurisdictions, beyond England and Wales. Clearly, the implications of efforts to guide sentencers in responding to MO cases need to be carefully considered when developing and introducing sentencing policies. In the final section of the chapter, we summarize the main points raised thus far and suggest that sentencing policy ought to be informed by empirical evidence on the advantages and limitations of existing sentencing practice.

Conclusions

It is clear that the approaches to sentencing MO cases currently in operation across several common law jurisdictions simplify the sentencer's task by making it more cognitively similar to the task of sentencing SO cases, which while also cognitively complex is perhaps less so. All of the approaches result in criminal penalties that are more lenient than that would follow a simple cumulative approach. Thus, these jurisdictions avoid disproportionately harsh sentences; do not blur distinctions between more and less serious offense types; reduce the likelihood that a sentence devastates the future life of a MO offender upon release from custody; and lessen the resource and cost burden associated with long-term imprisonment. However, these approaches to sentencing MO cases lack some transparency, and it may be difficult for people to understand exactly how the final sentence was reached.

In addition, the approaches to sentencing MO cases currently in operation have implications for the search for justice. The approach that simplifies a MO case by reconfiguring the offenses into one more serious offense may have appeal for some people but requires that the offenses in a MO case are commensurate so the harms are measurable to enable aggregation. The approach that minimizes the other offenses in a MO case but leads to a more severe penalty for the focal (most serious) offense may satisfy relatively more people but may still leave many thinking that offenders are "getting away with it". Finally, the approach that deals with offenses in a MO case in their totality may be similarly perceived as being "soft on crime."

Indeed, Dhami (2022) revealed that application of the totality principle in England and Wales often resulted in offenses in MO cases receiving a similar (and not harsher) penalty than in comparable SO cases. The quantitative analyses of Appeal Court judgments from the same jurisdiction, as described in the present chapter, appear to indirectly support this observation. Specifically, there were fewer appeals against sentence in MO cases after the totality guideline was introduced than before, potentially implying that offenders did not perceive their sentence as unduly excessive. In addition, the analyses suggest that appeals against sentence in MO cases were less likely to be successful after the guideline was introduced, suggesting that sentences in these MO cases were considered to be "just and proportionate". However, the main basis for the Appeal Court's opinion as to whether or not the totality principle was applied appears to be through the original sentencing court imposing concurrent sentences. This raises concerns about whether victims and the public would perceive the sentences served by offenders in MO cases as just and proportionate, especially in light of comparable SO cases. We argue that research on sentencing in MO cases, comparisons of sentencing outcomes in MO and SO cases, as well as perceptions of sentences ought to be used to inform the development of future sentencing policies.

In the present chapter, we have not presented an alternative approach to sentencing MO cases because we believe that the sentencing policy and practice ought to be evidence-based (see also Belton & Dhami, 2024; Dhami et al., 2015; Dhami, 2013a, 2013b). While much of that evidence ought to be focused on how sentences are reached, there is also an argument for examining how those sentences are perceived, given that both crime and our response to it are a social construction which differs from time and place. To that end, it is currently unclear what the public, offenders, and victims perceive as just penalties for offenses appearing in MO cases as opposed to SO cases. Similarly, it is unknown to what extent these perceptions alter when the sentence is to be served concurrently as opposed to consecutively. Knowledge of such issues could help construct a sentencing regime that results in increased satisfaction in the sentencing system as well as confidence in the courts.

Additionally, if the goals of sentencing are to be achieved, then research ought to be directed at identifying "what works" for offenders in MO cases as opposed to SO cases. The lack of differentiation between these two types of offenders in both the development of (prison and community) interventions and in the evaluation of the efficacy of such interventions might explain the mixed findings regarding their ability to successfully reduce reoffending (e.g., Koehler & Lösel, 2024; Pappas & Dent, 2023).

Finally, effort also needs to be directed at ensuring that the reasoning process underlying the choice of penalties meted out in MO cases is transparent and clearly understood by offenders, victims, and the public. According to procedural justice theory, perceived fairness is influenced by process-based criteria which include decision quality (see Tyler, 2003). Decision quality comprises the unbiased or neutrality of decisions based on objective information as well as the consistency of decisions.

Beyond filling the research gap, it is also important to consider how the sentencer may be helped to perform the cognitively complex task of sentencing (MO or SO cases). While some jurisdictions continue to eschew the utility of sentencing guidelines, other jurisdictions have implemented guidance that is ambiguous or overly rigid (see Dhami et al., 2015). The development of guidance itself ought to be informed by relevant empirical evidence such as from the field of human judgment and decision-making (e.g., see Dhami, 2013a). For instance, taking an information processing view of the sentencer would suggest a need to aid sentencers not only in paying attention to the "legally" relevant factors but also in advising them on the relative weight to be attached to such factors and the rule used to integrate them. The growing application of Artificial Intelligence in expert domains may also present a potential avenue for consideration of how such guidance is implemented.

It is imperative that we understand sentencing in MO cases, since they represent common court business. The findings would be of practical benefit to resource-stretched criminal justice agencies such as the prisons and probation who must plan for workload and allocation of resources. Similarly, differentiating between MO and SO cases in sentencing research generally could aid in more reliable and valid determination of the efficacy of criminal punishments. Finally, our knowledge of the sentences meted out to offenses in MO cases (especially relative to comparable offenses in SO cases) could fundamentally change our perceptions of, and confidence in, the justice system (see e.g., House of Commons Justice Committee, 2023). Indeed, public opinion surveys ask if sentences are "too tough, about right, or too lenient" (e.g., Jansson, 2015; Jones et al., 2008; McCarthy, 2016), and reasons for low confidence in the system include perceptions of biased and unfair court practices (Hough and Roberts, 2004). Perceived fairness and confidence are necessary for smooth functioning of the system.

References

Adriaenssen, A., Paoli, L., Karstedt, S., Visschers, J., Greenfield, V. A., & Pleysier, S. (2020). Public perceptions of the seriousness of crime: Weighing the harm and the wrong. *European Journal of Criminology, 17*(2), 127–150. https://doi.org/10.1177/1477370818772768

Albers, W. (2001). Prominence theory as a tool to model doundedly rational decisions. In G. Gigerenzer & R. Selten (Eds.), *Bounded rationality: The adaptive toolbox* (pp. 297–317). MIT Press.

Algom, D. (2021). The Weber–Fechner law: A Misnomer that persists but that should go away. Psychological Review, 128(4), 757–765. https://doi.org/10.1037/rev000027

Ashworth, A. (2015). *Sentencing and criminal justice* (6th ed.). Cambridge University Press.

Bagaric, M., & Alexander, T. (2013). Rehabilitating totality in sentencing: From obscurity to principle. *University of New South Wales Law Journal, 36*(1), 139–167.

Baird, J. C., & Noma, E. (1975). Psychophysical study of numbers: I. Generation of numerical responses. *Psychological Research, 37*(4), 281–297.

Belton, I. K., & Dhami, M. K. (2024). The role of character-based personal mitigation in sentencing judgments. *Journal of Empirical Legal Studies*. https://doi.org/10.1111/jels.12376

Bottoms, A. (1998). Five puzzles in von Hirsch's theory of punishment. In A. Ashworth & M. Wasik (Eds.), *Fundamentals of sentencing theory: Essays in honour of Andrew von Hirsch* (pp. 53–102). Oxford University Press.

Calanchini, J., Lai, C. K., & Klauer, K. C. (2020). Reducing implicit racial preferences: III. A process-level examination of changes in implicit preferences. *Journal of Personality and Social Psychology, 121*(4), 796–818. https://doi.org/10.1037/pspi0000339

Crawley, E., & Sparks, R. (2006). Is there life after imprisonment? *Criminology & Criminal Justice, 6*(1), 63–82. https://doi.org/10.1177/1748895806060667

Dehaene, S. (2003). The neural basis of the Weber–Fechner law: a logarithmic mental number line. *Trends in Cognitive Sciences, 7*(4), 145–147. https://doi.org/10.1016/s1364-6613(03)00055-x

Dhami, M. K. (2003). Psychological models of professional decision-making. *Psychological Science, 14*, 175–180. https://doi.org/10.1111/1467-9280.01438

Dhami, M. K. (2013a). A 'decision science' perspective on the old and new sentencing guidelines in England and Wales. In A. Ashworth & J. V. Roberts (Eds.), *Structured sentencing in England and Wales: From guidance to guidelines* (pp. 165–181). Oxford University Press.

Dhami, M. K. (2013b). Sentencing guidelines in England and Wales: Missed opportunities? *Law and Contemporary Problems, 76*, 287–305. https://scholarship.law.duke.edu/cgi/viewcontent.cgi?article=4355&context=lcp.

Dhami, M. K. (2022). Sentencing multiple- versus single-offence cases: Does more crime mean less punishment? *British Journal of Criminology, 62*(1), 55–72. https://doi.org/10.1093/bjc/azab030

Dhami, M. K., & Ayton, P. (2001). Bailing and jailing the fast and frugal way. *Journal of Behavioral Decision Making, 14*, 141–168. https://doi.org/10.1002/bdm.371

Dhami, M. K., Belton, I., & Goodman-Delahunty, J. (2015). Quasi-rational models of sentencing. *Journal of Applied Research on Memory and Cognition, 4*, 239–247. https://doi.org/10.1016/j.jarmac.2014.07.009

Dhami, M. K., Belton, I., Merrall, E. L. C., McGrath, A., & Bird, S. M. (2020). Criminal sentencing by preferred numbers. *Journal of Empirical Legal Studies, 17*(1), 139–163. https://doi.org/10.1111/jels.12246

Drapul, J. (2023). Sentencing multiple conviction offenders. *European Journal of Criminology, 20*(1), 142–160. https://doi.org/10.1177/1477370821996903

Englich, B., Mussweiler, T., & Strack, F. (2006). Playing dice with criminal sentences: The influence of irrelevant anchors on experts' judicial decision making. *Personality and Social Psychology Bulletin, 32*(2), 188–200. https://doi.org/10.1177/0146167205282152

FitzGerald, C., Martin, A., Berner, D., & Hurst, S. (2019). Interventions designed to reduce implicit prejudices and implicit stereotypes in real world contexts: A systematic review. *BMC Psychology, 7*(1), 29.

Folger, R. (1977). Distributive and procedural justice: Combined impact of voice and improvement on experienced inequity. *Journal of Personality and Social Psychology, 35*(2), 108–119. https://doi.org/10.1037/0022-3514.35.2.108

Frase, R. S. (2017). Principles and procedures for sentencing of multiple current offenses. In J. Ryberg, J. V. Roberts, & J. W. de Keijser (Eds.), *Sentencing multiple crimes* (pp. 189–210). Oxford University Press.

Hough, M., & Roberts, J. V. (2004). Confidence in justice: An international review. https://webarchive.nationalarchives.gov.uk/20110218143212/http://rds.homeoffice.gov.uk/rds/pdfs04/r243.pdf.

House of Commons Justice Committee. (2023). *Public opinion and understanding of sentencing*. https://committees.parliament.uk/publications/41844/documents/207521/default/.

Jansson, K. (2015). Public confidence in the criminal justice system—findings from the crime survey for England and Wales (2013/14). https://assets.publishing.service.gov.uk/government/uploads/system/uploads/attachment_data/file/449444/public-confidence.pdf.

Jareborg, N. (1998). Why bulk discounts in sentencing? In A. Ashworth & M. Wasik (Eds.), *Fundamentals of sentencing theory: Essays in honour of Andrew von Hirsch* (pp. 129–140). Oxford University Press.
Johansson, P., Hall, L., Sikström, S., Tärning, B., & Lind, A. (2006). How something can be said about telling more than we can know: On choice blindness and introspection. *Consciousness and Cognition, 15*, 673–692. https://doi.org/10.1016/j.concog.2006.09.004
Johansson, P., Hall, L., Tärning, B., Sikström, S., & Chater, N. (2013). Choice blindness and preference change: You will like this paper better if you (believe you) chose to read it! *Journal of Behavioral Decision Making, 27*, 281–289. https://doi.org/10.1002/bdm.1807
Jones, C., Weatherburn, D., & McFarlane, K. (2008). Public confidence in the New South Wales criminal justice system. https://pdfs.semanticscholar.org/7e41/20283c5151b17d446642744747128eb7c5aa.pdf.
Kelly, R. (2022). Totality: Principle and practice. *Criminal Law Review, 7*, 562–580.
Koehler, J., & Lösel, F. (2024). A meta-evaluative synthesis of the effects of custodial and community-based offender rehabilitation. *European Journal of Criminology*. https://doi.org/10.1177/14773708241256501
Konečni, V. J., & Ebbesen, E. B. (1982). *The criminal justice system—a social-psychological analysis*. Freeman.
Krasnostein, S., & Freiberg, A. (2013). Pursuing consistency in an individualistic sentencing framework: If you know where you're going, how do you know when you've got there. *Law & Contemporary Problems, 76*, 265.
Lai, C. K., Marini, M., Lehr, S. A., Cerruti, C., Shin, L., Joy-Gaba, J. A., Ho, A. K., et al. (2014). Reducing implicit racial preferences: I. A comparative investigation of 17 interventions. *Journal of Experimental Psychology: General, 143*(4), 1765–1785. https://doi.org/10.1037/a0036260
Lind, E. A., & Tyler, T. R. (1988). *The social psychology of procedural justice*. Plenum Press.
Lippke, R. (2011). Retributive sentencing, multiple offenders, and bulk discounts. In M. D. White (Ed.), *Retributivism: Essays on theory and policy* (pp. 212–231). Oxford University Press.
Liu, Y. (2023). A literature review of a cognitive heuristic: The anchoring effect. *Highlights in Business, Economics and Management, 11*, 271–279. https://doi.org/10.54097/hbem.v11i.8110
Lovegrove, A. (2000). Proportionality, sentencing and the multiple offender: Towards a numerical framework. *Punishment & Society, 2*(4), 453–469. https://doi.org/10.1177/14624740022228105
Manson, A. (2013). Some thoughts on multiple sentences and the totality principle: Can we get it right? *Canadian Journal of Criminology and Criminal Justice, 55*(4), 481–495.
McCarthy, J. (2016). American's views shift on toughness of justice system. https://news.gallup.com/poll/196568/americans-views-shift-toughness-justice-system.aspx.
McLaughlin, O., & Somerville, J. (2013). Choice blindness in financial decision making. *Judgment and Decision making, 8*, 577–588. https://doi.org/10.1017/S1930297500003673
Mitchell, O. (2005). A meta-analysis of race and sentencing research: Explaining the inconsistencies. *Journal of Quantitative Criminology, 21*(4), 439–466. https://doi.org/10.1007/s10940-005-7362-7
National Judicial College of Australia. (2018). *Taking into account other offences*. https://csd.njca.com.au/principles-practice-general_sentencing_principles-s16a_specific_relevant_factors-other-offences/.
National Judicial College of Australia. (2022). *Cumulative and concurrent sentences*. https://csd.njca.com.au/concurrent_consecutive_2/.
National Judicial College of Australia. (2023). *Totality principle*. https://csd.njca.com.au/totality/.
Nisbett, R. E., & Wilson, T. D. (1977). Telling more than we can know: Verbal reports on mental processes. *Psychological Review, 84*, 231–259. https://doi.org/10.1037/0033-295X.84.3.231
Pappas, L. N., & Dent, A. L. (2023). The 40-year debate: A meta-review on what works for juvenile offenders. *Journal of Experimental Criminology, 19*(1), 1–30. https://doi.org/10.1007/s11292-021-09472-z
Rachlinski, J. J., Wistrich, A. J., & Guthrie, C. (2015). Can judges make reliable numeric judgments? Distorted damages and skewed sentences. *Indiana Law Journal, 90*, 695–739.
Rawls, J. (1971). *A theory of justice*. Belknap Press/Harvard University Press.

Reaves, B. A. (2009). Felony defendants in large urban counties, 2009-statistical tables. Retrieved from https://www.bjs.gov/content/pub/pdf/fdluc09.pdf.

Roberts, J., Pina-Sánchez, J., & Marder, I. (2018). Individualisation at sentencing: The effects of guidelines and 'preferred' numbers. *Criminal Law Review, 2*, 123–136.

Ryberg, J. (2005). Retributivism and multiple offending. *Res Publica, 11*, 213–233. https://doi.org/10.1007/s11158-005-3522-8

Ryberg, J., Roberts, J. V., & de Keijser, J. W. (Eds.). (2017). *Sentencing multiple crimes*. Oxford University Press.

Sentencing Act. (2020). https://www.legislation.gov.uk/ukpga/2020/17/contents.

Sentencing Council. (2007). *Reduction in sentence for a Guilty Plea.* https://www.sentencingcouncil.org.uk/overarching-guides/crown-court/item/reduction-in-sentence-for-a-guilty-plea-first-hearing-before-1-june-2017/.

Sentencing Council. (2011). A short guide. Sentencing for multiple offences (Totality). https://www.sentencingcouncil.org.uk/wp-content/uploads/public_guide_totality_for_web.pdf.

Sentencing Council. (2012a). Allocation, offences taken into consideration and totality. Response to consultation. https://www.sentencingcouncil.org.uk/wp-content/uploads/Response_to_consultation_-_allocation_TICs_totality_final_web.pdf.

Sentencing Council. (2012b). Offences taken into consideration and totality. *Definitive Guideline.* https://www.sentencingcouncil.org.uk/wp-content/uploads/Offences-Taken-into-Consideration-and-Totality-definitive-guideline-Web.pdf.

Sentencing Council. (2015). Crown Court Sentencing Survey Annual Publication 2014. https://www.sentencingcouncil.org.uk/wp-content/uploads/CCSS-Annual-2014.pdf

Sentencing Council. (2021). *Exploring sentencers' views of the sentencing council's totality guideline.* https://www.sentencingcouncil.org.uk/wp-content/uploads/2021-09-17-Totality-guideline-report.pdf.

Sentencing Council (2023a). Revisions to the totality guideline. *Response to Consultation.* https://www.sentencingcouncil.org.uk/html-publication/item/revisions-to-the-totality-guideline-response-to-consultation/.

Sentencing Council. (2023b). *Totality.* https://www.sentencingcouncil.org.uk/overarching-guides/magistrates-court/item/totality/.

Sentencing Council (2024). *Types of sentence.* https://www.sentencingcouncil.org.uk/sentencing-and-the-council/types-of-sentence/.

Spohn, C. (2015). Race, crime, and punishment in the twentieth and twenty-first centuries. *Crime & Justice, 44*(1), 49–557. https://doi.org/10.1086/681550

Thomas, D. A. (1970). *Principles of sentencing: The sentencing policy of the Court of Appeal Criminal Division*. Heinemann.

van Ginneken, E. F., & Hayes, D. (2017). 'Just' punishment? Offenders' views on the meaning and severity of punishment. *Criminology & Criminal Justice, 17*(1), 62–78. https://doi.org/10.1177/1748895816654204

Tversky, A., & Kahneman, D. (1974). Judgment under uncertainty: Heuristics and biases: Biases in judgments reveal some heuristics of thinking under uncertainty. *Science, 185*(4157), 1124–1131. https://doi.org/10.1126/science.185.4157.1124

Tyler, T. (2003). Procedural justice, legitimacy, and the effective rule of law. In M. Tonry (Ed.), *Crime and justice: A review of research V30* (pp. 283–357). University of Chicago Press.

United States Sentencing Commission. (2023). *Guidelines manual.* https://www.ussc.gov/sites/default/files/pdf/guidelines-manual/2023/GLMFull.pdf.

Wasik, M. (2012). Concurrent and consecutive sentences revisited. In L. Zedner & J. V. Roberts (Eds.), *Principles and values in criminal law and criminal justice: Essays in honour of Andrew Ashworth* (pp. 285–306). Oxford University Press.

Wyse, J. (2018). Older men's social integration after prison. *International Journal of Offender Therapy and Comparative Criminology, 62*(8), 2153–2173. https://doi.org/10.1177/0306624X16683210

Does Ideology Undermine Procedure-Based Legitimacy?

Tom R. Tyler

Introduction

Watching the news today makes it clear that American politics are in turmoil. A key focus of this turmoil is a core feature of democracies: the capacity of procedures to produce outcomes that will be accepted by both those who benefit from them and those who do not. A prime example is the use of elections to legitimate authority to both winners and losers. This long-standing feature of Western democracies recently seems to be in question, at least in the United States. People do not like to lose, and a central element shaping the viability of democracies is that those who lose nonetheless will acquiesce to the leadership of someone they did not support. There are many possible procedures that might be used to legitimate a new leader, but in democracies, elections are often the preferred mechanism. Why? Because elections are widely judged to be a fair procedure.

The 2020 election failed to gain "loser's consent", a noteworthy departure from the American past during which election results, even in the contested Bush–Gore 2000 election, were widely accepted (Ackerman, 2002; Price & Romantan, 2004; Sunstein & Epstein, 2001). It is striking that in July 2023 an SSRS national poll indicated that 38% of Americans did not believe that Biden legitimately won the Presidency in 2020. A striking 69% of Republicans held that view. A December 2023 Washington Post poll similarly found that 36% of Americans did not think that Biden was "legitimately" elected President in 2020, up from 29% in December of 2021. Does this mean that fair procedures have lost the capacity to gain deference from losers?

T. R. Tyler (✉)
Yale Law School, New Haven, CT, USA
e-mail: tom.tyler@yale.edu

R. L. Wiener, D. J. Hansen (eds.), *Legal Judgment and the Motivation for Justice*, Nebraska Symposium on Motivation 71,
https://doi.org/10.1007/978-3-031-98812-7_6

This issue has particular relevance to social scientists because the idea of procedural justice-based legitimacy is an important example of a contribution of social science theory to understanding an important aspect of political dynamics. Framed in social science terms, it has been theorized that elections legitimate a winner and lead to a general acceptance of the responsibility to defer to their decisions and policies among both winners and losers because they accord with the principles of procedural justice. This argument encapsulates the social science concepts of legitimacy and social justice.

Political scientists and legal scholars label this idea obtaining the "loser's consent" (Anderson et al., 2005; Halliday et al., 2007; Tamanaha, 2004). And they focus on elections because they are a central basis of public evaluations of government. As an example, Broderstad (2023) used data from the European Social Survey to compare a variety of factors that might shape the evaluations of democratic governments. He found that perceived election fairness was the second most important factor shaping overall government evaluations, surpassed only by satisfaction with the economy. Of particular importance was his finding that whether respondents thought elections were fair was of more importance than whether their party had won or lost in recent elections.

This focus on elections as a legitimating mechanism receives similar support within social psychology. The classic experiment by Lewin et al. (1939) showed that electing a group leader enhanced the voluntary deference to that leader and to pursuing shared goals. Lewin was not concerned with political authority. His study was of leadership in work groups involving children. And he did not talk about legitimacy. However, his study set up a framework that continues to this day. If a group chooses its own leader and discusses its tasks, members feel personally responsible for engaging in those tasks and do so even when the leader is not present. They have internalized an obligation to the group. That internalization occurs because fair procedures are used in choosing a leader and defining the group's goals. In other words, procedural justice legitimates group norms and the group's leader.

Procedural Justice and Legitimacy

More recently, the suggestion that procedural justice is a basis for deference to the group has been given a theoretical explanation and supported empirically by a large literature on procedural justice. This literature argues both that people are motivated by justice concerns and that institutional authorities are particularly strongly evaluated in terms of the fairness of procedures (Thibaut & Walker, 1975). While this literature has generally focused on the implementation of decisions by existing authorities, a broader model such as that outlined by Leventhal (1980) also emphasizes the importance of using just procedures when choosing leaders (Gonzalez & Tyler, 2008).

As we approach the 50th anniversary of the publication of Thibaut and Walker's book, *Procedural Justice* (1975), we recognize that a major contribution of social psychology has been the demonstration that people are motivated by their justice-based judgments, distinct from their evaluations of their individual or group self-interest. Further, social psychologists have shown that people distinguish between distributive and procedural justice and authority relations are especially responsive to procedural justice (Tyler et al., 1997).

The extension of these findings to discussions of governance has led to the articulation of a justice-based model of authority that is an alternative to the traditionally dominant rational actor model that reflects the ideas of economics (Tyler, 2006a, 2006b). The rational actor model suggests that people respond to laws and policies from the perspective of potential gains and losses and not through a lens of justice. In contrast, psychological theories suggest that people are centrally concerned with issues of justice in their dealings with legal and political authority. Through empirical research, the psychological argument has gained traction within governance and has led authorities to recognize that people are concerned about justice. In particular, people believe that authorities need to exercise their authority through just procedures.

The social psychological model of authority has three components, each of which is discussed in a study by Tyler (2006a). First, people's law-related behavior, in particular their adherence to the rules, is shaped by their views about the legitimacy of law and legal authority. Such views about legitimacy are distinct from judgments about the risk of being caught and punished for rule-breaking. This argument draws upon the rich history of discussions about legitimacy in social psychology by scholars ranging from French and Raven (1959) to Milgram (1975) and Kelman (2006).

Second, people's judgments about the legitimacy of an authority are not primarily responsive to either the favorability or the fairness of their outcomes. These factors matter but are frequently less important than people's evaluations of the justice of the procedures authorities use to create and implement rules and policies (Leventhal, 1980; Lind & Tyler, 1988; Thibaut & Walker, 1975). This is referred to as procedural justice. It involves judgments about the process through which an authority exercises their authority. This work has focused primarily on the implementation of existing rules and decisions by established authorities. More recent applications to political authority have extended concern to the procedures through which societies determine who will lead (Gonzalez & Tyler, 2008).

Procedural justice includes four elements: whether people have an opportunity to speak and provide evidence (voice); whether they believe that the forum is unbiased, consistent, and fact-based (neutrality); whether they are treated with dignity and courtesy (respect); and whether they believe that the authorities involved are benevolent and sincere, trying to do what is best for the people involved (trust). Furthermore, there are several motives underlying the desire for procedural justice. Issues of voice and neutrality are associated with the quality of decision-making and address the concern for a procedure that produces the fairest outcomes in terms of the needs and concerns of the parties. Respect and trust are referred to as relational concerns because they communicate information about people's inclusion and status within a community. As members of a group, people are entitled to treatment with dignity and respect and to have their problems taken seriously by benevolent and sincere authorities. If people do not feel this is occurring, it sends a negative message about their relationship to the group, impacting feelings of self-worth and undermining self-esteem (Bradford, 2014; Bradford & Jackson, 2024; Tyler, 1997).

Taken together, these ideas form the basis for an alternative form of order management that is more consensual and cooperative than the one based upon incentives and sanctions. As the empirical literature has developed in the field, it has become clear that legitimacy is as, or more, effective in promoting compliance with rules as is a sanction-based approach. The benefit of legitimacy-based authority lies in the change in the relationship between people and authorities that underlies this form of authority. When they view authorities as legitimate, people believe that it is appropriate for them to defer. The motivation comes from people's internal values and is not a reaction to the incentives and sanctions in the environment. This leads to voluntary rule following. Further, people are more willing to cooperate with the authorities, helping them to co-manage the problems of social order and in the political arena to co-governance. Finally, when people believe that the authorities are more legitimate, people more actively engage in their communities economically, politically, and socially (Tyler & Nobo, 2022). This means that legitimacy-based authority can both maintain order in the immediate moment and promote development in the long term (Tyler & Nobo, 2022).

Much of the literature applying procedural justice and legitimacy has involved studies of legal authorities such as the police and the courts. In this arena, broad support has been found for a set of empirical propositions: (1) legitimacy shapes compliance, cooperation, and engagement; (2) procedural justice is a key antecedent of legitimacy; and (3) evaluations of the procedural justice of a process involve both decision-making and interpersonal (relational) elements. The ideas of legitimacy-based authority have significantly broadened the scholarly framework around examinations of the motivations for obeying (or breaking) the law. As an example, while in 2004 legitimacy was largely a novel idea in criminology (Skogan & Frydl, 2004), a recent review of major criminology/criminal law journals indicates that four of the top ten top cited scholars in the field of criminology today work on issues related to legitimacy (Farrington et al., 2022).

A similar set of ideas illuminate legitimacy-based governance. Procedural justice is found to be associated with attitudes toward politicians, political institutions, and the political system (Gulevich et al., 2024). Studies show that losers view existing political institutions as less legitimate (Anderson et al., 2005; Grimes, 2006; Hibbing & Theiss-Morse, 1995, 2001, 2002; Hooghe & Stiers, 2016; Moehler, 2009; Norris, 2014; Powell, 2000; Thomassen, 2014), but that impact is mitigated when they view election procedures as fair.

Why should threats to legitimacy-based governance be of concern? Legitimacy-based governance supports democracy and pluralism. Democratic governance depends upon widespread voluntary cooperation with government and law, and procedure-based legitimacy is an effective way to gain such deference. It is central to the capacity to make the type of universal appeals central governing to a pluralistic society. Creating social mechanisms that lead to deference is particularly central for democracies because they rely heavily on willing deference. Procedures bridge across pluralism and motivate voluntary deference. Hence, it is important to have fair procedures.

Elections are not the only procedure that can be viewed as just. Communities can use direct democracy in which every member votes on issues, and recently societies have used referendums as a direct mechanism to legitimate policies. More complex societies typically use some form of representative governance, which requires a procedure for choosing representatives. The varying structure of democracies leads different societies to use different types of election procedures. For example, some groups use rank ordering, and others a simple expression of preference. Nonetheless, there has been widespread use of some type of elections as a tool for legitimating government authorities. What matters is that whatever procedures are used are viewed as just by the people in a political community. Beyond facilitating democracy, legitimacy is important because it promotes pluralism. Societies composed of people belonging to different social groups contain a variety of social norms and moral codes. Legitimacy bridges over such diversity because deference is linked to a shared view that an authority is entitled to make decisions for the community. Similar arguments have been made about ideology, with liberals and conservatives sharing a commitment to defer to legitimate authorities.

To be viable as a mechanism for legitimacy-based governance, procedural justice must be effective across diversity (Tyler et al., 2015; Yancy-Bragg, 2020). In the past, the literature on legal authority has addressed this concern by testing the "invariance hypothesis" across demographic diversity. Invariance means that people who differ on some dimension, for example, men versus women, place similar weight on procedural justice when making legitimacy judgments and/or place similar weight on legitimacy when making decisions about whether to comply or cooperate. This hypothesis has focused on race/ethnicity, gender, and income. Studies in this vein suggest that procedural mechanisms are generally robust across those dimensions, although groups that do not identify with a society are less influenced by how they are treated by its authorities (Brown & Reisig, 2019; Fox et al., 2020; Tyler, 2005; Tyler & Huo, 2002; Wheelock et al., 2019; Wolfe et al., 2016; Zahnow et al., 2021).

Invariance and Ideology

The recent attention to political extremity raises similar invariance concerns across ideology. If ideology undermines commitment to process-based legitimacy, it undermines pluralistic democratic societies. Van den Bos (2024) addresses this issue and argues that the fair process effect provides a bridge across distrust, extremity, and conspiratorial thinking. This argument is optimistic and hopeful, but is it true? This is the question that is the focus of this chapter. What aspects of ideology might matter? This analysis will focus on two. First, ideological extremity. Second, autocratic values (authoritarianism and a commitment to antidemocratic values).

Ideology also has a long history within both psychology and political science and is intertwined with the idea of polarization. Ideology can be studied as the property of a person or it can be approached as a collective property of a community or state. On a personal level, ideology reflects the shift in political attitudes toward extremes. It can involve ideas and/or affect. In this analysis, aggregate polarization at the collective level will be distinguished from individual ideological extremity. Ideology is typically conceived as ranging from liberal to conservative, so this analysis is concerned with the issue of extreme ideology in either direction. Discussions of the political landscape argue for the growth of extremity among both the left and the right (Jost & Benaji, 1994; Jost et al., 2003).

There is also a long history of concern about autocratic values within political psychology (Hetherington & Weiler, 2009, 2018; Stenner, 2012). This includes values such as authoritarianism and the endorsement of antiprocedural norms. This chapter tests the argument that the procedural justice basis of legitimacy is robust against both extreme ideologies and autocratic values.

Legitimacy declines In the political arena, legitimacy is typically conceptualized as political trust. This encompasses "citizen's feelings about their governments. It overlaps with confidence, system support, and legitimacy on the positive side and with cynicism, political disaffection, and alienation on the negative" (Citrin & Stoker, 2018, p. 50). The issue of legitimacy has taken on new urgency because people in the United States and perhaps the overall Western world are losing trust in legal and political authorities. Public opinion polls indicate declines in trust in all three branches of national government (Citrin & Stoker, 2018). In addition, trust in the courts and the police is declining (Tyler et al., 2015). All of these declines have occurred over decades.

In national surveys of trust and confidence, declines are widely documented (Citrin & Skoker, 2018). Using data from the Gallup poll, it is possible to examine whether trust in government has declined in the period 1974–2023. A regression equation suggests that the proportion of people who express high trust in Congress has declined over time (unstandardized regression coefficient = −.73, SE =−0.06), as has trust in the Supreme Court (unstandardized regression coefficient = −.43, SE =−0.06). Legitimacy has declined. The decline in legitimacy is worrying in itself but also highlights concern about the potential influence of extreme ideologies and antidemocratic values. It may be the case in the future that at the same time that legitimacy-based authority has increasingly been shown to work in the sense that whether people follow rules and cooperate is responsive to legitimacy judgments, and legitimacy judgments are responsive to procedural justice judgments, and to have advantages, the requisite conditions for its successful application are progressively disappearing. If people do not think the government or legal authorities are legitimate, appeals to legitimacy are likely to fail. If people do not think political or legal authorities exercise their authority justly, appeals to procedural justice will similarly fail.

The issue of stability has not escaped the attention of political theorists and researchers, and an empirical literature has developed examining the loser's consent. The 2000 Bush–Gore election controversy drew attention to the issue of how to determine the winner of a Presidential election, as have more recent events involving Donald Trump's loss to Joseph Biden in 2020. The finding that many Americans distrust Biden's well-documented victory in 2020 highlights the challenges of bringing those who lose on board in legitimating the winner.

Empirical Evidence

The current project examines the impact of procedural justice on legal/political legitimacy at two levels. First, in the context of specific elections. Here, the focus is on American Presidential elections. Second, in terms of overall views about the justice of government procedures, including elections.

This empirical review tests several hypotheses across multiple studies:

1. Those who are more ideologically extreme or have stronger autocratic values will view political authority as less legitimate.
2. Procedural justice legitimates a winner in an election.
3. Procedural justice is less important to those who are more ideological or have more strongly autocratic values
4. Post-election judgments of procedural justice will be less strongly linked to pre-election procedural justice among those who are more ideological or autocratic.

Five datasets based on surveys are analyzed. The focus of each is on the legitimacy of political authorities. In each case, the question is the degree of legitimation via perceptions of procedural justice. The analysis then considers whether and how ideology moderates this relationship. Studies 1 and 2 are representative pre–post samples of Americans and focus on two national Presidential elections: 2000 (Bush–Gore) and 2020 (Biden–Trump). They explore impact on trust in political authorities. Study three uses a smaller sample to explore the 2008 (Obama–McCain) election. Study four examines a broad sample using the 2017–2021 World Value Survey (wave 7; n = 153,716). Study five considers general political legitimacy in the European Union using the 2010 European Social Survey (wave 5; n = 54,673). The Appendix to this chapter summarizes the methods and measures for each of the five studies.

Operationalizing Legitimacy In law, legitimacy is most directly conceptualized as the obligation to obey (Tyler, 2006a). However, in studies of political authority, a parallel concept of trust and confidence is often utilized. Because this study is focused on political authority and because trust and confidence are the indexes used in national election studies, that is the focus of this study. A broader operationalization of legitimacy would include obligation to obey, trust and confidence, and normative alignment, but these issues are not widely measured in survey research (Tyler & Jackson, 2014).

Ideology and Ideological Extremity When people talk about ideology, they include both individual beliefs and collective judgments. An individual is more are less extreme. A society is more or less polarized. This study focused on individual beliefs. There are two ways to operationalize extremity: self-report-based and issue-based. In discussing ideology, it is important to distinguish having an ideology (right–left) from being extreme, which involves having extreme views on either the left or the right. This can be conceptualized as the total amount of distance from moderate, and it is possible to distinctly assess either left or right extremity. In the studies discussed here, ideological extremity will be measured by distance from moderate in self-placement scales anchored in moderate and extending to extremely liberal and extremely conservative.

Issue-Based Ideology It is also possible to classify people's ideology based upon their issue positions. Such efforts typically recognize distinct elements of economic, political, and social ideology. Economic liberalism is associated with income and wealth equality. Political liberalism is associated with support for principles of democracy. Finally, social liberalism is connected to support for minority groups and a variety of lifestyles, for example, homosexuality. An extremely liberal person endorses liberal positions on all of these issues, and an extremely conservative person endorses conservative positions on all of them.

Autocratic Values Authoritarians frame issues of political authority as being about compliance (Stenner, 2012). They are less likely to utilize legitimacy as a framework for understanding political behaviors and focus more on unquestioning support for a leader. Liberals on the other hand are argued to be more highly motivated by legitimacy. Succinctly put, the argument is that conservatives are more concerned with following rules, while liberals care more about whether rules and authorities are legitimate (Feldman, 2003; Feldman & Johnston, 2014; Stenner, 2012). This study extends this line of argument to suggest that extremity may further shape the degree to which legitimacy is based upon procedural justice, which reflects a critical judgment about authority, and not on unquestioned compliance.

Lack of Support for Democratic Norms Another potentially relevant set of autocratic values involve support for or lack of support for democratic values. What does that mean? There are many definitions. They include being tolerant of political opponents; believing the state should be constrained by legality; and supporting basic democratic rights like free speech and democratic elections (Dahl, 1971, 1989). These are related to accepting losing an election and deferring to the winners, so a lack of these values is of concern in terms of legitimacy-based authority.

Level of Ideology: Is Ideology a Rising or an Ongoing Threat?

The first question to address is whether there is evidence to support the argument that extreme ideologies exist and/or are rising. This is the premise upon which the concerns raised are based in the case of extremity in self-reported liberalism–conservatism. The same question can be asked about autocratic values. Autocratic values are defined as (1) an increase in support for unquestioning acceptance of authorities and obedience toward rules and/or (2) lack of support for democratic values, as indicated by lack of tolerance for allowing diverse groups to speak or otherwise participate in politics.

Ideological Extremity Ideological extremity can be examined over time using the General Social Survey (GSS). To do so, the proportion indicating they are extremely liberal or extremely conservative can be calculated for each year. During the period 1974–2022, the proportion of the population that is extremely liberal has risen (unstandardized regression coefficient = 0.09, SE = 0.01), as has the proportion that is extremely conservative. (unstandardized regression coefficient = 0.06, SE = 0.01). Extremity has increased. Further, because there is both growing left and growing right extremity at a societal level, there is higher polarization. In 2022, the General Social Survey indicated that 6% of Americans classified themselves as extremely liberal; 5% as extremely conservative. This is an increase from 1974 when 2% classified themselves as extreme in either direction. Nonetheless, it is a small number as a proportion of the population. For this reason, this study operationalized ideological extremity as distance from moderate, which allows for several levels of extremity.

Autocratic Values A second aspect of ideology is autocratic values. One is authoritarianism. Surveys do not typically include a complete index of the multidimensional concept of authoritarianism or its related partner dogmatism, each of which has a history within psychology. However, it is possible to measure some potentially relevant ideas, for example, whether obedience is viewed as a key virtue and whether people say that rules should be followed without question. Stenner, a leading scholar on authoritarian tendencies, defines authoritarianism as being centered around an individual predisposition concerned with the appropriate balance between group authority and uniformity, on the one hand, and individual autonomy, on the other (Stenner, 2012).

Because of their importance to authoritarianism, studies consider the importance of different values about how to raise children and the parenting behavior they produce (Kohn & Schooler, 1983). The GSS has asked whether obedience is an important virtue for children from 1986 to 2022. The results suggest that support for obedience is declining (unstandardized regression coefficient = −.77, SE = 0.08). A less frequently asked question is whether it is important to unquestioningly follow laws. In 1985, 43% agreed, and in 2012, 40% agreed. These data all suggest that authoritarianism is declining.

Democratic Values What about support for democratic values? One measure is of willingness to allow free speech to a variety of unpopular groups as part of the political process, Recent studies suggest that the answer is complex. The General Social Survey tracks tolerance, and results indicate more tolerance for leftists and militarists but less tolerance for racist speech. Political scientists argue that there have been changes in the target of intolerance, with more disapproval of racism, but not the overall level of tolerance (Chong et al., 2022). Communists were stimuli between 1972 and 2022, with the percentage believing they should be allowed to speak slowly rising (54% in 1972 and 70% in 2022, $F(1,28) = 88.44$, $p < .001$). Racists were rated between 1976 and 2022 with a decrease from 62% to 51%, $F(1, 25) = 4.53$, $p < .05$. In general, these findings suggest that there are no major overall changes in tolerance for unpopular groups although a particular group may become more or less acceptable over time. The bottom line is that there is evidence that the American population is becoming more ideologically extreme, but the evidence in the data considered here does not suggest that the American population is becoming more autocratic (more authoritarian or less accepting of democratic norms).

Studies on Elections[1] Three studies focus on a particular national election. Two important elections are the 2000 Bush–Gore election in which there were serious conflicts about election fairness and the 2020 Trump–Biden election, which involves widespread questioning of the justice of the election procedures. Finally, 2008 was not a contentious election, but the study includes a more complete analysis of the elements of procedural justice.

The first study uses data from the ANES 2000–2002 panel study of the Bush–Gore election. Respondents were drawn from a random sample of Americans who were in the pre–post 2000 election interviews of the National Election Study ($n = 786$). The 2000 Presidential election garnered considerable attention among scholars because of a widespread perception that the procedures used (The United States Supreme Court choosing the winner) were suspect. The concern here is that extreme ideology and/or autocratic values might undermine the role of procedural justice in legitimating a winner.

Study 2 is based on the ANES panel study pre–post 2020 campaign between Biden and Trump. Prior to and following the 2020 Presidential election, the ANES conducted interviews with samples of Americans. This chapter is based upon an unweighted analysis of the 7453 respondents who completed both waves.

Study 3 uses pre–post data from the 2008 election involving Obama and McCain. It uses an identical multi-item scale for procedural justice prior to and following the election to examine the impact of outcomes on post-election procedural justice.

The potential influence of the fairness of procedures does not need to be centered around a specific election event. It can also be a more general issue of how fairly government elections are conducted when they occur and/or how fair are the general

[1] See Appendix for a full description of the measures for each of the studies.

procedures through government operations. This is the focus of two international studies: the World Value Survey and the European Social Survey.

Study 4 uses data from the World Value Survey. This study was conducted from 2017 to 2021. This includes data from 153,716 people in 165 countries. The study is not linked to a specific election but rather to general judgments about the political system.

Study 5 uses Wave 5 of the European Social Survey (conducted in 2010). This dataset includes 27 countries from Europe. A sample of 54,673 respondents are asked how fair national elections are in their country.

Extremity and Autocratic Values

While the results for extremity and autocratic values will be discussed separately, the two are related. In the 2008 study, more extreme liberalism is associated with less authoritarianism ($r = -.35$) and more support for democratic values ($r = 0.30$). In contrast, more extreme conservatism is associated with more authoritarianism ($r = 0.33$) and less support for democratic values ($r = -.26$). In the 2020 study, more extreme liberalism is associated with less authoritarianism ($r = -.22$), more support for free speech ($r = 0.32$), and more support for democratic values ($r = 0.21$). In contrast, more extreme conservatism is associated with more authoritarianism ($r = 0.27$), less support for free speech ($r = -.27$), and less support for democratic values ($r = -.26$).

In addition, while this study focuses on trust in confidence in political authorities, the underlying assumption is that trust and confidence have behavioral implications. There is considerable evidence that procedural justice encourages political participation (Grillos et al., 2021), promotes peaceful negotiations (Druckman & Wagner, 2019), and lessens political violence (Cruz & Kloppe-Santamaria, 2023; Tyler et al., 2012; Moore, 1978; Muller, 1979). This includes both support for particular authorities and for political institutions and systems. Further, it is true for both democratic and nondemocratic governments (Gulevich et al., 2024). Legitimacy promotes normative political activity, heightening engagement in the political system. As Moehler (2009) argues "elections have the potential to confer legitimacy, moderate dissent, engender compliance and heighten citizen efficacy (p. 345)".

The 2020 national survey contains a scale of political participation, and the results indicate that both procedural justice ($r = 0.31$) and legitimacy ($r = 0.12$) are positively related to participation. Further, as liberals become more extreme, they participate more ($r = 0.26$), while more extremity in conservatives leads to less participation ($r = -.17$). In addition, the study shows that nonauthoritarians participate more ($r = 0.32$), as do those who support democratic norms ($r = 0.27$).

Hypothesis 1. Extremity Undermines Mean Legitimacy

The first question is whether ideological extremity and/or autocratic values influences the level of legitimacy. Table 1 examines extreme ideology. In the case of election studies, the connection between extreme ideology and legitimacy is linked to outcomes. In 2008 and 2020, liberals won, and conservatism is linked to lower legitimacy. In 2000, conservatives won, and liberalism is linked to lower legitimacy. In each case, it is the losing side that declines in legitimacy, while the winning side increases. These tendencies are stronger among those whose ideologies are more extreme. It is also the case that losing lessens the belief that the procedures of the election were fair (see Table 2), and this also intensifies with extremity. In each case, those who are more extreme shift to a greater degree toward viewing procedures as fairer if they win and unfairer if they lose. Hence, procedural justice judgments are not entirely separate from outcomes, especially after there is an outcome, and the impact of outcomes on procedural justice judgments is stronger among the more extreme.

The findings concerning the relationship between autocratic values and legitimacy are consistent (Table 3). Being authoritarian and having nondemocratic values is associated with lower ratings of legitimacy. Further, being authoritarian and having nondemocratic values is associated with lower ratings of the procedural fairness of elections (Table 4).

Table 1 Correlation of ideological extremity with the mean level of legitimacy

	Who won?	Left extremity	Right extremity
Study 1, 2000	Conservatives	−.08*	0.18***
Study 2, 2020	Liberals	0.13***	−.14***
Study 3, 2008	Liberals	0.45***	−.51***

Note. Entries are Pearson correlations. *$p < .05$; **$p < .01$; ***$p < .001$

Table 2 Correlation of ideological extremity with estimates of the procedural justice of election procedures

	Who won?	Left extremism	Right extremism
Study 1, 2000	Conservatives	−.07*	0.13***
Study 2, 2020	Liberals		
Pre-election		0.19***	−.22***
Post-election		0.38***	−.44***
Study 3, 2008	Liberals		
Pre-election		−.07	0.10*
Post-election		0.35***	−.41***

Note. Entries are Pearson correlations. *$p < .05$; **$p < .01$; ***$p < .001$

Table 3 Influence of autocratic values on legitimacy

	Correlation of values to legitimacy
Study 2, 2020	
Authoritarianism	−.11***
Nondemocratic values	−.06***
Study 2, 2008	
Authoritarianism	0.05
Nondemocratic values	−.19***
Do not value free speech	−.15***

Note. Entries are Pearson correlations. *p < .05; **p < .01; ***p < .001

Table 4 Influence of autocratic values on procedural justice

	Correlation of values to procedural justice	
	Pre-election	Post-election
Study 2, 2020		
Authoritarianism	−.14***	−.25***
Nondemocratic values	−.23***	−.26***
Study 2, 2008		
Authoritarianism	−.09	0.07
Nondemocratic values	−.09	−.19***
Do not value free speech	−.16**	0.05

Note. *p < .05; **p < .01; ***p < .001

Table 5 Correlation of procedural justice to post-election legitimacy

	Procedural justice	Did your side win?
Study 1, 2000	0.30***	0.27***
Study 3, 2008	0.69***	0.57***
Study 2, 2020	0.23***	0.18***

Note. Entries are Pearson correlations. *p < .05; **p < .01; ***p < .001

Hypothesis 2. Does Procedural Justice Continue to Matter When People Are More Ideologically Extreme?

Does procedural justice continue to motivate people to accept the results of an election when they are more ideologically extreme or have more autocratic values? Table 5 reports the correlation between procedural justice judgments and legitimacy in the studies in which there is a specific winner. The findings support hypothesis 2. Procedural justice is consistently associated with legitimacy. Further, it is at least as powerful as outcomes. The evidence suggests that this effect is not as strong in 2020 as it is in 2008. However, in each case, the influence of procedural justice is stronger than that of being on the winning or losing side.

Hypothesis 3. Does Extremity Change the Association of Procedural Justice with Legitimacy?

The finding that procedural justice continues to matter is especially important in the case of extreme ideology, since the data presented indicates that extreme ideology is rising in America. Does extreme ideology lessen the influence of procedural justice, which is supposed to be able to legitimate an outcome among winners and losers? Hypothesis 3 argues that it does.

Table 6 reports the results of tests of the interaction hypothesis that extremity lessens the magnitude of the procedural justice effect. It has already been shown that the procedural justice of election procedures shapes post-election legitimacy. The question is whether this influence is stronger or weaker among those who are more or less ideologically extreme. This is revealed in the data by looking at the interaction term. If the interaction term is statistically significant, then the weight of procedural justice in shaping legitimacy varies depending on the level of a person's ideological extremity.

The results across two election studies (2000 and 2020) are very consistent. When they lose, those who are more extreme put less weight on procedural justice when making legitimacy assessments. Consider the 2000 election, which conservatives won. Among conservatives, more extremity increased the weight placed on procedural justice (beta = 0.34, $p < .05$). Among liberals, more extremity decreased

Table 6 Interaction of ideological extremism and procedural justice in shaping legitimacy

	Left extremism		Right extremism	
	Pre	Post	Pre	Post
Study 1, 2000 (Conservatives won)				
Procedural justice (Pre)	0.27***		0.30***	
Outcome	0.26***		0.11**	
Extremity (Post)	0.12**		–.29***	
Interaction of procedural justice with extremity	–.06		0.34*	
Multiple correlation coefficient	15%***		15%***	
Study 2, 2020 (Liberals won)				
Procedural justice				
Pre	0.26***	—	0.32***	—
Post	—	0.38***	—	0.47***
Outcome	—	–.02	—	0.01
Extremity	–.03	–.20***	0.01	0.10*
Interaction of procedural justice with extremity	0.11***	0.24***	–.09*	–.09*
Multiple correlation coefficient	10%***	19%***	10%***	19%***

Note. Entries are beta weights and the multiple correlation coefficients. *$p < .05$; **$p < .01$; ***$p < .001$

the weight placed on procedural justice (beta = −.06, not significant). The opposite pattern was found in 2020, which liberals won.

What accounts for the differences between 2000 and 2020? It is not possible to separate the direction of extremity from the election results, since the data is dependent on who wins the election. But the two elections with different winners show similar findings in terms of the argument made in this analysis. Extremity lessens the capacity of just election procedures to mitigate losses in legitimacy when one's candidate loses. This interaction effect is stronger in 2020 when conservatives are the losers.

What about autocratic values? As in Table 6, the argument here is that procedural justice influences legitimacy, but the strength of that influence could differ among people with different values and norms. This would be revealed in significant interaction effects between values/norms and procedural justice in the regression equations.

Table 7 indicates that respondents who hold highly authoritarian values or non-democratic norms are consistently found to put less weight on procedural justice when making judgments about legitimacy. For example, in 2020, respondents with antidemocratic norms put less weight on procedural justice when making legitimacy judgments (beta = −.36, p < .001), as did those with more highly authoritarian values (beta = −.37, p < .001).

Table 7 Influence of autocratic values on legitimacy

	Norms	Values	Free speech
Study 2, 2020			
Procedural justice	−.01	0.15***	
Outcome	0.11***	0.08***	
Antidemocratic norms	0.20***	—	
Authoritarian values	—	0.27***	
Interaction of procedural justice	−.36***	−.37***	
Multiple correlation coefficient	11%	11%	
Study 3, 2008			
Procedural justice	0.77***	0.62***	0.13
Outcome	0.52***	0.53***	0.53***
Antidemocratic norms	−.23	—	—
Authoritarian values	—	−.09	—
Want free speech	—	—	−.38***
Interaction of procedural justice	−.43*	−.24	−.48*
Multiple correlation coefficient	44%***	44%***	44%***

Note. Entries are beta weights and multiple correlation coefficients. *p < .05; **p < .01; ***p < .001

Hypothesis 4. Does Extremity Decrease the Influence of Pre-election Procedural Justice on Post-election Procedural Justice?

The final hypothesis is that ideologically extreme people will put less weight on pre-election judgments of procedural justice when making post-election judgments of procedural justice. In a purely procedural-based world, pre-election judgments about procedures should determine post-election judgments about procedures completely. The results indicate that post-election judgments are instead also influenced by the outcome (see Table 8). However, there is no interaction between either left or right extremity and the weight placed on pre-election procedural justice in making assessments of post-election procedural justice in either of the studies considered. In other words, extremity does not intensify the general tendency to view procedures as less fair after they produce an undesired outcome.

General Assessments

The last two studies focus general governance procedures, not on a single election. In addition, they are broad in scope and include people from a number of countries. Finally, the World Value Survey also provides an opportunity to compare

Table 8 Influence of pre-election procedural justice on post-election procedural justice

	Left extremity	Right extremity
	Study 1, 2008 (Liberals won)	
Pre-election procedural justice	0.38***	0.44***
Outcome	0.55***	−.44***
Extremism	−.15	0.17
Interaction of procedural justice with extremity	0.18	−.06
Multiple correlation coefficient	43%***	43%***
	Study 3, 2020 (Liberals won)	
Pre-election procedural justice	0.34***	0.31***
Outcome	0.42***	−.39***
Extremism	0.01	0.09*
Interaction of procedural justice with extremity	0.01	−.06
Multiple correlation coefficient	11%***	11%***

Note. Entries are beta weights and the multiple correlation coefficient. *p < .05; **p < .01; ***p < .001

self-reported and issue-based ideology. Across the broad range of societies, these two studies suggest that liberal extremity lowers legitimacy, while conservative extremity raises the level of legitimacy (see Table 9). This suggests that the influence of extremity on mean legitimacy is based upon the direction of the extremity, and there is no general finding about the influence of extremity on the level of legitimacy.

In the case of autocratic values, these studies suggest that antidemocratic norms are associated with lower levels of legitimacy. No significant connection is found between authoritarian values and legitimacy in the European Social Survey (see Table 10).

Both international studies suggest that procedural justice judgments are linked to legitimacy judgments. Because there is no specific election involved, it is not possible to have a simple measure of winning and losing. However, general performance evaluations can be computed and compared to the influence of procedural justice. This comparison suggests that both matter (see Table 11). Whether procedures are viewed as fair also influences legitimacy.

Table 9 Correlation of ideological extremity with legitimacy

	Self-reported extremity	Issue-based extremity
Study 4. World Value Survey		
Left extremity	–.07***	–.01***
Right extremity	0.07***	0.05***
Study 5. European Social Survey		
Left extremity	–.07***	—
Right extremity	0.13***	—

Note. Entries are Pearson correlations. *p < .05; **p < .01; ***p < .001

Table 10 Correlation of autocratic values with legitimacy

Study 5. European Social Survey	
Antidemocratic norms	–.21***
Authoritarian values	–.07
Want free speech	0.00

Note. Entries are Pearson correlations. *p < .05; **p < .01; ***p < .001

Table 11 Correlation of procedural justice with legitimacy

Study 4. World Value Survey	
Procedural justice	0.41***
Study 5. European Social Survey	
Procedural justice	0.44***
Performance	0.44***

Note. Entries are Pearson correlations. *p < .05; **p < .01; ***p < .001

Does extremity change the weight given to procedural justice in judgments about legitimacy? The World Value Survey allows this issue to be addressed using both self-reported and issue-based extremity. The World Value Survey analysis suggests that among those whose extremity is in the direction of liberalism, more extremity leads to more weight on procedural justice. Among conservatives, the results are unclear. Using self-report, more extremity leads to more weight on procedural justice, using issues less weight (Table 12). The results for conservative extremity are therefore unclear in that the direction depends upon which index of extremity is used. Liberals in contrast are generally found to put more weight on procedural justice as they become more extreme.

Autocratic values (authoritarianism and democratic norms) are reliably found to be related to the weight given to procedural justice. Autocratic respondents put less weight on procedural justice when making assessments about legitimacy (Table 13). This is shown by the significant interactions found with more authoritarian values and judgments that it is not important for the government to be democratic and the belief that being free is not among one's most important values.

Table 12 Interaction of ideological extremity and procedural justice on legitimacy

	Left extremism	Right extremism
Study 4, World Value Survey		
Self-reported extremity		
Procedural justice (Pre)	0.40***	0.39***
Ideological extremity	0.02	–.19***
Interaction of procedural justice with extremism	0.05***	0.12***
Multiple correlation coefficient	17%***	18%***
Issue-based extremity		
Procedural justice (Pre)	0.43***	0.38***
Ideological extremity	–.18***	0.21***
Interaction of procedural justice with extremism	0.24***	–.21***
Multiple correlation coefficient	18%***	17%***

Note. Entries are beta weights and multiple correlation coefficients. *p < .05; **p < .01; ***p < .001

Table 13 Influence of autocratic values on legitimacy

	Norms	Values	Free speech
Study 5. European Social Survey			
Procedural justice	0.55***	0.55***	0.25***
Antidemocratic norms	–.07	—	—
Authoritarian values	—	–.01	—
Want free speech	—	—	–.13***
Interaction of procedural justice	–.31***	–.13***	–.22***
Multiple correlation coefficient	21%***	20%	20%

Note. Entries are beta weights and multiple correlation coefficients. *p < .05; **p < .01; ***p < .001

Why Does Extremity Matter?

The results of study 4 (the World Value Survey) provide some suggestions about why we find the differences observed. The study measures materialist versu post-materialist values (i.e., values that feature quality of life rather than materialistic goals). Post-materialist values connect with liberalism and conservatism in different ways, with liberals being more post-materialist. An analysis of the World Value Survey data suggests that people with post-materialist values place greater weight on procedural justice in making legitimacy judgments. Hence, one reason that liberal extremity may be linked to procedural justice is that it is associated with post-materialist values.

There is also a suggestion in the distinction between fixed and fluid values. This distinction is between two types of values: the desire for social conformity and the desire for personal autonomy (Feldman, 2003; Feldman & Johnston, 2014). Feldman draws upon this idea and suggests that studies across different societies (Schwartz, 1992) identify two clusters of ideals: social conformity (obedient, have self-discipline, politeness, and honor parents/elders) and self-direction (creative, free, choose own goals, curious, and independent). Feldman highlights the tension between individual freedom and the need for social control. He argues that there are several mechanisms that maintain social order, including force and adherence to a common set of norms. The first reflects sanctions and incentives, and the second one is a value-based orientation consistent with legitimacy-based authority. People with fixed values prefer safety (e.g., security, rule following, proper behavior, and follow traditions), while those with fluid values prefer freedom (i.e., freedom, think new ideas, do new things, and understand different people). Extreme liberalism is linked to more fluid values ($r = 0.07$) and less fixed values ($r = -.11$), while extreme conservatism is linked to more fixed values ($r = 0.07$). People with more fluid values put greater weight on procedural justice in making legitimacy judgments (beta = 0.09, $p < .001$), while those with fixed values put less weight on procedural justice when making legitimacy judgments (beta = −.05, $p < .05$). These connections suggest that extremity is connected to people's values, with more materialistic and more fixed values being associated with less concern with procedural justice-based legitimacy.

What psychological models might help to understand extremity effects? One is the literature on social identity and cooperative behavior (Tyler, 2011; Tyler & Blader, 2000). That literature theorizes and supports empirically the argument that the impact of values on behavior is moderated by the degree to which people share a perceived social bond with the authority, institutions, and society making and implementing the rules. The reason for this connection is that ideology and identity are intertwined, and if people feel that their identity is connected to a group, their connection to that group affects their sense of self and their feelings of self-worth. Directives from outsiders are responded to instrumentally, while directives from insiders evoke a value-based response.

The social identity perspective suggests that to the degree extreme ideology lessens feelings of connection to society and social authorities, it should lead to people putting less weight on procedural justice when making legitimacy judgments. Consistent with this argument, in the World Value Survey, more extreme liberalism is associated with higher trust in other people ($r = 0.04$), while more extreme conservatism is associated with less trust in other people ($r = -.06$). Similarly, an index of general trust in others (i.e., neighbors, people you know, strangers, people of other religions, and people from other countries) suggests that liberal extremity leads to more trust ($r = 0.04$), while more conservative extremity leads to less trust ($r = -.07$). In other words, extremity leads liberals to connect more to others and conservatives to connect less to others. This suggests that community identification becomes more important to liberals.

In contrast to this general effect argument, it is possible to draw upon a different psychological literature to make a second argument. That literature is the moral foundation literature of Haidt (2001, 2012). Haidt distinguishes between individualizing (harm/care; fairness)and binding (in-group loyalty; respect for authority; purity/sanctity) morality. Individualizing morality is associated with liberalism, and binding morality with conservatism (Graham et al., 2009). If people become more liberal, we would expect them to lean more heavily on individualizing morality (harm reduction and fairness). A key antecedent of legitimacy is fairness, so we would predict that the focus on the legitimacy of authorities would become stronger as ideology becomes more extremely liberal (i.e., individuating). Individualizing morality leads to a focus on fairness and harm, so those who are more extreme should be more interested in evaluating the fairness of authorities to decide if they are being harmful.

What about extreme conservatives? The elements of binding morality are the unquestioned acceptance of authority and a heightened focus on in-group loyalty. This suggests that extreme conservatives would be less concerned about the legitimacy of authorities, since they are following their orders, not evaluating them. Extremity should motivate conservatives to bind themselves more tightly to rules, not to more strongly question them.

Is morality relevant to ideology? D'Amore et al. (2024) recently used panel data to demonstrate that when people view the political landscape as more polarized, they are more motivated to engage in value-protective responses, which include strengthening "attitude moralization". If people become more moralized in their political attitudes, this would cause liberals and conservatives to embrace their own distinct moral foundations, consistent with the results of this study.

Conclusion

Four hypotheses were put forward. After reviewing the data of the studies considered, what can we say about those hypotheses?

Hypothesis 1. Those who are more ideologically extreme will view political authority as less legitimate.

In the case of elections, being on the losing side is associated with lower legitimacy, and this tendency is stronger for those with extreme ideologies in either direction. Similarly, ideological extremity increases the degree to which winners think the procedures are fair and losers think the procedures are unfair. In other words, extremity intensifies the impact of winning or losing on judgments about legitimacy and procedural justice.

Studies involving elections suggest that having autocratic values is generally associated with lower levels of legitimacy. It is also associated with lower levels of perceived procedural justice, both prior to and following an election.

In international studies involving general government evaluations, left extremity lowers legitimacy and right extremity raises legitimacy. In studies of general government evaluations involving norms and values, autocratic values are found to lead to lower evaluations of legitimacy. This indicates two opposing tendencies since right extremity and more autocratic values are positively associated.

Overall, these findings suggest two conclusions. First, ideological extremity leads judgments of procedural justice and legitimacy to be more strongly linked to winning and losing. Second, autocratic values are generally related to lower evaluations of procedural justice and legitimacy.

Hypothesis 2. Procedural justice legitimates a winner in an election.

Across all of the election studies (2000–2020), procedural justice continues to legitimate authorities. The general studies of government also find that procedural justice legitimates authority. Whatever are the undermining influences of ideological extremity and autocratic values, they have not eliminated the legitimating influences of procedural justice on legitimacy.

Hypothesis 3. Procedural justice is less important to those who are more ideological.

In the case of elections ideological extremity lessens the capacity of just election procedures to mitigate losses in legitimacy when one's candidate loses. In the case of elections, extreme values and norms lessens the weight people put on procedural justice when evaluating elections.

In the case of general government evaluations, ideological extremity has an inconsistent effect on the weight conservative extremity has, but suggests that more extreme liberals put more weight on procedural justice. In the case of general government evaluations, autocratic values lead to putting less weight on procedural justice.

The overall finding is that when a specific event is involved (i.e., an election), both ideological extremity and more autocratic values decrease the weight given to procedural justice in shaping legitimacy. However, when general government evaluations are involved, the dynamics are more complex. It is primarily left extremity that is influential, with more extreme left ideology increasing the weight put on procedural justice. Autocratic values continue to decrease the weight associated with procedural justice.

Hypothesis 4. Post-election judgments of procedural justice will be less strongly linked to pre-election procedural justice among those who are more ideological.

Extreme ideology does not influence how much weight is placed on pre-election procedural justice judgments when forming post-election procedural justice judgments.

What does all of this suggest? Authority dynamics are not found to be invariant across ideology and autocratic values. In particular, there are clear indications that both ideological extremity and more autocratic values are at least sometimes associated with a weaker connection of procedural justice judgments to legitimacy, especially in the context of elections.

Discussion

What does this study show? It shows that the procedural justice–legitimacy connection does not exist in a vacuum. It is impacted by outside societal forces. Two are considered here: ideological extremity and autocratic values. At their current levels, these background factors do not undermine the legitimacy-based model of authority, but they do limit it. This is particularly troublesome in the case of ideological extremity since there is evidence that levels are rising. Like the melting ice caps, this signals a worrying sign for the future. These findings are important to legal and political psychologists because the extension of psychological theories into the arena of political and legal authorities is a major contribution of social psychology to society. Legitimacy-based governance has gained broad support and recognition in recent decades facilitated by the work of social psychologists.

As noted, legitimacy-based authority has important advantages. It enables pluralism and democratic government. It also has two other advantages. First, by enabling voluntary deference and willing cooperation, it lessens the tensions associated with management using sanctions. Second, legitimacy provides a framework within which people are more willing to engage in their communities politically, economically, and socially. Social psychology has something valuable to give society. However, this gift is less valuable to the degree that because of societal factors outside the model it does not work. Rather than simply speculating about the impact of such societal factors, this study tries to directly measure that impact.

Why is this issue interesting to political and legal theorists? There have been two general models of authority that have dominated policy discussions, economic theory-based rational choice and legitimacy. Both are argued to bridge across differences in demographics, social norms, and moral values. The advantages of power are clear: it is under the control of authorities and has immediate effects. Legitimacy is an improvement and has advantages. The key question is whether it is sustainable.

Remedies

Having identified the problems of procedural justice-based authority as an issue; it is important to also identify proactive remedies which might be undertaken to preserve this desirable form of authority. The author suggests five: emphasizing procedural justice impacts; distinguishing procedural elements; building identification with the community; personalizing authority; and focusing on multiple stages of authority.

Emphasizing procedural justice impacts The model outlined argues for links between procedural justice and legitimacy. There is abundant evidence for this model. However, the myth of self-interest is a strongly held part of American culture. The instrumental model dominates legal and political culture. People persist in an image of human nature that views people as self-interested. The instrumental model fits human biases and social motivations. Authorities have enhanced views of their competence and benevolence. It seems wise and natural to concentrate power in their hands, pushing policies down using dominance and sanctions.

In other words, the procedural justice model is counterintuitive, and its acceptance is based upon weighting evidence above intuition. This is particularly an issue in law, which is a highly intuitive field, in contrast to political science or psychology. The task here is one of education. Since economics dominates legal and political studies, and economics is focused on behavior (revealed preferences), it is especially important that legitimacy is linked to behavior. In this case, as noted, legitimacy shapes political participation. Education would involve efforts to communicate to authorities the central role that procedural justice plays in shaping legitimacy, as well as the distinct advantages of legitimacy-based authority.

One avenue to increasing the power of procedural justice is to expand the framework for considering the creation of authority structures (Barrett-Howard & Tyler, 1986; Tyler & Degoey, 1995). This chapter focuses on elections which is one such structure. However, it has already been noted that there are many forms of procedure for creating authorities and making decisions. As an example, Tyler and Markell (2010) ask residents of a Florida community how they would like to make decisions about land use. Five procedures are evaluated: private party negotiations; public hearings; public referendums; administrative law hearings; and judicial adjudication. The key finding is that people wanted third-party involvement and picked third-party procedures based upon procedural justice criteria, not in terms of their likelihood of prevailing under any given procedure. Respondents put weight on three values: neutrality, respect, and voice.

Disaggregating procedural elements As noted, procedural justice contains elements of just decision-making and just interpersonal treatment. Drawing from their legal backgrounds, authorities often emphasize just decision-making when they talk about procedural justice (for example, Thibaut & Walker, 1975). However, members of the public emphasize interpersonal treatment. For example, Rottman and Tyler (2014) found that when residents of California were asked to evaluate the courts, their trust judgments included judgments about both just decision-making and fair interpersonal treatment. However, the primary issue of importance to members of the public was interpersonal treatment. Hence, it is important to redirect the authorities toward this element of procedural justice.

This is not only an American issue. According to Van De Walle and Raine (2008), when explaining attitudes toward the justice system in the UK and EU, the crucial issue to the public was: "Feeling that the courts are out of touch with common people. That judges do not care about everyday people and their needs and concerns (p. 12).". Similarly, Rosenvallon (2011) argues that early links between impartiality (i.e., neutrality) and legitimacy have been replaced by an emphasis on proximity. This means citizens want to be listened to and reckoned with. They expect the government to be attentive to their problems and to show genuine concern with their everyday experiences. Everyone wants his or her particular situation to be taken into account, and no one wants to be subject to inflexible and impersonal rules. People want to deal with attentive, fair, respectful authorities who listen to the arguments of the people they govern.

This argument can be extended by considering how ideological extremity shapes reactions to losing. The 2008 election study allowed an examination of how losers' (Conservatives) degree of extremity shaped how they evaluated post-election winner legitimacy. Moderate conservatives evaluated the legitimacy of the winner post-election by focusing primarily on the neutrality of election procedures. Extreme conservatives primarily focused on trust and respect. In other words, they were more focused on the quality of treatment, relative to moderates.

Why would this matter? A recent study addressed misinformation as a concern arising from extremity and looked at ways to correct errors (Martel et al., 2024). These findings suggest that it might be more profitable to focus on identity issues. As an example, consider identity affirmation. It is possible to lessen threat by identity affirmation, and, in response, people are more open to persuasion about ideological issues (Cohen & Sherman, 2014).

Building identification with the community It is also possible to focus on building the community. Procedural justice theories emphasize that concern about procedural justice is linked to identification with a community. This connection works in two ways. People care more about procedural justice when they identify with a community and its authorities. Treatment by authorities has impact because people draw important messages of status and standing from group authorities. Conversely, when people are treated justly, it builds their identification with the authorities and the community. Hence, an indirect path forward is to build identification with communities and indirectly strengthen governance based upon the relational aspects of procedural justice. As an example, a society could address grievances about inequity in employment opportunities or healthcare provision. That would heighten identification with society. Although political-legal authorities would not be the target of such changes they would benefit because people would then identify more strongly with the society and care more about the actions of all government authorities.

A focus on communities reveals that the level of trust in others in one's community is also generally declining, a trend parallel to declines in trust in authorities. This is important because interpersonal trust is one element of identification with the community and has an important direct influence on people's behavior. For example, Dieleman (2022) found that variations in the level of trust in others explained around 40% of the variance in the rate of COVID deaths around the world. These declines in trust in others in the community undermine identification and undermine the influence of procedural justice on the part of community authorities.

Data supports the argument that procedural justice promotes identification. Data from a sample of Americans (Tyler & Jackson, 2014) shows that procedural justice is associated with community identification, as well as promoting social connections with others and higher levels of economic and political engagement. As would be expected, interpersonal fairness is especially strongly connected to identification and social engagement. As identification develops, the influence of procedural justice will further increase. The key point is that the focus is on building identification with the community and not on directly addressing trust in political or legal authorities.

Personalizing authority If a person or group is alienated from state authority, they can still respond to personal experiences with specific authorities. Hence, one path forward is to personalize authority. As Aronson et al. (2023) suggest: "A personalized public administration emphasizes individual decisionmakers and seeks legitimacy through familiarity with the character, identity, and virtues of individual agents (p. 833)". The value of this strategy is supported by findings that people who are less identified with their communities make overall legitimacy judgments by putting more weight on whether they have been personally treated fairly and less upon whether people in the community are generally treated fairly. On the other hand, Aronson et al. (2023) find that personalization undermined perceived objectivity, suggesting that personalization is a complex legitimation strategy which may enhance trust but lower perceived neutrality. However, in marginalized communi ties with low trust personalization is a strategy for beginning to build legitimacy on a person by person basis.

Focusing on multiple stages of authority As noted, most research is on the procedural justice of policy implementation. This chapter focuses on fairness in creating the initial authority structure which then creates and implements policy. A final stage of procedures involves the redress of grievances (appeals and responsiveness to them). A study of the residents of New York city found that each of these three stages contributes distinctively to overall legitimacy (creation beta = 0.30; implementation beta = 0.42; and redress beta = 0.27). These findings validate the virtue of a focus on implementation but at the same time highlight the value of expanding the range of the framework within which the procedural justice - legitimacy connection is studied.

Conclusion

The results of these analyses are at the same time reassuring and concerning. First, as predicted, procedural justice continues to shape legitimacy. It is distinct from and more important than winning or losing. Second, however, the strength of this mechanism is moderated by background values. In general people who have more extreme ideology or who have more autocratic values reply less strongly upon procedural justice when making post-election judgments. This is particularly troubling in the case of ideological extremity because time series analyses indicate that the prevalence of intense ideologies is increasing in America. Autocratic values, in contrast, seem to be more a stable characteristic of a minority of Americans than an increasing threat to legitimacy-based authority.

The findings at the general level echo the more specific findings about elections. Liberal extremity leads to more focus on whether election procedures are just when making judgments about political legitimacy. Conservative extremity is unclear in these studies, with some suggestion that conservative extremity leads to less focus on procedural justice when making judgments about political extremity. Thus, the examination of changes in public views over time suggests that to the degree that there is a rising challenge to democratic governance, it is coming at least in part from increasing ideological extremity. On the other hand, the results of this analysis indicate that the strongest negative impact on procedural justice-based governance come from autocratic values. Hence, one contribution of these studies is to suggest that the most productive focus might be on efforts at understanding why people hold autocratic values. The fact of rising extremity is mitigated to some degree by the weak magnitude of the impact of that rise in undermining procedure-based legitimacy. The decline of procedural-based legitimacy is not inevitable in the face of societal level changes in values and ideology. The key is proactive strategies focused on building the framework within which procedural justice-based legitimacy is viable and effective. This analysis points to five such strategies and provides evidence of their likely effectiveness.

Appendix

Study One. National Election 2000

The first study uses data from the ANES 2000–2002 panel study. The 2000 Presidential election garnered considerable attention among scholars because of a widespread perception that the procedures used (The United States Supreme Court choosing the winner) were suspect. The concern here is with the possibility that ideological extremity might undermine the role of procedural justice in legitimating a winner.

Respondents were drawn from a random sample of Americans who were in the pre–post 2000 election interviews of the National Election Study (*n* = 786). The sample had a mean age of 50; was 44% male; and 84% White. It was 33% liberal; 61% conservative; and 6% moderate. The median annual family income was $50–65,000. Thirty-one percent had a high school diploma or less; 54% had some college up to a college degree; and 15% had more education.

Post-election Measures

Liberal/conservative extremity Respondents place themselves on a seven-point strongly liberal to strongly conservative scale. This was used to create two extremity scales ranging from 1 (*moderate*) to 4 (*extreme*). The proportions who were at the most extreme level were 2% left and 5% right.

Election outcome Respondents were asked who they voted for and how strongly they felt about that person. These two questions were used to create a scale of outcome desirability ranging from 2 (voted for a person they felt strongly in favor of and they won) to −2 (voted for a person they felt strongly in favor of and they lost).

Procedural justice of the election 2000 Respondents were asked: "In some countries, people believe their elections are conducted justly. In other countries, people believe that their elections are conducted unjustly. Thinking about the Presidential election we've just had, do you believe it was very fair, somewhat fair, neither fair nor unfair, somewhat unfair, or very unfair?" Participants rated this item on a five-point scale, and because this is a single item, reliability cannot be calculated.

Legitimacy Measured as institutional trust. Four items: "How much can the government be trusted?"; "How much of taxes does government waste?"; "Is the government run by big interests or for the benefit of the people?"; and "How many in government are crooked?" (Coefficient alpha = 0.61).

Study Two. ANES Panel Study Pre–Post 2020 Campaign

Prior to and following the 2020 Presidential election, the ANES conducted interviews with samples of Americans. This chapter is based upon an unweighted analysis of the 7453 respondents who completed both waves. Again, the question is whether procedural justice legitimates the winner.

Pre-election

Fairness of the election process Two questions. "How accurately are votes counted? (not at all–completely)" and "How much do you trust election officials (not at all–a great deal)". These items were combined into a scale of the fairness of the election process (coefficient alpha = 0.75).

Liberalism This scale ranges from a self-placement from *extremely liberal* (1) to *extremely conservative* (7). People who did not respond were followed up with "if you had to choose question". This scale was anchored at the moderate point in the liberalism scale. Moving from that point, deviations in both directions led to scales ending in "extremely liberal" and "extremely conservative".

Post-election

Government legitimacy Four agree–disagree items were combined: "Public officials do not care what people think"; "I have no say in government"; "Most politicians are trustworthy;" and "Politicians only care about the rich" (coefficient alpha = 0.69).

Post-election rating of fairness Two items were combined: "How often are votes counted fairly?" and "Corruption is widespread among politicians.". This is a weak scale (coefficient alpha = 0.37).

Did your candidate win? Respondents were asked (yes vs. no) if the person they preferred won the election.

Recent political participation In the past 12 months, have you: (1) gotten into a political argument; (2) joined a protest march, rally, or demonstration; (3) signed a petition; (4) given money to an organization. (5) posted political content online; (6) contacted a political official; (7) worked on a political issue facing your community; (8) done any volunteer work; and (9) contacted any Federal official. The scale is the number of activities in which the respondent engaged.

Values

Authoritarianism Authoritarianism was measured by asking respondents what they felt was important in terms of values for children: "independence or respect"; "curiosity or good manners"; "obedience or self-reliance"; and "considerate or well-behaved." A four-item scale was constructed based upon these four choices (coefficient alpha = 0.66).

Support for democratic norms Respondents were asked whether "The press needs to be free to criticize government."; "It is important to balance power among the branches."; and "There should be serious consequences for misconduct." A three-item scale was created (coefficient alpha = 0.66).

Study Three. Knowledge Networks 2008 Election Study

The study uses panel respondents from a Knowledge Networks panel. A sample of 310 was selected for heightened partisanship, divided between Strong Democrats (136) and Strong Republicans (174). Respondents completed a questionnaire prior to and following the election. The respondents were 62% high-school graduates; 85% White; 50% over 54; 54% female; and 49% with an annual family income of over $60,000.

Pre-election

Procedural fairness of the election process The items were: "In some countries people believe their elections are conducted in fair ways. In other countries people believe that their elections are conducted in unfair ways. Do you believe the recent Presidential election was conducted using procedures that are fair?"; "Do you agree there was a fair procedure used to decide who would be the new President?"; "Do you agree the campaign was as honest and open as others have been?"; "Did the campaign give people the type of information they needed to make informed decisions?"; "Did the campaign provide people with accurate facts?"; "Did the campaign give equal consideration to the views of all the different groups in America?"; "Did the campaign protect the rights of all Americans?"; "Did the campaign address the need and concerns of the average voter?"; "Did the campaign give voters an opportunity to choose the most trustworthy candidate?"; and "Did the campaign give people an adequate voice?" All of the items were four-point scales (agree strongly to disagree strongly) (coefficient alpha = 0.91).

Ideological extremity The original scale was: *extremely liberal* (1) to *extremely conservative* (7). Two scales were created, each neutral: slightly polarized to extremely polarized.

Support for free speech "If a person wanted to make a speech in your community against churches and religion, they should be allowed to speak" and "If a person wanted to make a speech in your community in favor of Muslim radicals like Osama bin Laden they should be allowed to speak." All of the items were four-point scales (agree strongly to disagree strongly) (coefficient alpha = 0.68).

Authoritarianism "To compromise with political opponents is dangerous because it usually leads to the betrayal of one's ideals" and "A group which tolerates too many differences of opinion among its own members cannot exist for long." All of the items were four-point scales (agree strongly to disagree strongly) (coefficient alpha = 0.56).

Support for democratic norms "People in the minority should be free to try to win majority support"; "Public officials should be chosen by majority vote"; "No matter what a person's political beliefs are, he is entitled to the same rights and protections as anyone else"; "There should be free speech for all no matter what their views might be." All of the items were four-point scales (agree strongly to disagree strongly) (coefficient alpha = 0.71).

Post-election

Procedural fairness of the election process The items were: "In some countries people believe their elections are conducted in fair ways. In other countries people believe that their elections are conducted in unfair ways. Do you believe the recent Presidential election was conducted using procedures that are fair?"; "Do you agree there was a fair procedure used to decide who would be the new President?"; "Do you agree the campaign was as honest and open as others have been?"; "Did the campaign give people the type of information they needed to make informed decisions?"; "Did the campaign provide people with accurate facts?"; "Did the campaign give equal consideration to the views of all the different groups in America?"; "Did the campaign protect the rights of all Americans?"; "Did the campaign address the need and concerns of the average voter?"; "Did the campaign give voters an opportunity to choose the most trustworthy candidate?"; and "Did the campaign give people an adequate voice?" All of the items were four-point scales (agree strongly to disagree strongly) (coefficient alpha = 0.93).

Legitimacy "You can usually trust the government in Washington to do what is right."; "You can usually trust them to make fair decisions."; "You can usually trust them to do what is best for the country."; "Many of our political leaders are dishonest."; "Many of our political leaders are more concerned about special interests than they are about the average voter."; "You willingly accept the results of this most recent Presidential election."; "You think that this President was legitimately elected and deserves your support."; "You trust the new President to do what is good for our country."; "You think the new President will do a good job while in office."; "You will willingly follow the policies established by the President."; "You will follow

Presidential policies even when you do not agree with them."; "You do not support challenging the results of this election." and "You do not support efforts by Congress to limit the power of the new President." All of the items were four-point scales (agree strongly to disagree strongly) (coefficient alpha = 0.90).

Study Four. World Value Survey. 2017–2021. n = 153,716. (90 Countries)

Ideology The scale of self-reported liberalism (0 = *left*; 10 = *right*) was used to create two distinct scales: extreme liberalism and extreme conservatism. The extreme liberalism scale ranged 0–5: 0 (45%); 1 (29%); 2 (8%); 3 (8%); 4 (4%), and 5 (7%). The extreme conservatism scale ranged from 0 to 5: 0 (55%); 1 (13%); 2 (10%); 3 (9%); 4 (4%), and 5 (9%).

Issue-based ideology Respondents were asked about three aspects of ideology: economic ideology: "How much do you favor income equality? (scale of 1–10, strongly yes to strongly no)"; political ideology: "Is having a strong leader a good idea? (scale of 1–4, good to bad)," and social ideology: "Are homosexual couples good parents? (1–5, agree strongly to disagree strongly)".

The two scales constructed, reflecting self-reported liberalism and conservatism ($r = -.57$) were correlated, as were liberal and conservative issue-based ideology ($r = -.62$). Self-reported liberalism was correlated with issue-based liberalism ($r = 0.20$), and self-reported conservatism was correlated with issue-based conservatism ($r = 0.19$).

Political legitimacy A five-item scale was used: how much trust in the police; in the justice system/courts; in Parliament; in the civil services and in the government (1–4 item scale; a great deal to none at all) (coefficient alpha = 0.87).

Values Respondents were coded for materialism–postmaterialist values using a framework provided in the theory. Twenty-eight percent were materialism; 59% mixed; and 13% post-materialist. Post-materialism was linked to liberal extremity ($r = 0.10$) and to conservative extremity ($r = -.08$).

Study Five. European Social Survey

There were 54,673 respondents (the recommended post-stratification weight was used in the analysis).

Election fairness Respondents were asked how much this applies in their country:

"In [your] country national elections are free and fair (0 = *does not apply at all*) (10 = *completely applies*). Overall, 71% of respondents were in the positive range (6 thru 10)."

Ideology Self-placement (0–10) was used to create separate scales of left and right ideological extremity.

Political legitimacy Respondents were asked about their level of trust in their countries' legal system: parliament, politicians, and political parties. The scale ranged from 0 (*no trust at all*) to 10 (*complete trust*). Overall, 41% of responses were in the positive range (6–10). (coefficient alpha = 0.91).

Authoritarianism Agreement with five items: "How important is it to do what is told and follow rules"; "To behave properly"; "That government is strong and ensures safety"; "To live in secure and safe surroundings"; and "To follow traditions and customs" (coefficient alpha = 0.71).

Democracy is important How important is it to you to live in a democratically governed society? (1–10; not at all important to extremely important).

Democratic norms How important is it to have these democratic elements?: "Opposition parties are free to criticize the government"; "The media are free to criticize the government"; "The rights of minority groups are protected"; "The courts treat everyone the same"; "The courts able to stop the government acting beyond its authority"; and "The government explains its decisions to voters" (1–10; not at all important to extremely important) (coefficient alpha = 0.83).

References

Ackerman, B. (2002). *Bush v. Gore: The question of legitimacy*. Yale.

Anderson, C. J., Blais, A., Bowler, S., Donovan, T., & Listhaug, O. (2005). *Loser's consent: Elections and democratic legitimacy*.

Aronson, O., Elad-Strenger, J., Kessler, T., & Feldman, Y. (2023). Does personalization of office-holders undermine the legitimacy of the office? *Regulation and Governance, 17*, 833–850. https://doi.org/10.1111/rego.12495

Barrett-Howard, E., & Tyler, T. R. (1986). Procedural justice as a criterion in allocation decisions. *Journal of Personality and Social Psychology, 50*, 296–304. https://doi.org/10.1037/0022-3514.50.2.296

Bradford, B. (2014). Policing and social identity: Procedural justice, inclusion and cooperation between police and public. *Policing and Society, 24*(1), 22–43. https://doi.org/10.1080/10439463.2012.724068

Bradford, B., & Jackson, J. (2024). Legitimacy, relational norms and reciprocity. In R. Hollander-Blumoff (Ed.), *Research handbook in law and psychology. Research handbooks in law and society* (pp. 343–360). Elgar.

Broderstad, T. S. (2023). An empirical evaluation of explanations for political system support. *Political Research Quarterly, 76*, 1542–1554. https://doi-org.libproxy.unl.edu/10.1177/10659129231156388
Brown, K. L., & Reisig, M. D. (2019). Procedural injustice, police legitimacy, and officer gender: A vignette-based test of the invariance thesis. *Behavioral Sciences & The Law, 37*(6), 696–710. https://doi.org/10.1002/bsl.2439
Chong, D., Citrin, J., & Levy, M. (2022). The realignment of political tolerance in the United States. *Perspectives on Politics*. Online. https://doi.org/10.1017/S1537592722002079.
Citrin, J., & Stoker, L. (2018). Political trust in a cynical age. *Annual Review of Political Science, 21*, 49–70. https://doi.org/10.1146/annurev-polisci-050316-092550
Cohen, G. L., & Sherman, D. K. (2014). The psychology of change: Self-affirmation and social psychological intervention. *Annual Review of Psychology, 65*, 333–371.
Cruz, J. M., & Kloppe-Santamaria, G. (2023). Determinants of support for extralegal violence in Latin America and the Caribbean. *Latin American Research Review, 56*, 50–68.
Dahl, R. A. (1971). *Polyarchy*. Yale.
Dahl, R. A. (1989). *Democracy and its critics*. Yale.
D'Amore, C., van Zomeren, M., & Koudenburg, N. (2024). How perceived polarization predicts attitude moralization. *Journal of Personality and Social Psychology*. https://doi-org.libproxy.unl.edu/10.1177/01461672211047375
Dieleman, J. L. (2022). Pandemic preparedness and COVID-19. *Lancet, 399*, 1489–1512. https://doi.org/10.1016/S0140-6736(22)00172-6
Druckman, D., & Wagner, L. (2019). Justice matters: Peace negotiations, stable agreements, and durable peace. *Journal of Conflict Resolution, 63*, 287–316. https://doi.org/10.1177/0022002717739088
Farrington, D. P., Cohn, E. G., & Skinner, G. C. M. (2022). Changes in the most cited scholars in five international journals between 2006 and 2020. *Asian Journal of Criminology*. https://doi.org/10.1007/s11417-022-09362-x
Feldman, S. (2003). Enforcing social conformity: A theory of authoritarianism. *Political Psychology, 24*, 41–74. https://doi.org/10.1111/0162-895X.00316
Feldman, S., & Johnston, C. (2014). Understanding the determinants of political ideology. *Political Psychology, 35*, 337–358. https://doi.org/10.1111/pops.12055
Fox, B., Moule, R. K., Jaynes, C., & Parry, M. (2020). Are the effects of legitimacy and its components invariant? *Journal of Research in Crime and Delinquency, 58*(1), 3–40. https://doi.org/10.1177/0022427820926228
French, J. R. P., Jr., & Raven, B. H. (1959). The bases of social power. In D. Cartwright (Ed.), *Studies in social power* (pp. 150–167). University of Michigan Institute for Social Research.
Gonzalez, C., & Tyler, T. R. (2008). The psychology of enfranchisement: Engaging and fostering inclusion of members through voting and decision-making procedures. *Journal of Social Issues, 64*, 447–466. https://doi.org/10.1111/j.1540-4560.2008.00572.x
Graham, J., Haidt, J., & Nosek, B. A. (2009). Liberals and conservatives rely on different sets of moral foundations. *Journal of Personality and Social Psychology, 96*, 1029–1046. https://doi.org/10.1037/a0015141
Grillos, T., Zarychta, A., & Nunez, J. N. (2021). Water scarcity and procedural justice in Honduras. *World Development, 142*, 105451. https://doi.org/10.1016/j.worlddev.2021.105451
Grimes, M. (2006). Organized consent: The role of procedural fairness in political trust and compliance. *European Journal of Political Research, 45*, 285–315. https://doi.org/10.1111/j.1475-6765.2006.00299.x
Gulevich, O., Borovikova, J., & Rodionova, M. (2024). The relationship between political procedural justice and attitudes toward the political system. *Political Psychology, 45*, 537–557.
Haidt, J. (2001). The emotional dog and its rational tail: A social intuitionist approach to moral judgment. *Psychological Review, 108*, 814–834.
Haidt, J. (2012). *The righteous mind*. Pantheon.

Halliday, T. C., Karpik, L., & Feeley, M. M. (2007). Fighting for political freedom: Comparative studies of the legal complex and political liberalism.

Hetherington, M. J., & Weiler, J. D. (2009). *Authoritarianism and polarization in American politics.*

Hetherington, M. J., & Weiler, J. D. (2018). *Prius or pickup? How the answers to four simple questions explain America's great divide.*

Hibbing, J. R., & Theiss-Morse, E. (1995). *Congress as public enemy: Public attitudes toward American political institutions.* Cambridge University Press.

Hibbing, J. R., & Theiss-Morse, E. (2001). *What is it about government that Americans dislike?* Cambridge University Press.

Hibbing, J. R., & Theiss-Morse, E. (2002). *Stealth democracy: Americans' beliefs about how government should work.*

Hooghe, M., & Stiers, D. (2016). Elections as a democratic linkage mechanism: How elections boost political trust in a proportional system. *Electoral Studies, 44*, 46–55.

Jost, J. T., Glaser, J., Kruglanski, A. W., & Sulloway, F. J. (2003). Political conservatism as motivated social cognition. *Psychological Bulletin, 129*, 339–375. https://doi.org/10.1037/0033-2909.129.3.339

Jost, J. T., & Banaji, M. R. (1994). The role of stereotyping in system-justification and the production of false consciousness. *British Journal of Social Psychology, 33*, 1–27. https://doi.org/10.1111/j.2044-8309.1994.tb01008.x

Kelman, H. C. (2006). Interests, relationships, identities: Three central issues for individuals and groups in negotiating their social environment. *Annual Review of Psychology, 57*, 1–26. https://doi.org/10.1146/annurev.psych.57.102904.190156

Kohn, M. L., & Schooler, C. (1983). *Work and personality.* Ablex.

Leventhal, G. S. (1980). What should be done with equity theory? New approaches to the study of fairness in social relationships. In K. J. Gergen, M. S. Greenberg, & R. H. Willis (Eds.), *Social exchange* (pp. 27–55). Plenum Press.

Lewin, K., Lippitt, R., & White, R. K. (1939). Patterns of aggressive behavior in experimentally created social climates. *The Journal of Social Psychology, 10*, 271–299.

Lind, E. A., & Tyler, T. R. (1988). *The social psychology of procedural justice.* Plenum.

Martel, C., Rathje, S., Clark, C. J., Pennycook, G., Van Bavel, J. J., Rand, D. G., & van der Linden, S. (2024). On the efficacy of accuracy prompts across partisan lines. *Psychological Science, 35*, 435–450. https://doi.org/10.1177/09567976241232905

Milgram, S. (1975). *Obedience to authority.* Harper Colophon.

Moehler, D. C. (2009). Critical citizens and submissive subjects: Election winners and losers in Africa. *British Journal of Political Science, 39*, 345–366. https://doi.org/10.1017/S0007123408000513

Moore, B., Jr. (1978). *Injustice: The social bases of obedience and revolt.* Sharpe.

Muller, E. N. (1979). *Aggressive political participation.* Princeton University Press.

Norris, P. (2014). *Why electoral integrity matters.*

Powell, G. M. (2000). *Elections as instruments of democracy.* Yale.

Price, V., & Romantan, A. (2004). Confidence in institutions before, during, and after "Indecision 20002". *Journal of Politics, 66*, 939–956.

Rosenvallon, P. (2011). *Democratic legitimacy.*

Rottman, D., & Tyler, T. R. (2014). Thinking about judges and judicial performance. *Onati Socio-legal series, 4*, 1046–1070. https://opo.iisj.net/index.php/osls/article/view/343

Schwartz, S. H. (1992). Universals in the content and structure of values. *Advances in Experimental Social Psychology, 25*, 1–65. https://doi.org/10.1016/S0065-2601(08)60281-6

Skogan, W. G., & Frydl, K. (Eds.). (2004). *Fairness and effectiveness in policing: The evidence.* The National Academies Press.

Stenner, K. (2012). *The authoritarian dynamic.*

Sunstein, C. R., & Epstein, R. A. (2001). The Vote: Bush, Gore and the Supreme Court.

Tamanaha, B. Z. (2004). *On the rule of law: History, politics, theory.* Cambridge University Press.

Thibaut, J., & Walker, L. (1975). *Procedural justice*. Erlbaum.
Thomassen, J. (Ed.). (2014). *Elections and democracy*.
Tyler, T. R. (1997). The psychology of legitimacy: A relational perspective on voluntary deference to authorities. *Personality and Social Psychology Review, 1*, 323–345. https://doi.org/10.1207/s15327957pspr0104_4
Tyler, T. R., & Blader, S. (2000). *Cooperation in groups: Procedural justice, social identity, and behavioral engagement*. Psychology Press.
Tyler, T. R. (2005). Policing in Black and White: Ethnic group differences in trust and confidence in the police. *Police Quarterly, 8*, 322–342. https://doi.org/10.1177/1098611104271105
Tyler, T. R. (2011). *Why people cooperate*. Princeton University Press.
Tyler, T. R. (2006a). *Why people obey the law: Procedural justice, legitimacy, and compliance*. Princeton University Press.
Tyler, T. R. (2006b). Psychological perspectives on legitimacy and legitimation. *Annual Review of Psychology, 57*, 375–400. https://doi.org/10.1146/annurev.psych.57.102904.190038
Tyler, T. R., Boeckmann, R., Smith, H. J., & Huo, Y. J. (1997). *Social justice in a diverse society*. Westview.
Tyler, T. R., & Degoey, P. (1995). Collective restraint in social dilemmas: Procedural justice and social identification effects on support for authorities. *Journal of Personality and Social Psychology, 69*(3), 482–497. https://doi.org/10.1037/0022-3514.69.3.482
Tyler, T. R., Goff, P., & MacCoun, R. (2015). The impact of psychological science on policing in the United States: Procedural justice, legitimacy, and effective law enforcement. *Psychological Science in the Public Interest, 16*(3), 75–109. https://doi.org/10.1177/1529100615617791
Tyler, T. R., & Huo, Y. J. (2002). *Trust in the law: Encouraging public cooperation with the police and courts*. Russell-Sage Foundation.
Tyler, T. R., & Jackson, J. (2014). Popular legitimacy and the exercise of legal authority: Motivating compliance, cooperation, and engagement. *Psychology, Public Policy, and Law, 20*(1), 78–95. https://doi.org/10.1037/a0034514
Tyler, T. R., Jackson, J., Huq, A., & Bradford, B. (2012). *Going outside the law: The role of the state in forming attitudes toward extralegal violence*. University of Chicago. Working papers.
Tyler, T. R., & Markell, D. (2010). The public regulation of land-use decisions. *Journal of Empirical Legal Studies, 7*, 538–573. https://doi.org/10.1111/j.1740-1461.2010.01188.x
Tyler, T. R., & Nobo, C. (2022). *Legitimacy-based policing and the promotion of community vitality*. Cambridge University Press: Cambridge Elements.
Van De Walle, S., & Raine, J. W. (2008). *Explaining attitudes toward the justice system in the UK and Europe*. Ministry of Justice.
Van den Bos, K. (2024). *The fair process effect*.
Washington Post-University of Maryland poll. (2023, December). *Center for Democracy and Civil Engagement*. University of Maryland.
Wheelock, D., Stroshine, M. S., & O'Hear, M. (2019). Disentangling the relationship between race and attitudes toward the police: Police contact, perceptions of safety, and procedural justice. *Crime & Delinquency, 65*(7), 941–968. https://epublications.marquette.edu/socs_fac/262
Wolfe, S. E., Nix, J., Kaminski, R., & Rojek, J. (2016). Is the effect of procedural justice on police legitimacy invariant? Testing the generality of procedural justice and competing antecedents of legitimacy. *Journal of Quantitative Criminology, 32*(2), 253–282. https://doi.org/10.1007/s10940-015-9263-8
Yancy-Bragg, N. (2020, December 8). Americans' confidence in police fall to historic law. Gallup poll shows. *USA Today*.
Zahnow, R., Mazerolle, L., & Pang, A. (2021). Do individual differences matter in the way people view police legitimacy? A partial replication and extension of invariance thesis. *Policing: A Journal of Policy and Practice, 15*(2), 665–685. https://doi.org/10.1093/police/paz066

Motives for Civil Justice

Jennifer K. Robbennolt

What motivates people to sue? Tort claimants have a variety of justice motives. Indeed, an injured person's inclination to litigate tends to be associated with the degree to which they perceive an injustice (Trost et al., 2016). So, too, are there a variety of motives that may inhibit claiming. In addition, an array of processes and remedies are available by which claimants can attempt to fulfill their goals. Claimants must manage this mix of goals in the context of a system that focuses on money damages, but also creates the possibility for other remedies via settlement, and that offers them multiple possible methods for resolving their disputes. This chapter explores the mix of justice motives that claimants report and how money damages and apologies, and trial or settlement, fit with or are incompatible with these motivations for justice.

Motives for Claiming

Compensation through money damages is important to many claimants and is the primary legal remedy available to civil claimants. Claimants may have bills to pay, lost wages to replace, future bills or lack of earning capacity to plan for, and other out-of-pocket expenses to compensate. Many are moved to initiate litigation when they realize that they will need funds to cover expenses. Claiming is more likely for those who are more severely injured or have experienced greater economic losses and less likely for those who have other resources that can be used to cover expenses (Hensler et al., 1991; May & Stengel, 1990; Pleasence et al., 2011; Sloan & Hsieh,

J. K. Robbennolt (✉)
University of Illinois College of Law, Champaign, IL, USA
e-mail: jrobbenn@illinois.edu

R. L. Wiener, D. J. Hansen (eds.), *Legal Judgment and the Motivation for Justice*, Nebraska Symposium on Motivation 71,
https://doi.org/10.1007/978-3-031-98812-7_7

1995). In a system involving legal costs and contingency fees, sufficient compensation is necessary to cover the costs of bringing suit (see, e.g., Shepherd, 2014). Cases involving low financial stakes are unlikely to be brought, and reforms like caps on noneconomic damages have reduced the frequency of certain kinds of cases with low economic damages (Daniels & Martin, 2010). Ultimately, compensation is one key goal that has an important influence on litigation decision-making (see, e.g., Kritzer, 1991; Reinders Folmer et al., 2019).

But claimant motives for justice are broader than financial compensation. Indeed, many claimants will readily declare that their lawsuit is not about money. Beyond money damages, many claimants have in mind a range of nonfinancial goals. These nonmaterial interests play a key role in decisions about whether to claim, claimants' approach to and decision making in settlement negotiations, and their satisfaction with the outcomes of the process (see, e.g., Curhan et al., 2006; Hensler, 2003).

Some tort claimants, for example, are motivated by a desire for information or explanations—they want to understand what has happened to them and why and to obtain information or explanations about their injuries and what led to them (see, e.g., Antonsdóttir, 2020; Hickson et al., 1992; Relis, 2007; see also Quinney et al., 2022). In the medical context, for example, patients who receive timely information about an adverse event are less likely to sue (Sloan & Hsieh, 1995). When the desired information is not received, tort litigation can provide an information-forcing function (Burch & Lahav, 2021; Freeman Engstrom, 2018; Wagner, 2007). Sometimes, information is sufficient to end the claim. Golann (2011), for example, found that forcing the disclosure of information was a key reason that many medical malpractice claimants filed suit and that it was not uncommon for them to drop their lawsuits once they obtained that information.

Tort claimants are also motivated by deterrence or reform, to generate behavioral or institutional change to prevent the recurrence of harm. They bring claims, in part, to try to prevent similar tortious behavior and harmful consequences from happening in the future (Antonsdóttir, 2020; Hickson et al., 1992; Relis, 2007; Tumelty, 2020; van Dijck, 2018; Vincent et al., 1994; see also Friele & Sluijs, 2006). Even if their own harm cannot be repaired, claimants want to protect others from a similar fate. Medical malpractice claimants, for example, often want reforms to processes to prevent similar mistakes (see, e.g., Gallagher et al., 2003). Survivors of sexual harassment and sexual violence want to be safe from future mistreatment and to prevent harm to future victims (Antonsdóttir, 2020; Des Rosiers et al., 1998; Koss, 2014). Mock claimants are also more hesitant to settle with repeat offender defendants suggesting concerns about ongoing wrongful behavior (Bachar, 2024).

The need for there to be some form of accountability also motivates claiming. Many claimants want the harm-doer to take responsibility for their behavior and the harm that it caused (e.g., Antonsdóttir, 2020). Indeed, responsibility-taking has been identified as a key nonmaterial need of injured persons (Reinders Folmer et al., 2019). Accountability may also be provided through a court verdict or a settlement. Some claimants also hope that accountability will include punishment of the harm-doer (Relis, 2007; Vincent et al., 1994).

Wrapped up with the desire for financial compensation or reform or accountability is a need for acknowledgment. Claimants desire recognition of the wrong and its consequences, support for the legitimacy of the violated rule, and confirmation of their standing as a rights bearer and valued member of the community (e.g., Antonsdóttir, 2020; Relis, 2007; Tumelty, 2020; van Dijck, 2018). Many want the harm-doer to acknowledge the harmful behavior and the harm done (e.g., Antonsdóttir, 2020). Acknowledgment from the harm-doer speaks to claimants' desire for the harm-doer to understand what they did and how it affected the claimant. And it signals that there is potential for changed behavior going forward. As with accountability, when such acknowledgment from the offender is not forthcoming, claimants value such acknowledgement from the court, as a representative of the community. Whether it comes from the harm-doer or a court, acknowledgment is an indication that the claimant is taken seriously and that they were wronged.

Along with the justice motives of compensation, deterrence, information, accountability, and acknowledgement, claimants desire to be treated in a procedurally just manner, wanting voice, respect, trust, and a neutral decision-maker (Lind & Tyler, 1988). They may want to have their "day in court." They may hope to have control over how their dispute is resolved (Shestowsky, this volume). They want to have their claim addressed in a timely manner, to find meaning in their experience or loss, and to heal and move beyond the incident.

Motives That Limit Claiming

Injured persons, then, are motivated to claim by a range of factors. Few injured persons, however, actually bring tort lawsuits (Engel, 2016; Hart & Peters, 2008; Hensler et al., 1991; Miller & Sarat, 1981; Sloan & Hsieh, 1995). Those who do not claim often have similar motives for justice but face a variety of barriers to claiming as well.

The transformation of an injury into a tort claim is a complicated psychological process with many opportunities for significant attrition along the way (Felstiner et al., 1980–1981). Many claimants choose to "lump it," never entering or choosing to exit the process of claiming redress for their injuries. They may fail to recognize that they have been injured. They may not attribute the source of the harm to the fault of another, recognize their right not to have been injured in this way, or engage in self-blame (see, e.g., Engel, 2016; Hensler et al., 1991; Kritzer, 1991). They may not take steps toward a process of claiming, lacking information or resources or confidence about how to claim or find legal representation or not having sufficient feelings of self-efficacy (e.g., Sandefur, 2008). People may differ in their underlying propensity to file a claim—an individual difference known as "claim consciousness" (Vidmar & Schuller, 1987). Claiming may seem futile or, even worse, as having the potential to make things worse (Bumiller, 1987). As a practical matter, the monetary stakes of a potential claim matter as well, with claimants and lawyers unlikely to pursue claims when the costs of litigation will be greater than any eventual recovery (Daniels & Martin, 2010; Kritzer, 1997).

Injured persons, too, may be dissuaded from claiming by social norms or their estimation of how tort plaintiffs might be perceived. Norms of "individual responsibility" and plaintiff blaming, for example, may create a barrier to claiming (see Robbennolt & Hans, 2016), with potential claimants attuned to the ways in which litigants are negatively perceived. Interviews with civil jurors, for example, demonstrate that jurors are frequently critical of plaintiffs' behavior and motives, and surveys of laypeople and jurors find a considerable degree of skepticism about the legitimacy of plaintiffs' lawsuits (Hans, 2000). Other studies have found that people have relatively negative attitudes toward tort plaintiffs, even when they view the underlying claims as nonfrivolous, with plaintiffs who are injured and not themselves at fault (Barnes et al., 2023a, 2023b; see also Major & Kaiser, 2005; Neubauer & Meinhold, 1994). Injured people themselves, then, may not see litigation as an appropriate approach to dispute resolution, as something that is done by people like them (Engel, 1984; see also Ellickson, 1986; Macaulay, 1963).

In similar ways, the fact that money is the hallmark remedy in a tort suit may give rise to concerns about being seen as greedy or as a "gold-digger." Survivors of sexual violence, for example, express "discomfort in relation to the compensation claim" and worried that "they were playing into the myth of women pressing charges for sexual violence for monetary gain" (Antonsdóttir, 2020). Potential claimants worry about attacks on their credibility and their inability to live up to the standard of an ideal plaintiff (Wexler, 2017; Wexler et al., 2019).

Goal Management—Multiple Goals, Multiple Pathways

Just as claimants and potential claimants have myriad goals, so too are there a variety of processes and remedies through which they can attempt to fulfill those goals. They may pursue remedies through the legal system or outside it. They may choose to litigate or to lump it. They may engage in "alternative" dispute resolution processes—processes that may or may not be court-connected. They may decide to settle their case or proceed to trial. A settlement may come early or late in the process. Claimants may receive money damages or other remedies, or not.

A useful metaphor is of a dispute "tree" in which the branches represent the many different avenues by which disputes can be resolved, along with "truncated branches for injuries named and blamed but not claimed, and fruitless tips for grievances that were pursued without remedy then abandoned" (Albiston et al., 2014). Branches may be more or less accessible and may "produce flowers, fruit, or both, or they may wither and die. Flowers represent symbolic indicia of justice, such as the public opportunity to be heard, the recognition of injuries and responsibility (e.g., a formal apology), and the like. Fruit, by contrast, represents material remedies such as reinstatement at work or financial compensation for injury" (Albiston et al., 2014). Different branches may be more or less supportive of different types of remedies. For example, nonmonetary remedies are less central as formal tort remedies but are possible as tort claimants and defendants negotiate settlements.

How do people go about managing this broad set of goals—goals that are sometimes congruent and sometimes conflicting—in the context of a system that has multiple possible paths? Goal systems theory suggests that people engage in behaviors to the extent that those behaviors will serve as means to accomplish their goals and recognizes that people will often hold multiple goals at the same time and may consider multiple courses of action as possible means for accomplishing those goals (Ajzen & Kruglanski, 2019). Consider some fundamental principles of goal management (Robbennolt et al., 2003; see also Kruglanski et al., 2002). First, the principle of equifinality holds that in some instances it may be possible to satisfy a particular goal via more than one pathway. Similarly, it may be possible for a particular pathway to accomplish multiple goals at the same time—the principle of multifinality. At the same time, however, some pathways may be better suited to fulfilling some goals than they are to accomplishing other goals. This is the principle of best fit. And, finally, it must be recognized that sometimes goals may conflict in ways that make it difficult or impossible to satisfy them all. This is the principle of goal incompatibility.

System Focused on Money Damages

The civil justice system is centered on money damages as the remedy. An award of money is the remedial option available to judges and juries in cases that go to trial. And a financial payment is often the central part of any settlement agreement (Judicial Conference, 2022; see also Robbennolt et al., 2023a, 2023b). Money damages are intended to compensate plaintiffs for any harm caused by the defendant in an attempt to make them "whole." According to the principle of multifinality, it can be possible to accomplish multiple goals via a single pathway, and this is surely true of money damages. Financial compensation is an important goal of the system and of many tort claimants. Money damages would seem to be the best fit to accomplishing the goal of compensating for a variety of consequences attendant to an injury—medical bills, lost wages or earning capacity, the need to repair or replace property, and rehabilitative or accommodative equipment (e.g., ramps and special vehicles).

Money damages may also serve to fulfill other aspects of claimant motives for compensation. Money damages, for example, are expected to compensate for nonfinancial harms such as pain and suffering, disfigurement, loss of enjoyment of life, or damage to reputation. Money damages may not be the best fit for compensating these injuries. Indeed, a remedy calculated in dollars is less commensurable with these sorts of general damages than it is with economics harms. Money itself cannot relieve physical or emotional pain, cannot restore a damaged reputation, cannot reestablish lost privacy, cannot erase scars, and cannot bring back the ability to play the violin or hug a grandchild. As the Restatement (Third) of Torts (2023) recognizes, "money is an especially poor substitute for the absence of pain or distress." Moreover, the task of translating these sorts of injuries into an appropriate damage award in dollars is difficult. More pessimistically, money damages for intangible harm is "at best an indirect means towards these ends and at worst irrelevant, distracting, and inconsistent" (Abel, 2006, p.266).

At the same time, however, various theories have been offered for how money damages can compensate for these nonfinancial injuries in some way. As Judge Posner has noted: "No one likes pain and suffering and most people would pay a good deal of money to be free of them." (Kwasny v. U.S., 1987). Money damages might compensate by restoring the injured person to their "pre-accident level of utility" even if that utility is a substitute that is different in kind (see, e.g., Viscusi, 1996, p. 147). Or money damages might provide a means by which the injured person's flourishing or capacity to flourish is restored even if the means of flourishing differs from what came before (Feldman, 1997). As noted by one court:

> [R]ecovery for noneconomic losses such as pain and suffering and loss of enjoyment of life rests on the legal fiction that money damages can compensate for a victim's injury.... We accept this fiction, knowing that although money will neither ease the pain nor restore the victim's abilities, this device is as close as the law can come in its effort to right the wrong. We have no hope of evaluating what has been lost, but a monetary award may provide a measure of solace for the condition created .... (McDougald v. Garber, 1989, pp. 374–75).

Similarly, the Restatement (Third) of Torts (2023) takes the position that "[a]ny tort system committed to the rightful-position standard and make-whole relief must recognize that full compensation includes compensation for the physical and emotional pain and related harms accompanying bodily harm. Such compensation is essential to corrective justice. . . . [P]ain and suffering is a real harm, as deserving of compensation as harms that can be measured by market prices." Although monetary damages "for pain and suffering can rarely be used to eliminate the pain," they are thought to be able to "enable plaintiffs to improve their lives in other ways, providing pleasures and benefits that may to some extent offset the pain. In any event, once a serious injury has occurred, this is a close to even as the law can come."

Some scholars have argued that it is useful to think of "compensation" not as providing a monetary equivalent for noneconomic harm or as making the injured person whole but instead as a mechanism for counterbalancing or evening out the harm caused, offsetting or putting it right, atoning or making amends for having caused harm, or "correctifying" the rupture (e.g., Antonsdóttir, 2020; Ingber, 1985; Zavos, 2009). In this way, noneconomic damages are "a meaningful, symbolic sum, whereby a defendant can show the appropriate respect to the plaintiff for a loss he tortiously caused and is unable to fix" (Zavos, 2009, pp. 246–247).

Beyond compensation, money damage awards can also operate to accomplish other claimant goals (Rabin, 2005). To hold the harm-doer responsible for compensating for the harm caused is to hold them accountable. Money damages are also thought to be one way to effectuate deterrence, both general and specific. The sting of a high damages award is expected to incentivize the defendant to engage in safer behavior going forward. And the risk of such an award is expected to incentivize others to conform their behavior to the boundaries set by the law as well.

Money damages can also serve as an acknowledgement. Money awarded by a court can communicate the court's recognition that the claimant was harmed, validate community norms of appropriate behavior, and recognize the rights of the claimant as a valued member of that community (Antonsdóttir, 2020; Carroll & Witzleb, 2011; Holder & Daly, 2018; Hulst & Akkermans, 2011; Okimoto, 2008). In addition to satisfying financial needs, greater levels of material compensation have been found to increase the satisfaction of needs related to responsibility-taking, interpersonal treatment and respect, and the desire for closure (Reinders Folmer et al., 2019). In an adjacent context, Hulst and Akkermans (2011) found that family members of people seriously injured by tortious or criminal conduct who received a modest monetary payment from the state in recognition of their emotional harm understood the award as both acknowledging the harm-doer's responsibility and legally recognizing their emotional injury, appreciating the symbolism of such a payment.

Even nominal damages—like the $1 sought by and awarded to Taylor Swift against a radio host who groped her during a photo shoot—can communicate this recognition. During his closing argument to the jury, Swift's lawyer referred to "a single symbolic dollar, the value of which is immeasurable to all women in this situation" (Flanagan, 2017).

> Requiring payment is a way both to bring the wrongdoer to recognize that she has done wrong and to make redress to the victim. Redress is not restitution or rectification. Redress instead means showing the victim that her rights are taken seriously. It is accomplished by affirming that some action is required to symbolize public respect for the existence of certain rights and public recognition of the transgressor's fault in disrespecting those rights. (Radin, 1993, p. 61).

This recognition is accomplished, in part, by "requiring something important to be given up on one side and received on the other, even if there is no equivalence of value possible" (Radin, 1993). In the case of the tort system, the "something of value" is money. Although money is the medium by which the gravity of the harm and the worth of the claimant are signaled, the "core concepts are rights and wrongs, not dollars and exchange" (Radin, 1993).

In cases that settle rather than going to trial, the monetary payment can serve similar purposes. Even if it is not the court ordering the damages and even if the settlement is purely monetary, the payment of money tends to send similar signals. Speaking of monetary settlements, commentators have noted: "dollars speak loudly" (Ellison et al., 2023) and "money is accountability" (Press Conference, 2023). Even as observers recognize an array of motivations and reasons for settlement, there is a tendency to read a settlement as a tacit acknowledgement of responsibility (Bregant et al., 2021).

The payment of *any* damages via verdict or settlement may do some of this acknowledgment work. So, too, may the *amount* of the award (Bregant et al., 2021). The reaction to a large verdict or settlement is often along the lines of: "[y]ou don't pay that kind of money unless you know you've done something horribly wrong" (Boykin, 2023). And a large verdict or settlement can speak volumes to the injured party and the public. Consider, for example, a $1 billion verdict in favor of a young woman who was raped by a security guard (Victor, 2018). The young woman recognized that the award would not be collectable in that amount, nor would any amount of money remove the harm, but she found value in the symbolism of the amount: "Twelve strangers feel like what I went through and my story and how I feel . . . is worth a billion dollars. That is life-changing, history-making, just beautiful news to know" (Victim, 2018). Money damages can also serve as a measure of punishment (Sherwin, 2003). This is certainly true for punitive damage awards—which are rare—but there can also be a punitive element to some compensatory damage awards (e.g., Anderson & MacCoun, 1999).

Finally, it is worth noting that there are instances in which money damages are discordant with the justice goals of claimants (the principle of incompatibility). A recent study of sexual violence survivors, for example, found significant ambivalence in how they thought about monetary compensation (Antonsdóttir, 2020). Survivors valued the role of money damages in recognizing their harm and found it important that the offender (and not the state) pay compensation. At the same time, however, "[m]any expressed the view that putting a price tag on what had been done to them was ridiculous at best and offensive at worst," with some referring to money damages as "disgusting money," "dirty money," "blood money," or "hush money." Relatedly, some claimants may find monetary compensation incompatible with other goals such as public acknowledgment or some measure of prevention when they face defendants who are willing to settle but only in conjunction with a confidentiality clause (see, e.g., Albiston, 1999; Bachar, 2022). Or some may reject monetary settlements that come without the information or public reckoning that they desire (e.g., Hadfield, 2008; Lawless & Robbennolt, 2024).

Thus, while money damages serve both compensatory and deterrence goals and have symbolic meaning that can address an array of claimants' nonfinancial goals, money may not always be the most aligned to addressing each of these goals. That is, the financial awards that are central to tort law may not be the path with the "best fit" to or may even be incommensurable (principle of incompatibility) with the full array of claimant motives. Money damages, by themselves, then, may speak to but not satisfactorily address some of these relational and nonmonetary interests, making it important to consider other branches of the dispute tree.

Apologies and Justice Motives

Unlike money damages, apologies are not formally available as a remedy in tort. But they may be offered informally or as part of a settlement agreement (Cohen, 1999; Robbennolt, 2003, 2006, 2008, 2013). Good apologies acknowledge the wrongdoing and the harm that has resulted and communicate regret. They take responsibility for the wrongful behavior and its consequences and promise that it will not happen again. And they offer to make up for the harm caused through monetary compensation or some other means of restoration (see Goffman, 1971; Kirchhoff et al., 2012; Lewicki et al., 2016; Scher & Darley, 1997; Slocum et al.,

2011; Smith, 2008; Tavuchis, 1991). Some apologetic statements fall short of this ideal but at least convey sympathy for the harm caused (Cohen, 1999; Robbennolt, 2003).

Apologies have been shown to have a range of effects on parties to conflict, including their physical responses, affective reactions, cognitions, and behavior. Both giving and receiving apologies can have positive physiological effects on the body—including positive impacts on blood pressure and heart rate (Whited et al., 2010; Witvliet et al., 2002, 2020). Apologies tend to moderate negative emotions like anger and help to cultivate more positive emotions, such as sympathy (e.g., Gold & Weiner, 2000; Ohbuchi et al., 1989; Weiner et al., 1991). Those who apologize are perceived more favorably than those who do not, are seen as less responsible, and are thought to be less likely to behave in a similar way going forward (Davis & Gold, 2011; Gold & Weiner, 2000; Hodgins & Liebeskind, 2003; Pace et al., 2010; Weiner et al., 1991; see also Schumann, 2019). Ultimately, apologies are associated with increased forgiveness, reduced aggression, and more lenient recommendations for punishment (Darby & Schlenker, 1982; Ohbuchi et al., 1989; Robbennolt, 2013; Weiner et al., 1991).

Considering the nature and effects of apologies alongside tort claimant goals reveals some noteworthy intersections. These connections suggest that apologies can play an important role in addressing some of these justice concerns. Indeed, tort claimants often report that they want apologies and that the desire for apologies or lack of apology motivated their initiation of legal action (Gallagher et al., 2003; Mazor et al., 2004; Relis, 2007; Tumelty, 2020; Vincent et al., 1994; Witman et al., 1996). The greater the nonmaterial needs held by claimants, the more they desire apologies (e.g., Reinders Folmer et al., 2019). Claimants may even value apologies when they are required of the harm-doer or negotiated as part of a settlement deal (Jehle et al., 2012; Robbennolt, 2013). Apologies may influence the willingness to participate in settlement negotiations or may be a focal point of those negotiations (e.g., Babula, 2003; Henry, 2004; Schneider, 2000).

Apologies can also change the claimant's orientation to the monetary aspects of settlement negotiations and make it easier to reach agreement. Experimental work, for example, has found that mock claimants are more likely to accept a settlement offer when they have received an apology, particularly when the apology takes responsibility for the behavior that has caused harm, as compared to when they did not (Robbennolt, 2003; see also Korobkin & Guthrie, 1994). In addition, apologies have been shown to change people's approach to settlement, affecting key settlement levers that tend to influence final negotiated outcomes, including bottom-line financial goals, financial aspirations, and assessments of what settlement amount is fair. In particular, mock claimants who received apologies set lower values for these settlement levers (Robbennolt, 2006).

Apologies are valued by claimants for a variety of reasons. Good apologies address many of the justice goals held by claimants (multifinality). In particular, at their best, apologies acknowledge the wrongful behavior and take responsibility for it, acknowledge the harm that was done, recognize the validity of the rule that was violated, bolster the standing of the injured person, provide information, and signal that the offender will not engage in similar conduct in the future. Note the correspondence between these functions and claimant motivations (best fit).

Just as with money damages, it is important to recognize that sometimes apologies will be incompatible with the claimants' justice goals. Apologies, for example, will not pay the bills or the lawyer (Kritzer, 1991; Sternlight, 1999). In addition, although insincere or forced apologies can sometimes be valuable to claimants, a lack of sincerity may also limit the ability of such apologies to meet the claimant goals (see, e.g., Hubbard et al., 2013; Saulneir & Sivasubramaniam, 2015; Tomlinson et al., 2004).

Trial and Settlement

Trial and settlement as modes of dispute resolution may each provide a path for accomplishing a variety of justice goals (multifinality). Each may be a path by which to obtain money damages. And each may be a way to get acknowledgment. So, too, might trial and settlement each be more compatible with some claimant motives than others. In the abstract, the desire to have a "day in court" is perhaps more compatible with trial processes than with a negotiated settlement. In practice, however, trial does not necessarily provide claimants with the day in court that they imagine, and, conversely, the settlement negotiation process could be structured to be sensitive to some of the relevant interests (Hollander-Blumoff & Tyler, 2008). Trial might be better suited to public acknowledgment than settlement, particularly if that settlement comes with a nondisclosure agreement (Bachar, 2024). In contrast, moving on from an injury is not easily compatible with a lengthy litigation process.

When it comes to money damages, trial offers the possibility of "full" compensation but coupled with the risk of losing. Settlements, in contrast, are a sure thing, but "by their nature, rarely confer complete relief" (In re Takata Airbag Products Liability Litig, 2022) and are inherently compromise agreements (Robbennolt et al., 2023a, 2023b). The financial recoveries involved in a settlement, therefore, may not fully compensate the claimant for their losses.

Settlement, however, makes room for a broader array of remedies, allowing for creative options that address claimant interests (best fit). To take one example, consider a settlement reached by two Black men who were arrested when a Starbucks employee called the police because the men had not ordered anything. The men's case against the City of Philadelphia settled for $1 to each of them and a commitment by the city to fund a program on entrepreneurship for public high school students (Fortin, 2018). Or consider the settlement reached between USA Gymnastics and gymnasts abused by Larry Nassar. The settlement included a large monetary payment ($380 million). But it also included a series of nonmonetary commitments, including a host of changes to bylaws and policies, the requirement that at least one survivor would serve on USA Gymnastics' board of directors, the establishment of a permanent "Safe Sport" committee, new reporting mechanisms, and processes to provide for "historical accountability" (In re USA Gymnastics, 2021). In another example, the actor James Woods and the hospital at which his brother died reached a settlement when the CEO of the hospital admitted to errors by the hospital, offered an apology, and established the Michael J. Woods Institute to study medical error and patient safety. According to Woods: "It was all I ever needed to see in my life, one human being saying to another human being 'I'm sorry for your loss.'" (WPRI, 2009). The settlement between the City of Uvalde, Texas and the families of children who were shot at Robb Elementary School included a permanent memorial to the victims, improved maintenance of the cemetery where many of the children were buried, and to designate the anniversary of the shooting as a day or remembrance in addition to the monetary and procedural reform aspects of the settlement (Sandoval & Goodman, 2024; see also McClurg, 2005).

Priorities, Trade-Offs, and a Mix of Remedies and Processes

Claimants may well be able to accomplish some of their justice goals through either money damages or apologies and through either trial or settlement (equifinality). And they may be able to accomplish multiple goals through money damages or through apologies and through either trial or settlement (multifinality). Acknowledgment, for example, could be obtained via trial decision or settlement, through money damages or apology.

As we have seen, however, some remedies may be a better fit for some goals than for others. That is, money damages and apologies might each be better or less well suited to serving particular claimant goals. Money damages are surely better than apologies for addressing the material needs of claimants. And, although both money damages and apologies can address claimant desires for acknowledgement from the offender, apologies may be able to do this more directly. Similarly, there may be aspects of different processes that fit better with some claimant goals. So, too, will some claimant goals be more difficult to satisfy simultaneously (incompatibility). Additional research to better parse these differences would be quite valuable.

Which of these interrelated motives are prioritized by claimants will likely vary. When goals are incompatible or when negotiation requires claimants to make trade-offs among goals, different motives may take precedence. In the abstract, interviews with and surveys of claimants suggest that certain motives—preventing future harm, getting answers, and obtaining admissions or apologies—tend to be described more often than others (Relis, 2007; Vincent et al., 1994). These aggregate priorities, however, are likely to elide variation among claimants and cases. Indeed, goals are likely to fluctuate based on the characteristics of the situation or due to associations that bring certain goals to the fore while deactivating others (Ajzen & Kruglanski, 2019).

One study, for example, found that money damages were less important for claimants who were family members of someone who had died (Vincent et al., 1994), cases in which economic damages are often lower and in which money can seem particularly incommensurable with the loss of life. Another study found that claimants who reported a lack of communication or feeling that they had been misled were particularly likely to report being motivated by a desire for information (Hickson et al., 1992). In contrast, those claiming over an injury that involved treatment in an intensive care unit were more likely to report that they were motivated to sue by a need for money (Hickson et al., 1992). Other researchers have found that claimants who report greater material needs have a greater desire for compensation and those who report greater nonmaterial needs have a greater desire for apology (Reinders Folmer et al., 2019).

But there is much more to be learned about the circumstances in which particular motives come to the fore and how claimants prioritize different goals. Because much of the existing research explores the motives of claimants in particular types of cases and involving particular types of injuries (most predominantly in medical malpractice and sexual harassment or violence cases), attention should be broadened to other types of cases and injuries as well. Similarly, although there have been some studies comparing motives like deterrence and just deserts with regard to punishment (e.g., Carlsmith et al., 2002), there has been less attention to these sorts of comparisons when it comes to making civil claims. Lawyers, too, have influence over how their clients understand their disputes and claims, the processes available to them, and their expectations about what might be achieved. These understandings may change over the course of the claim as may claimant goals (see generally, e.g., Guthrie & Korobkin, 1997; Kritzer, 1998; Menkel-Meadow, 1985; Shewstowsky, this volume). How claimant justice motives interact with their process choices has also been understudied.

Given the myriad goals that claimants have, a mix of remedies might often be ideal. Interviews with injured persons reveal that they do not see apologies as a "substitute" for compensation but that apologies and compensation are seen as complements (Moore & Mello, 2017). Monetary compensation and apologies may also have interactive effects (see, e.g., Ohtsubo, 2020; see also Witvliet et al., 2020). As Martha Minow (2002, p. 23) noted in the context of reparations: "reparations without apologies seem inauthentic, and apologies without reparations seem cheap." Apologies or acknowledgment may give meaning to money damages (Okimoto, 2008; Okimoto & Tyler, 2007), and money damages may give credibility to an apology (Bottom et al., 2002; DiFonzo et al., 2018; Jeter & Brannon, 2017; Zechmeister et al., 2004). Each may have the potential to fill in the gaps left by the other (see, e.g., Haesevoets et al., 2013; Reinders Folmer et al., 2019; see also Carlisle et al., 2012).

Of course, money damages and apologies are only two remedial options. Other nonmonetary remedies might appropriately be part of this mix and may provide the "best fit" for remedying some kinds of harms and addressing some kinds of goals (see, e.g., Lewinsohn-Zamir, 2013). Similarly, going to trial and negotiating a settlement are only two possible processes that might be used during the course of a dispute (see, e.g., Shestowsky, this volume). Different mechanisms for dispute resolution—whether such procedures are connected to courts, involve lawyers, make use of neutrals, or entail other design choices—may be appropriate "best fitting" fora for different claimants or disputes or at different stages of a claim (see, e.g., Sander & Goldberg, 1994).

The dispute tree metaphor encompasses each of these myriad mechanisms for dispute resolution—the tree branches—as well as a range of potential remedies—both fruit and flowers (Albiston et al., 2014). Researchers ought to continue to map the ways in which claimants choose a branch or move from branch to branch, including both branches that are truncated and those that bear fruit and flowers. So, too, should research continue to assess the ways in which different branches do and do not support different types of fruit and flowers. These efforts are necessary to enhancing our understanding of the interconnections among claimant motives, dispute resolution processes, remedies, and justice.

References

Abel, R. (2006). General damages are incoherent, incalculable, incommensurable, and inegalitarian (both otherwise a great idea). *DePaul Law Review, 55*, 253–329.

Ajzen, I., & Kruglanski, A. W. (2019). Reasoned action in the service of goal pursuit. *Psychological Review, 126*(5), 774–786. https://doi.org/10.1037/rev0000155

Albiston, C. R. (1999). The rule of law and the litigation process: The paradox of losing by winning. *Law and Society Review, 33*, 869–910. https://doi.org/10.2307/3115153

Albiston, C. R., Edelman, L. B., & Milligan, J. (2014). The dispute tree and the legal forest. *Annual Review of Law and Social Science, 10*(1), 105–131. https://doi.org/10.1146/annurev-lawsocsci-110413-030826

Anderson, M. C., & MacCoun, R. J. (1999). Goal conflict in juror assessments of compensatory and punitive damages. *Law and Human Behavior, 23*(3), 313–330. https://doi.org/10.1023/A:1022308515445

Antonsdóttir, H. F. (2020). Compensation as a means to justice? Sexual violence survivors' views on the tort law option in Iceland. *Feminist Legal Studies, 28*, 277–300. https://doi.org/10.1007/s10691-020-09442-2

Babula, J. (2003, September 24). Letter ends lawsuit, patient says. *Las Vegas Review-Journal*, p. 1B.

Bachar, G. J. (2024). Just tort settlements. *Arizona State Law Journal, 56*, xx–xx. forthcoming.

Bachar, G. J. (2022). The psychology of secret settlements. *Hastings Law Journal, 73*, 1–48.

Barnes, J., Hevron, P., & Menounou, E. (2023a). Tort tales and total justice: Exploring attitudes toward everyday tort claims for workplace injuries. *Law and Society Review, 57*(4), 508–530. https://doi.org/10.1111/lasr.12684

Barnes, J., Menounou, E., & Hevron, P. (2023b). Turning on those who turn to the courts: Experimental evidence of backlash against personal injury litigants. *Journal of Law and Courts*, 1–22. https://doi.org/10.1017/jlc.2023.9

Bottom, W. P., Gibson, K., Daniels, S. E., & Murnighan, J. K. (2002). When talk is not cheap: Substantive penance and expressions of intent in rebuilding cooperation. *Organization Science, 13*(5), 497–513. https://doi.org/10.1287/orsc.13.5.497.7816

Boykin, K. (2023). https://twitter.com/keithboykin/status/1648422895578906624?ref_src=twsrc%5Etfw

Bregant, J., Robbennolt, J. K., & Winship, V. (2021). Perceptions of settlement. *Harvard Negotiation Law Review, 27*, 93–167.

Bumiller, K. (1987). Victims in the shadow of the law: A critique of the model of legal protection. *Signs, 12*, 421–439. https://www.jstor.org/stable/3174330

Burch, E. C., & Lahav, A. D. (2021). Information for the common good in mass torts. *DePaul Law Review, 70*, 345–394.

Carlisle, R. D., Tsang, J.-A., Ahmad, N. Y., Worthington, E. L., vanOyen Witvliet, C., & Wade, N. (2012). Do actions speak louder than words? Differential effects of apology and restitution on behavioral and self-report measures of forgiveness. *The Journal of Positive Psychology, 7*(4), 294–305. https://doi.org/10.1080/17439760.2012.690444

Carroll, R., & Witzleb, N. (2011). "It's not just about the money"—Enhancing the vindicatory effect of private law remedies. *Monash University Law Review, 37*, 216–240.

Carlsmith, K. M., Darley, J. M., & Robinson, P. H. (2002). Why do we punish? Deterrence and just deserts as motives for punishment. *Journal of Personality and Social Psychology, 83*(2), 284–299.

Cohen, J. R. (1999). Advising clients to apologize. *Southern California Law Review, 72*, 1009–1069.

Curhan, J. R., Elfenbein, H. A., & Xu, H. (2006). What do people value when they negotiate? Mapping the domain of subjective value in negotiation. *Journal of Personality and Social Psychology, 91*(3), 493–512. https://doi.org/10.1037/0022-3514.91.3.493

Daniels, S., & Martin, J. (2010). "It's no longer viable from a practical and business standpoint": Damage caps, "hidden victims," and the declining interest in medical malpractice cases. *International Journal of the Legal Profession, 17*, 59–82. https://doi.org/10.1080/09695951003588923

Darby, B. W., & Schlenker, B. R. (1982). Children's reactions to apologies. *Journal of Personality and Social Psychology, 43*, 742–753. https://doi.org/10.1037/0022-3514.43

Davis, J. R., & Gold, G. J. (2011). An examination of emotional empathy, attributions of stability, and the link between perceived remorse and forgiveness. *Personality and Individual Differences, 50*, 392–397. https://doi.org/10.1016/j.paid.2010.10.031

Des Rosiers, N., Feldthusen, B., & Hankivsky, O. A. R. (1998). Legal compensation for sexual violence: Therapeutic consequences and consequences for the judicial system. *Psychology, Public Policy, and Law, 4*, 433–451. https://doi.org/10.1037/1076-8971.4.1-2.433

DiFonzo, N., Alongi, A., & Wiele, P. (2018). Apology, restitution, and forgiveness after psychological contract breach. *Journal of Business Ethics, 161*, 53–69. https://doi.org/10.1007/s10551-018-3984-1

Ellickson, R. C. (1986). Of Coase and cattle: Dispute resolution among neighbors in Shasta County. *Stanford Law Review, 38*, 623–687.

Ellison, S., Dawsey, J., & Helderman, R. S. (2023, April 24). Fox was resigned to a tough trial. Then a secret mediator stepped in. *Washington Post*. https://www.washingtonpost.com/media/2023/04/19/mediator-fox-news-dominion-settlement/

Engel, D. M. (1984). The oven bird's song: Insiders, outsiders, and personal injuries in an American community. *Law and Society Review, 18*, 551–582. https://doi.org/10.2307/3053447

Engel, D. M. (2016). *The myth of the litigious society: Why we don't sue*. University of Chicago Press.

Freeman Engstrom, N. (2018). When cars crash: The automobile's tort law legacy. *Wake Forest Law Review, 53*, 293–336.

Feldman, H. L. (1997). Harm and money: Against the insurance theory of tort compensation. *Texas Law Review, 75*, 1567–1603.

Felstiner, W. L. F., Abel, R. L., & Sarat, A. (1980). The emergence and transformation of disputes: Naming, blaming, claiming.... *Law and Society Review, 15*(3/4), 631–654. https://doi.org/10.2307/3053505

Flanagan, A. (2017). Taylor Swift wins sexual assault lawsuit against former radio host. *NPR.org*. https://www.npr.org/sections/therecord/2017/08/14/543473684/taylor-swift-wins-sexual-assault-lawsuit-against-former-radio-host

Fortin, J. (2018, May 3). 2 Black men settle with Starbucks and Philadelphia Over Arrest. *New York Times*, p. B3. https://www.nytimes.com/2018/05/02/us/starbucks-arrest-philadelphia-settlement.html

Friele, R., & Sluijs, E. M. (2006). Patient expectations of fair complaint handling in hospitals: Empirical data. *BMC Health Services Research, 6*, 106. https://doi.org/10.1186/1472-6963-6-106

Gallagher, T. H., Waterman, A. D., Ebers, A. G., Fraser, V. J., & Levinson, W. (2003). Patients' and physicians' attitudes regarding the disclosure of medical errors. *Journal of the American Medical Association, 289*(8), 1001–1007. https://doi.org/10.1001/jama.289.8.1001

Goffman, E. (1971). *Relations in public: Microstudies of the public order*. Routledge.

Golann, D. (2011). Dropped medical malpractice claims: Their surprising frequency, apparent causes, and potential remedies. *Health Affairs, 30*(7), 1343–1350. https://doi.org/10.1377/hlthaff.2010.1132

Gold, G. J., & Weiner, B. (2000). Remorse, confession, group identity, and expectancies about repeating a transgression. *Basic and Applied Social Psychology, 22*, 291–300. https://doi.org/10.1207/S15324834BASP2204_3

Guthrie, C., & Korobkin, R. (1997). Psychology, economics, and settlement: A new look at the role of the lawyer. *Texas Law Review, 76*, 77–141.

Haesevoets, T., Reinders Folmer, C., De Cremer, D., & Van Hiel, A. (2013). Money isn't all that matters: The use of financial compensation and apologies to preserve relationships in the aftermath of distributive harm. *Journal of Economic Psychology, 35*, 95–107. https://doi.org/10.1016/j.joep.2013.02.003

Hadfield, G. K. (2008). Framing the choice between cash and the courthouse: Experiences with the 9/11 Victim Compensation Fund. *Law and Society Review, 42*, 645–682. https://doi.org/10.1111/j.1540-5893.2008.00354.x

Hans, V. P. (2000). *Business on trial: The civil jury and corporate responsibility*. Yale University Press.

Hart, K. D., & Peters, P. G. (2008). Cultures of claiming: Local variation in malpractice claim frequency. *Journal of Empirical Legal Studies, 5*, 77–107. https://doi.org/10.1111/j.1740-1461.2007.00119.x

Henry, B. (2004, January). It's rarely too late to say you're sorry. *The Practical Litigator*, pp. 31–40.

Hensler, D. (2003). Money talks: Searching for justice through compensation for personal injury and death. *DePaul Law Review, 53*, 417–456.

Hensler, D. R., Marquis, M. S., Abrahamse, A., Barry, S. H., Ebener, P. A., Lewis, E., Lind, E., MacCoun, R. J., Manning, W. G., Rogowski, J., & Vaiana, M. E. (1991). *Compensation for accidental injuries in the United States*. RAND.

Hickson, G. B., Clayton, W., Githens, B., & Sloan, F. A. (1992). Factors that prompted families to file medical malpractice claims following perinatal injuries. *JAMA, 267*(10), 1359–1363. https://doi.org/10.1001/jama.267.10.1359

Hodgins, H. S., & Liebeskind, E. (2003). Apology versus defense: Antecedents and consequences. *Journal of Experimental Social Psychology, 39*, 297–316. https://doi.org/10.1016/S0022-1031(03)00024-6

Holder, R. L., & Daly, K. (2018). Recognition, reconnection, and renewal: The meaning of money to sexual assault survivors. *International Review of. Victimology, 24*(1), 25–46. https://doi.org/10.1177/0269758017739372

Hollander-Blumoff, R., & Tyler, T. R. (2008). Procedural justice in negotiation: Procedural fairness, outcome acceptance, and integrative potential. *Law and Social Inquiry, 33*(2), 473–500. https://doi.org/10.1111/j.1747-4469.2008.00110.x

Hubbard, A. S. E., Hendrickson, B., Fehrenbach, K. S., & Sur, J. (2013). Effects of timing and sincerity of an apology on satisfaction and changes in negative feelings during conflicts. *Western Journal of Communication, 77*(3), 305–322. https://doi.org/10.1080/10570314.2013.770160

Hulst, L., & Akkermans, A. J. (2011). Can money symbolize acknowledgment? How victims' relatives perceive monetary awards for their emotional harm. *Psychological Injury and Law, 4*(3), 245–262. https://doi.org/10.1007/s12207-011-9110-7

In re Takata Airbag Products Liability Litigation. (2022). S.D. Fla. Case No.14-cv-24009-MORENO. https://www.autoairbagsettlement.com/Volkswagen/Content/Documents/Volkswagen/Final%20Approval%20Order.pdf
In re USA Gymnastics. (2021). Case No. 18-09108-RLM-11, U.S. Bankruptcy Court, Southern District of Indiana. https://www.courthousenews.com/wp-content/uploads/2021/10/usa-gymnastics-chapter-11-plan.pdf
Ingber, S. (1985). Rethinking intangible injuries: A focus on remedy symposium: Alternative compensation schemes and tort theory. *California Law Review, 73*(3), 772–856.
Jehle, A., Miller, M. K., Kemmelmeier, M., & Maskaly, J. (2012). How voluntariness of apologies affects actual and hypothetical victims' perceptions of the offender. *The Journal of Social Psychology, 152*(6), 727–745. https://doi.org/10.1080/00224545.2012.697079
Jeter, W. K., & Brannon, L. A. (2017). 'I'll make it up to you:' Examining the effect of apologies on forgiveness. *The Journal of Positive Psychology, 20*, 1–8. https://doi.org/10.1080/17439760.2017.1291854
Judicial Conference of the U.S. Courts, Committee on Court Administration and Case Management. (2022). *Civil litigation management manual* (3rd ed.). Judicial Conference of the U.S. Courts.
Kirchhoff, J., Wagner, U., & Strack, M. (2012). Apologies: Words of magic? The role of verbal components, anger reduction, and offence severity. *Peace and Conflict: Journal of Peace Psychology, 18*(2), 109–130. https://doi.org/10.1037/a0028092
Korobkin, R., & Guthrie, C. (1994). Psychological barriers to litigation settlement: An experimental approach. *Michigan Law Review, 93*(1), 107–192. https://doi.org/10.2307/1289916
Koss, M. P. (2014). The RESTORE program of restorative justice for sex crimes: Vision, process, and outcomes. *Journal of Interpersonal Violence, 29*, 1623–1660. https://doi-org.libproxy.unl.edu/10.1177/0886260513511153
Kritzer, H. (1997). Contingency fee lawyers as gatekeepers in the civil justice system. *Judicature, 81*, 22–29.
Kritzer, H. (1998). Contingency fee lawyers and their clients: Settlement expectations, settlement realities, and issues of control in the lawyer-client relationship. *Law and Social Inquiry, 23*, 795–821. https://doi.org/10.1111/j.1747-4469.1998.tb00034.x
Kritzer, H. M. (1991). *Let's make a deal: Understanding the negotiation process in ordinary litigation*. University of Wisconsin Press.
Kruglanski, A. W., Shah, J. Y., Fishbach, A., Friedman, R., Chun, W. Y., & Sleeth-Keppler, D. (2002). A theory of goal systems. In M. P. Zanna (Ed.), *Advances in experimental social psychology* (Vol. 34, pp. 331–378). Academic Press. https://doi.org/10.1016/S0065-2601(02)80008-9
Kwasny v. U.S., 823 F.2d 194 (7th Cir. 1987).
Lawless, R. M., & Robbennolt, J. K. (2024, April/May). Procedural justice in the bankruptcy courts. *Monitor on Psychology*, p. 39.
Lewicki, R. J., Polin, B., & Lount, R. B. (2016). An exploration of the structure of effective apologies. *Negotiation and Conflict Management Research, 9*(2), 177–196. https://doi.org/10.1111/ncmr.12073
Lewinsohn-Zamir, D. (2013). Can't buy me love: Monetary versus in-kind remedies. *University of Illinois Law Review, 2013*, 151–194.
Lind, E. A., & Tyler, T. R. (1988). *The social psychology of procedural justice*. Plenum Press.
Macaulay, S. (1963). Non-contractual relations and business: A preliminary study. *American Sociological Review, 28*, 55–69. http://www.jstor.org/stable/2090458
Major, B., & Kaiser, C. R. (2005). Perceiving and claiming discrimination. In L. B. Nielsen & R. L. Nelson (Eds.), *Handbook of employment discrimination research* (pp. 285–301). Springer.
Mazor, K. M., Simon, S. R., Yood, R. A., Martinson, B. C., Gunter, M. J., Reed, G. W., & Gurwitz, J. H. (2004). Health plan members' views about disclosure of medical errors. *Annals of Internal Medicine, 140*(6), 409–418. https://doi.org/10.7326/0003-4819-140-6-200403160-00006
May, M. L., & Stengel, D. B. (1990). Who sues their doctors? How patients handle medical grievances. *Law and Society Review, 24*(1), 105–120. https://doi.org/10.2307/3053788

McClurg, A. J. (2005). Dead sorrow: A story about loss and a new theory of wrongful death damages. *Boston University Law Review, 85*, 1–52.
McDougald v. Garber, 536 N.E.2d 372 (N.Y. 1989).
Menkel-Meadow, C. (1985). The transformation of disputes by lawyers: What the dispute paradigm does and does not tell us. *Missouri Journal of Dispute Resolution, 1985*, 25–72.
Miller, R. E., & Sarat, A. (1981). Grievances, claims, and disputes: Assessing the adversary culture. *Law and Society Review, 15*, 525–566. https://doi.org/10.2307/3053502
Minow, M. (2002). *Breaking the cycles of hatred: Memory, law, and repair*. Princeton University Press.
Moore, J., & Mello, M. M. (2017). Improving reconciliation following medical injury: A qualitative study of responses to patient safety incidents in New Zealand. *BMJ Quality and Safety, 26*(10), 788–798. https://doi.org/10.1136/bmjqs-2016-005804
Neubauer, D., & Meinhold, S. S. (1994). Too quick to sue? Public perceptions of the litigation explosion. *The Justice System Journal, 16*(3), 1–14. https://doi.org/10.1080/23277556.1994.10871179
Ohbuchi, K., Kameda, M., & Agarie, N. (1989). Apology as aggression control: Its role in mediating appraisal of and response to harm. *Journal of Personality and Social Psychology, 56*(2), 219–227. https://doi.org/10.1037/0022-3514.56.2.219
Ohtsubo, Y. (2020). Does financial compensation need to be accompanied by verbal apologies? *Peace and Conflict: Journal of Peace Psychology, 26*, 96–99. https://doi.org/10.1037/pac0000433
Okimoto, T. G. (2008). Outcomes as affirmation of membership value: Material compensation as an administrative response to procedural injustice. *Journal of Experimental Social Psychology, 44*(5), 1270–1282. https://doi.org/10.1016/j.jesp.2008.04.009
Okimoto, T. G., & Tyler, T. R. (2007). Is compensation enough? Relational concerns in responding to unintended inequity. *Group Processes and Intergroup Relations, 10*(3), 399–420. https://doi.org/10.1177/1368430207078701
Pace, K. M., Fediuk, T. A., & Botero, I. C. (2010). The acceptance of responsibility and expressions of regret in organizational apologies after a transgression. *Corporate Communications: An International Journal, 15*(4), 410–427. https://doi.org/10.1108/13563281011085510
Pleasence, P., Balmer, N. J., & Reimers, S. (2011). What really drives advice seeking behaviour? Looking beyond the subject of legal disputes. *Oñati Socio-Legal Series, 1*(6).
Press Conference. (2023). https://news.sky.com/video/dominion-lawyer-money-is-accountability-and-we-got-that-today-from-fox-12860403
Quinney, B., Wenzel, M., & Woodyatt, L. (2022). Truth is its own reward: Completeness of information, the feeling of truth knowing, and victims' closure. *British Journal of Social Psychology, 61*(1), 389–409. https://doi.org/10.1111/bjso.12486
Rabin, R. L. (2005). Pain and suffering and beyond: Some thoughts on recovery for intangible loss. *DePaul Law Review, 55*(2), 359–378.
Radin, M. J. (1993). Compensation and commensurability. *Duke Law Journal, 43*(1), 56–86.
Reinders Folmer, C. P., Desmet, P. T. M., & Van Boom, W. H. (2019). Beyond compensation? Examining the role of apologies in the restoration of victims' needs in simulated tort cases. *Law and Human Behavior, 43*(4), 329–341. https://doi.org/10.1037/lhb0000335
Relis, T. (2007). It's not about the money: Theory of misconceptions of plaintiffs' litigation aims. *University of Pittsburgh Law Review, 68*(3), 701–746.
Restatement (Third) of Torts: Remedies § 20 TD No 2 (2023).
Robbennolt, J. K. (2003). Apologies and legal settlement: An empirical examination. *Michigan Law Review, 102*(3), 460–516. https://doi.org/10.2307/3595367
Robbennolt, J. K. (2006). Apologies and settlement levers. *Journal of Empirical Legal Studies, 3*(2), 333–373. https://doi.org/10.1111/j.1740-1461.2006.00072.x
Robbennolt, J. K. (2008). Attorneys, apologies, and settlement negotiation. *Harvard Negotiation Law Review, 13*, 349–397.

Robbennolt, J. K. (2013). The effects of negotiated and delegated apologies in settlement negotiation. *Law and Human Behavior, 37*(2), 128–135. https://doi.org/10.1037/lhb0000020

Robbennolt, J. K., Bregant, J., & Winship, V. (2023a, May 18). "We acknowledge the court's rulings" and other terrible apologies. *Verdict*. https://verdict.justia.com/2023/05/18/we-acknowledge-the-courts-rulings-and-other-terrible-apologies

Robbennolt, J. K., Bregant, J., & Winship, V. (2023b). Settlement schemas: How laypeople understand civil settlement. *Journal of Empirical Legal Studies, 20*, 488–533. https://doi.org/10.1111/jels.12360

Robbennolt, J., Darley, J., & MacCoun, R. J. (2003). Symbolism and incommensurability in civil sanctioning: Decision makers as goal managers. *Brooklyn Law Review, 68*(4), 1121–1158.

Robbennolt, J. K., & Hans, V. P. (2016). *The psychology of tort law*. NYU Press.

Sandefur, R. (2008). Access to civil justice and race, class, and gender inequality. *Annual Review of Sociology, 34*, 339–358. https://doi.org/10.1146/annurev.soc.34.040507.134534

Sander, F. E. A., & Golberg, S. B. (1994). Fitting the forum to the fuss: A user-friendly guide to selecting an ADR procedure. *Negotiation Journal, 10*, 49–68. https://doi.org/10.1111/j.1571-9979.1994.tb00005.x

Sandoval, E., & Goodman, J. D. (2024). Uvalde settles with victims' families over school shooting. *New York Times*. https://www.nytimes.com/2024/05/22/us/uvalde-lawsuit-settlement.html.

Saulnier, A., & Sivasubramaniam, D. (2015). Effects of victim presence and coercion in restorative justice: An experimental paradigm. *Law and Human Behavior, 39*(4), 378–387. https://doi.org/10.1037/lhb0000130

Scher, S. J., & Darley, J. M. (1997). How effective are the things people say to apologize? Effects of the realization of the apology speech act. *Journal of Psycholinguistic Research, 26*(1), 127–140. https://doi.org/10.1023/A:1025068306386

Schneider, C. D. (2000). What it means to be sorry: The power of apology in mediation. *Mediation Quarterly, 17*, 265–280. https://doi.org/10.1002/crq.3900170305

Schumann, K. (2019). Apologies as signals for change? Implicit theories of personality and reactions to apologies during the #MeToo movement. *PLoS ONE, 14*(12), Article e0226047.

Shepherd, J. (2014). Uncovering the silent victims of the American medical liability system. *Vanderbilt Law Review, 67*, 151–195.

Sherwin, E. (2003). Compensation and revenge. *San Diego Law Review, 40*, 1387–1413.

Sloan, F. A., & Hsieh, C. R. (1995). Injury, liability, and the decision to file a medical malpractice claim. *Law and Society Review, 29*(3), 413–435. https://doi.org/10.2307/3053973

Slocum, D., Allan, A., & Allan, M. M. (2011). An emerging theory of apology: An emerging theory of apology. *Australian Journal of Psychology, 63*(2), 83–92. https://doi.org/10.1111/j.1742-9536.2011.00013.x

Smith, N. (2008). *I was wrong: The meanings of apologies*. Cambridge University Press.

Sternlight, J. R. (1999). Lawyers' representation of clients in mediation: Using economics and psychology to structure advocacy in a non-adversarial setting. *Ohio State Journal on Dispute Resolution, 14*, 269–366.

Tavuchis, N. (1991). *Mea culpa: A sociology of apology and reconciliation*. Stanford University Press.

Tomlinson, E. C., Dineen, B. R., & Lewicki, R. J. (2004). The road to reconciliation: Antecedents of victim willingness to reconcile following a broken promise. *Journal of Management, 30*(2), 165–187. https://doi.org/10.1016/j.jm.2003.01.003

Trost, Z., Monden, K. R., Buelow, M., Boals, A., & Scott, W. (2016). Perceived injustice predicts intention to litigate: Findings from a spinal cord injury sample. *Psychological Injury and Law, 9*(1), 31–40. https://doi.org/10.1007/s12207-015-9245-z

Tumelty, M. (2020). Medical negligence litigation and apologies: An empirical examination. *European Journal of Health Law, 27*, 386–403. https://doi.org/10.1163/15718093-BJA10021

van Dijck, G. (2018). Victim-oriented tort law in action: An empirical examination of catholic church sexual abuse cases. *Journal of Empirical Legal Studies, 15*(1), 126–164. https://doi.org/10.1111/jels.12175

Victim of rape discusses jury's decision to make company pay $1 billion verdict. (2018). https://www.youtube.com/watch?v=njt-OFxl-Gc
Victor, D. (2018, May 23). Woman who was raped as a teenager is awarded $1 billion in damages. *New York Times*. https://www.nytimes.com/2018/05/23/us/georgia-assault-billion-dollars.html
Vidmar, N., & Schuller, R. A. (1987). Individual differences and the pursuit of legal rights: A preliminary inquiry. *Law and Human Behavior, 11*(4), 299–317. https://doi.org/10.1007/BF01044743
Vincent, C. B., Young, M., & Phillips, A. (1994). Why do people sue doctors—A study of patients and relatives taking legal action. *The Lancet, 347*, 1609–1613. https://doi.org/10.1016/s0140-6736(94)93062-7
Viscusi, W. K. (1996). Pain and suffering: Damages in search of sounder rationale. *Michigan Law and Policy Review, 1*, 141–178.
Wagner, W. (2007). When all else fails: Regulatory risky products through tort litigation. *Georgetown Law Journal, 95*, 693–732.
Weiner, B., Graham, S., Peter, O., & Zmuidinas, M. (1991). Public confession and forgiveness. *Journal of Personality, 59*, 281–312. https://doi.org/10.1111/j.1467-6494.1991.tb00777.x
Wexler, L. (2017, September 29). Ideal victims and the damage of a damage free victory. *Verdict*. https://verdict.justia.com/2017/09/29/ideal-victims-damage-damage-free-victory
Wexler, L., Robbennolt, J. K., & Murphy, C. (2019). #MeToo, Time's Up, and theories of justice. *University of Illinois Law Review, 2019*(1), 67–110.
Whited, M. C., Wheat, A. L., & Larkin, K. T. (2010). The influence of forgiveness and apology on cardiovascular reactivity and recovery in response to mental stress. *Journal of Behavioral Medicine, 33*(4), 293–304. https://doi.org/10.1007/s10865-010-9259-7
Witman, A. B., Park, D. M., & Hardin, S. B. (1996). How do patients want physicians to handle mistakes? A survey of internal medicine patients in an academic setting. *Archives of Internal Medicine, 156*, 2565–2569. https://doi.org/10.1001/archinte.1996.00440210083008
Witvliet, C. V. O., Root Luna, L., Worthington, E. L., & Tsang, J.-A. (2020). Apology and restitution: The psychophysiology of forgiveness after accountable relational repair responses. *Frontiers in Psychology, 11*. https://doi.org/10.3389/fpsyg.2020.00284
Witvliet, C. V., Ludwig, T. H., & Bauer, D. J. (2002). Please forgive me: Transgressors' emotions and physiology during imagery of seeking forgiveness and victim responses. *Journal of Psychology and Christianity, 21*, 219–233. http://caps.net/membership/publications/jpc
WPRI. (2009). *James Woods settled lawsuit with Kent Hospital*. https://www.youtube.com/watch?v=qXXySNBnJCs
Zavos, H. (2009). Monetary damages for nonmonetary losses: An integrated answer to the problem of the meaning, function, and calculation of noneconomic damages. *Loyola of Los Angeles Law Review, 43*(1), 193–272.
Zechmeister, J. S., Garcia, S., Romero, C., & Vas, S. N. (2004). Don't apologize unless you mean it: A laboratory investigation of forgiveness and retaliation. *Journal of Social and Clinical Psychology, 23*(4), 532–564. https://doi.org/10.1521/jscp.23.4.532.40309

Why Do People Use ADR?

Donna Shestowsky

Introduction

Although trials were once "the central institution of the law," statistical trends in the civil justice system suggest that they are "approaching extinction" (Galanter & Frozena, 2011). While trial remains a theoretical possibility in every filed case, real-life experiences of case resolution often take a different form. In 2023, less than 1% of cases filed in federal courts reached trial (United States Courts, 2023). Similar trends are observed in the state court system where most disputes in the United States are handled (Galanter, 2004; Shestowsky, 2016). Whereas some cases that do not resolve through trial end because they are voluntarily dismissed, or are disposed of by motions or hearings, others conclude through some form of Alternative Dispute Resolution ("ADR"), including negotiation, mediation, and arbitration (Galanter, 2004; Riskin et al., 2019). This shift to ADR has prompted the National Conference on Bar Examiners to begin testing ADR concepts on the bar exam starting in 2026 (Gundavaram, 2022), placing ADR into a strong new spotlight. As law professors and law students accordingly focus more attention on ADR, they might

Note: The Author wishes to thank David Hansen, John Lande, and Richard Wiener for helpful comments on early drafts of this chapter, research assistants Sydney Simon and Roxanne Camarena Castillo for their research support, and presenters and audience members at the 2024 Nebraska Symposium on Motivation for their thoughtful questions and suggestions. Research support was provided by a *Small Grant in Aid of Research* from the University of California, Davis, Academic Senate.

D. Shestowsky (✉)
University of California, Davis, CA, USA
e-mail: dshest@ucdavis.edu

R. L. Wiener, D. J. Hansen (eds.), *Legal Judgment and the Motivation for Justice*, Nebraska Symposium on Motivation 71,
https://doi.org/10.1007/978-3-031-98812-7_8

notice the glaring need for additional research investigating the subject from the litigant perspective, including on the foundational issue of what motivates litigants' interest in using ADR.[1] Understanding these motivations is critical for lawyers who advise clients on procedural options and court personnel who design ADR programs. And the topic offers rich opportunities to psychologists who are poised to further explore this important domain.

To set the stage for the future, it helps to reflect on the past. To that end, this chapter synthesizes three lines of psychological research that offer insights into why individuals opt for ADR: laypeople's knowledge of ADR, litigants' procedural preferences, and factors affecting litigants' procedural choices. Taken together, the literature highlights the dependance litigants have on lawyers. Accordingly, it should prompt psychologists to use a dyadic framework to examine motivations to use ADR, capturing the dynamics of the lawyer–client relationship. And it should motivate lawyers to recognize the need to counsel clients on ADR in ways that preserve client decision autonomy and self-determination. To provide context for my analysis, I begin by defining key terms and briefly tracing the history of ADR's emergence.

By "ADR," I refer to any procedure used to try to resolve legal disputes outside of trial or trial-adjacent procedures, such as hearings. ADR encompasses a wide range of procedures, with negotiation, mediation, and arbitration being among the most prevalent (Riskin et al., 2019). In contrast to trial and similar procedures, ADR options are generally informal, flexible, and subject to minimal legal constraints. Consequently, they offer a variety of structural possibilities. To frame the discussion, however, I will share some standard definitions of the prevalent procedures.

By "negotiation," I mean any type of communication (including in-person meetings, video conferences, and emails) between two or more parties directly or through their attorneys that attempts to resolve a dispute without third-party assistance. Compared to trial, it is a highly informal, conversational process. Moreover, the relevant law need not dictate the outcome—negotiators can use other factors, including their own notions of fairness, to shape the outcome of their case.

When I refer to "mediation," I imply negotiations that involve a "neutral" (i.e., a neutral third party) called a mediator who assists parties in resolving a dispute. The mediator does not determine the outcome—as in negotiation, that power lies with the parties themselves. As in negotiation, parties may rely on factors other than the applicable law to determine the outcome. Mediation is typically very informal and conversational in nature.

A third type of ADR, "arbitration," tends to be significantly more formal than mediation. In arbitration, one or more neutrals, referred to as "arbitrators," render a decision after hearing structured presentations based on arguments and evidence akin to those made in a trial setting. Arbitrators often base their decisions on the

[1] Academics often address the question of what motivates people to pursue justice in specific ways. For example, legal scholars have explored why people settle cases (Priest & Klein, 1984), and economists and psychologists have long debated this issue, with the former group supporting the rational actor model and the latter remaining skeptical of it (Watkins, 2010). This chapter does not address this subject.

applicable law but sometimes use other standards, such as industry norms. Arbitration can be either binding or nonbinding. In binding arbitration, under the Federal Arbitration Act which governs arbitration clauses in the realm of consumer disputes and disputes that nonunionized employees have with their employers (Gilles, 2016; Sternlight, 2015), arbitrators render a decision that is legally binding and, in most instances, not appealable (Federal Arbitration Act, 1947). Consequently, even if the arbitrators' decision clearly deviates from the applicable law, such a discrepancy would not invalidate the obligation of the losing party to comply with the decision. By contrast, in nonbinding arbitration, the arbitrators' decision is advisory, allowing either party to reject the outcome. When a court offers arbitration through its ADR program,[2] it is nonbinding arbitration (Hensler, 2003).

In contrast to trials and hearings, ADR procedures face minimal regulation. Mediation and arbitration, for instance, are not licensed professions, and practitioners in these fields are not necessarily lawyers.[3] Lawyers, who frequently take on the task of choosing neutrals for their clients' cases, however, often favor those with significant legal expertise, such as former judges (Goldberg et al., 2009; McAdoo & Welsh, 1997).

To understand how ADR procedures function, it helps to keep in mind the purposes they serve in the civil justice system. In the United States, the use of ADR procedures for civil cases evolved for primarily two reasons. First, the courts sought to use ADR to increase the time and cost efficiency of their operations (Welsh, 2001). Second, ADR was designed to provide parties with an alternative to the rigidities of trial, granting them what ADR scholars refer to as "self-determination"—increased control over the resolution of their disputes (Bingham, 2002), as disputes, ultimately, "belong to the parties" (Menkel-Meadow, 1995).

These distinct goals reflect the two-pronged history of modern ADR. The goal of promoting disputant self-determination originated from the community empowerment movement of the late 1960s and early 1970s (Hensler, 2003). Advocates of this movement viewed formal legal institutions, such as the courts, as tools that reinforced the power of the elite, enabling the exploitation of less powerful members of society (Hensler, 2003). They contended that it was essential to establish grassroots justice institutions so that individuals could shape the course of their lives and communities (Hensler, 2003). These institutions would apply community-based norms and involve community members in conflict resolution efforts. This conceptualization aligns with the perspective of contemporary ADR scholars who assert that disputes fundamentally belong to the disputants, and thus they should control how they are resolved (Menkel-Meadow, 1995; Shestowsky, 2008). A key objective of ADR, under this view, is to offer disputants greater self-determination opportunities than what they can exercise in a trial, allowing their subjective assessments and preferences to play a crucial role in shaping the process and determining

[2] Not all courts of general jurisdiction offer ADR programs, but many do (Riskin et al., 2019). Court ADR programs are discussed *infra*.

[3] However, some court ADR programs allow only licensed attorneys to be included on their lists of available neutrals (Shestowsky, 2017).

the outcome of their disputes. In ADR procedures that encourage collaboration, for example, like mediation and negotiation, outcomes that creatively meet the needs of both parties to a dispute are possible, unlike the win–lose outcomes mandated by court adjudication (Riskin & Welsh, 2008).

While community justice centers were evolving autonomously outside the court system, a parallel movement emerged within the courts, focused on promoting ADR as a tool for improving institutional efficiency (Hensler, 2003). Following World War II, the traditional "laissez-faire judicial system" (Hensler, 2003, p. 174) characterized by minimal oversight in judge assignments came under scrutiny (Hensler, 2003). Specifically, critics contended that the judicial system should take on a more business-oriented approach in the allocation of public resources, particularly judges' time (Hensler, 2003). This critique, coupled with shrinking court budgets and a surge in case filings, spurred the "court management" revolution, which included the introduction of professional "court administrators" to help judges manage their dockets effectively (Hensler, 2003). Courts began experimenting with strategies to ready cases for trial and expedite case resolution, with the overarching goal of saving the courts time and money (Hensler, 2003; Welsh, 2001). Many courts responded to this call by implementing mandatory nonbinding arbitration and mediation (Hensler, 2003), thereby allowing nonjudge neutrals to handle smaller dollar-value cases.

Even today, court-connected ADR programs echo these two originating values of ADR and the two-pronged history of its evolution in the judicial system. The preambles of statutes and local rules establishing some court ADR programs state that they were created to conserve the court's time and financial resources (Shestowsky, 2008). Other courts emphasize that their ADR offerings are designed to promote party self-determination (Shestowsky, 2008). Some courts assert that their programs are intended to achieve both objectives (Shestowsky, 2008).

Whereas the reasons that *courts* offer or promote ADR tend to be directly articulated in materials disseminated by those institutions, why *litigants* choose ADR is less obvious. What motivates *them* to use it?

Paths to ADR

Sometimes, individuals are required to use ADR. This situation arises when a contract (Stipanowich, 2001) or court (Shestowsky, 2008) requires them to use it. As an example of the latter pathway, individuals may be compelled to utilize ADR by court mandate. Some courts require parties to use ADR, allowing cases to proceed to trial only when ADR fails to resolve them, in an arrangement known as a "mandatory" court ADR (Katz, 1993; Quek, 2010). As an example of the former pathway, individuals may find themselves bound by arbitration clauses embedded in consumer contracts or employment agreements, frequently without their knowledge or awareness (Eisenberg & Miller, 2007; Drahozal, 2001). These clauses, which require the use of binding arbitration, have generated substantial controversy, especially in the context of consumer and employee rights. Critics contend that corporations include arbitration provisions in their agreements to restrict the ability of consumers and employees to exercise their constitutional rights to a jury trial, an impartial judge, and due process (Sternlight, 1997), as well as to limit corporate exposure to class action lawsuits (Gilles, 2016).

When ADR use is not required, disputants can use ADR as a matter of choice. Disputants may exercise the option to use ADR either before or after a lawsuit is initiated, or as an alternative to filing a court case. People resolving a dispute outside the court system can enlist the help of "private" ADR neutrals who offer ADR services (e.g., mediation or arbitration) outside the court system. Those who choose ADR for cases already filed in court may select a private neutral or they may utilize court-facilitated access to specific procedures or neutrals through a "voluntary" court ADR program, if their court has one (McAdoo & Welsh, 1997; Nolan-Haley, 1996; Watkins, 2010).

Many disputants have the freedom to choose among trial and various ADR procedures, and when they do, they do not relinquish that freedom when they have legal representation. Every state has adopted some version of Rule 1.2 of the ABA Model Rules of Professional Conduct (American Bar Association, n.d.), which outlines the scope of authority between the lawyer and client. This rule states, "A lawyer shall abide by a client's decisions concerning the objectives of representation and, as required by Rule 1.4, shall consult with the client as to the means by which they are to be pursued." Although these rules do not reference communications about ADR specifically, the framework they establish underscores the client's role in setting representation goals while requiring lawyers to consult with them to make decisions on procedural options (Shestowsky, 2024). Lawyers retain significant discretion in how they conduct these consultations. The client counseling literature, which lawyers may consult for general guidance on client communication, typically advocates for a client-centered approach, encouraging attorneys to assist clients in making informed decisions about their cases (Shestowsky, 2024) and preserving their decision autonomy. This client-centered model encourages lawyers to assist their clients in making choices that align with their interests, objectives, and priorities (Binder et al., 2019; Blankley et al., 2021).

Motivations for Using ADR

Having established the foundation for understanding common ADR procedures and their associated contexts, my focus will transition to individuals situated within the voluntary ADR framework. This context is where the psychological factors affecting motivation to use ADR take center stage.

While it is generally assumed that individuals engage with the civil justice system in pursuit of justice—however that may be defined or interpreted—the motivations behind their choice of resolution method, and why some choose ADR, are less straightforward. An analysis of the existing literature suggests that this foundational issue can be explored through three key questions, each tied to its own line of research.

First, are laypeople aware of ADR? People cannot choose ADR if they are unaware of its availability as an option. Second, when do litigants prefer ADR to trial and trial-adjacent procedures? This question is crucial, as ADR essentially "competes" with trial and trial-adjacent procedures for disputes that fall within the civil justice system. Third, what criteria drive procedure selection? Understanding this issue is essential for examining how litigants navigate situations where multiple procedures align with their preferences. We begin by addressing the first question: What does the prevailing empirical research reveal about the awareness of ADR?

Awareness and Knowledge

The notion that individuals must possess knowledge about ADR to use it seems banal. But when it comes to ADR, the link between awareness and usage has, historically, not been so simple. For instance, upon the introduction of voluntary mediation programs by courts, utilization rates often failed to meet expectations, even when mediation was offered free of charge or at minimal cost to the parties (Bingham, 2002; Wissler, 1997). Numerous theories emerged to explain this tepid response. Some observers speculated that it signaled a general aversion to mediation (Hensler, 2002). Consequently, many courts transitioned their voluntary initiatives into mandatory programs (Nolan-Haley, 1996; McAdoo & Welsh, 1997; McAdoo, 2007), ostensibly to eliminate barriers to participation that stemmed from individual preferences. Other scholars argued that under-utilized programs might not have been "fully implemented" (Bingham, 2002, p. 122), meaning that even if they were attractive, well-designed, and well-functioning, outreach campaigns to educate and entice parties may have been inadequate or nonexistent. This contention underscores the crucial connection between awareness and utilization rates.

The most relevant contemporary study regarding public familiarity with ADR is the project aptly titled "ADR is Not a Household Term" (Blankley et al., 2021). Using a large sample from the United States, Blankley and her colleagues assessed how much knowledge, familiarity, and experience that community members possessed concerning litigation and various ADR procedures including arbitration, negotiation, and two styles of mediation (i.e., evaluative and facilitative mediation).[4] To analyze familiarity, they categorized participants into two groups. One group included participants who indicated they had never heard of the procedure and those who were aware of the term but had no further knowledge; they considered these individuals as "lacking familiarity." A second group, who were deemed to be

[4] In evaluative mediation, mediators provide a legal assessment of the claims and may suggest specific resolutions. In contrast, in facilitative mediation, mediators do not offer opinions on the legal positions of the parties; instead, they help the parties reach their own resolution (Kovach & Love, 1996).

Table 1 Community participants categorized by familiarity

Dispute resolution process	% who lack familiarity	% who have at least some familiarity
Litigation	11.2%	88.7%
Arbitration	20.1%	79.7%
Evaluative mediation	75.9%	24.0%
Facilitative mediation	75.4%	24.5%
Negotiation	2.7%	97.2%

Note. Adapted from "ADR is Not a Household Term: Considering the Ethical and Practical Consequences of the Public's Lack of Understanding of Mediation and Arbitration" by K. Blankley, A. M. Votruba, L. Bartz, and L.M. PytlikZillig, 2021, *Nebraska Law Review, 99*(797), p. 817. Adapted with permission

familiar with the terms, was comprised of participants who reported at least a slight knowledge of the procedure, reflecting a conservative operationalization of "familiarity." As shown in Table 1, the data revealed that 11.2% of participants had no familiarity with litigation, 20.1% had no familiarity with arbitration, and over 75% lacked familiarity with either form of mediation. Overall, these statistics suggest that legal professionals should not assume that the public—the population from which most litigants originate—possesses familiarity with common legal procedures. They also emphasize the vital educational role that lawyers and court personnel can play in promoting public familiarity with ADR.

The researchers also asked participants to rate their overall knowledge of each procedure. The data revealed a noticeable skew toward responses, suggesting that participants were only "slightly" or "not knowledgeable" about these procedures, except for negotiation. Not surprisingly, when they were asked to rate their level of experience with the different options, this skew seemed even sharper, suggesting that the vast majority were only slightly or not at all experienced with the various procedures except for negotiation. Nearly half of the participants reported having engaged in some form of negotiation, although not necessarily for a legal dispute.[5] Overall, these self-report data suggest that the public has little familiarity, knowledge, or experience with ADR procedures.

Blankley and her colleagues (Blankley et al., 2021) then conducted a more nuanced examination by assessing laypeople's comprehension of fundamental aspects of legal procedures. To achieve this, they enlisted dispute resolution experts to evaluate the characteristics of the legal procedures and then compared those evaluations with parallel assessments made by lay participants who reported at least slight familiarity with all focal dispute resolution procedures. The analyses unveiled discrepancies in how community members and experts perceived the various procedures. For instance, community participants perceived arbitration and negotiation as

[5] Nearly half (47.2%) of the community participants reported having participated in a negotiation. Participants reported much lower levels of participation in litigation (17.6%), arbitration (10.9%), evaluative mediation (4.9%), and facilitative mediation (6.2%). For the community participants who had been involved in litigation, arbitration, evaluative mediation, or facilitative mediation, the vast majority had been involved in the listed dispute resolution procedure only once.

having significantly greater collaborative potential than experts did, while they evaluated facilitative mediation as significantly less collaborative than the experts did. Additionally, compared to the experts, community participants viewed evaluative mediation, facilitative mediation, and negotiation as allowing for significantly less party self-determination.

In subsequent writing about this research, Blankley et al. explained that "even when community members claim to be familiar with all five of the processes included in this study, their perception of important characteristics differs from the perception of those same characteristics by professionals performing those services" (Blankley et al., 2022, p. 83). These discrepancies may reflect misunderstandings on the part of the public or could arise from other sources. For instance, community members with prior experience with these procedures may possess differing perceptions due to their distinct roles in the underlying disputes (i.e., as disputants versus dispute resolution experts).

No matter the cause of these disparate perceptions, they yield several important implications. First, lawyers should avoid presuming that their lay clients share their understanding of procedures, even when clients seem familiar with ADR terminology. Second, it is essential that lawyers educate clients about the complexities of ADR procedures, even if they claim to be familiar with them. Third, lawyers should not expect their clients to initiate conversations about ADR. This implication aligns with earlier research findings which revealed that 67% of litigation attorneys reported their clients either "never" (40%) or "rarely" (27%) (McAdoo & Hinshaw, 2002). As Wissler noted, "the fact that litigants are unlikely to propose the use of alternative processes but often are willing to use them suggests that, in order to increase voluntary ADR use, the discussion of ADR needs to be initiated by the court or by the litigants' attorney" (Wissler, 2002b, p. 205). Lastly, a productive avenue for future research may involve exploring how disparities in roles (e.g., lawyer versus potential disputant) contribute to variations in perceptions concerning the traits that ADR procedures have and what they entail.

Familiarity and knowledge about procedural options for individuals involved in litigation are particularly crucial. And yet, only a few studies have directly studied this population on these issues. One study, by Stallworth and Stroh (1996), surveyed 211 disputants with Equal Employment Opportunity Act (EEOC) disputes pending before the Illinois Human Rights Commission, a state agency empowered to perform adjudicatory functions. None of the respondents classified themselves as "familiar" with ADR; 77% said they were "somewhat familiar," and roughly one-quarter (23%) indicated that they were "not familiar at all" (p. 36). It is notable that nearly one-quarter indicated a complete lack of familiarity with ADR when ADR was beginning to gain traction in the courts.

But even more recent studies corroborate this discouraging perspective. In 2010–2011, my research team studied litigant awareness of ADR from a different perspective—that of litigants who had court-connected ADR options (Shestowsky, 2017). We recruited litigants from three courts, from different states, that had mediation and nonbinding arbitration programs, surveying litigants whose cases made them eligible for both programs. Thus, these options, along with trial, were constant across all participants in the study. With the permission of each court, we downloaded civil case filings and randomly selected a subset of litigants with the goal of recruiting one litigant per case. Those litigants were mailed a survey shortly after their case was filed ("ex ante" survey), allowing us to assess perceptions at the start of litigation. Using court databases, we monitored their cases on a weekly basis.[6] Once a case was designated as "closed," we extended an invitation for participation in a second survey—the "ex post" phone survey—typically conducted within 3 weeks of the case's closure. This survey assessed their knowledge of their court's programs by asking two questions: "Did the court where your case was filed offer a mediation program?" and "Did the court where your case was filed offer an arbitration program?" The objectively correct response to both inquiries was "yes" for all participants.

The findings were discouraging. Fewer than one-quarter of participants accurately identified their court's mediation program, with less than 25% answering correctly with "yes." Nearly the same percentage (22%) responded incorrectly with "no," while the remaining 54.5% indicated that they did not know. A similar trend was observed for arbitration: only about a quarter accurately identified their court's arbitration program, while 22% incorrectly answered "no," and 50.7% admitted they did not know. When considering both mediation and arbitration together, only 15% of litigants said they were aware that their court offered both options. Thus, at most, a small percentage of litigants recognized the choices that their court aimed to provide.

We used regression analysis to understand the factors that predicted their ability to correctly identify their court's offerings. We incorporated several variables that are difficult to assess in a meaningful way in laboratory research, including court location (to examine differences in court program structure),[7] repeat experience as a litigant (i.e., whether they were a "repeat player"), and legal representation. Tables 2 and 3 depict the results for mediation, with the former reporting the analysis comparing those who said "yes" with those who answered incorrectly by saying "no," and the latter presenting the analysis comparing those who said they did not know whether the court offered mediation with those who correctly said "yes." One of the most unexpected findings was the absence of a significant difference in awareness between individuals with legal representation and those who were unrepresented.

Another interesting result was that repeat players exhibited an information (and confidence) advantage over first-time litigants. Although repeat players were not more likely to give the correct answer of "yes" as opposed to the incorrect answer of "no" to the questions about either program, they *were* significantly less likely

[6] A wide variety of case types were represented in the sample. The median amount in controversy was $35,000; the mean amount in controversy was $2,053,051.53. Sixteen percent of participants came from the California court, 47% came from the Oregon court, and 38% came from the Utah court.

[7] Although "court location" might seem like a proxy for participants' geographical region, litigants in these three courts had mailing addresses in 19 states; 7.02% of litigants had addresses external to the states where the courts were located (Shestowsky, 2014).

Table 2 Results from model with likelihood of choosing "no" versus "yes" response to whether the court offered mediation ($N = 164$)

Predictor	Estimate	SE	P	Odds Ratio
Intercept	1.286	0.962	0.181	
Lawyer representation	−0.917	0.623	0.141	0.400
Repeat player status	−0.147	0.469	0.754	0.863
Location: CA vs. OR	0.255	0.681	0.708	1.291
Location: CA vs. UT	−0.054	0.710	0.939	0.947
Impression of court	−0.215	0.111	**0.052**	0.806

Note. Bolded *p*-values represent significance at the $p = 0.05$ level. Adapted from "When Ignorance Is Not Bliss: An Empirical Study of Litigants' Awareness Of Court-Sponsored Alternative Dispute Resolution Programs" by D. Shestowsky, 2017, *Harvard Negotiation Law Review, 22*(189), p.214. Adapted with permission

Table 3 Results from model with likelihood of choosing "don't know" versus "yes" response to whether the court offered mediation ($N = 164$)

Predictor	Estimate	SE	P	Odds Ratio
Intercept	1.515	0.811	0.062	
Lawyer representation	−0.541	0.482	0.261	0.582
Repeat player status	0.793	0.389	**0.042**	2.209
Location: CA vs. OR	0.168	0.572	0.769	1.183
Location: CA vs. UT	0.072	0.587	0.902	1.075
Impression of court	−0.204	0.093	**0.029**	0.815

Note. Bolded p-values represent significance at the $p < 0.05$ level. Adapted from "When Ignorance Is Not Bliss: An Empirical Study of Litigants' Awareness Of Court-Sponsored Alternative Dispute Resolution Programs" by D. Shestowsky, 2017, *Harvard Negotiation Law Review, 22*(189), p.214. Adapted with permission

than first-time litigants to say "I don't know" as opposed to "yes," as shown in Table 3.[8] Thus, repeat players appeared to express less uncertainty or confusion compared to first-time litigants. A separate analysis of arbitration revealed similar results.[9]

We also found that awareness had important consequences. Specifically, when parties knew their court offered mediation, they had significantly more favorable

[8] We also examined the effect of court location on litigant awareness. It did not emerge as a significant predictor. This finding is noteworthy because, during the data collection period, Oregon civil cases involving an amount in controversy of less than $50,000 were statutorily required to undergo non-binding arbitration unless litigants or their attorneys affirmatively opted out of this default. Surprisingly, only 43% of litigants whose cases were affected by this rule correctly identified their court's arbitration program. This statistic raises questions about whether the affected litigants knew they could opt out of the arbitration default and whether informed consent supported their participation in whatever procedure they ultimately used.

[9] Repeat players were nearly 2.53 times more likely to provide a "yes" response over a "don't know" response for arbitration.

impressions of their court.[10] This finding is also catalogued in Table 3. Further, we found that when they knew their court offered arbitration, they were significantly more likely—2.62 times more likely—to indicate in the ex post survey that they had considered using arbitration.[11] This result suggests a link between knowledge and contemplated use.

In summary, an important step in motivating people to use ADR requires ensuring they know about it. Laypeople generally lack familiarity with ADR options. In addition, even *litigants*—people for whom awareness and knowledge have profound consequences—should not be presumed to know their procedural options. This holds true even for represented litigants. While enhancing public awareness of ADR represents an admirable policy objective, the lack of awareness among disputants actively engaged in the civil justice system—despite having direct access to these options through the courts[12]—presents a more urgent concern from a justice perspective. Moreover, this issue persists even among represented litigants, raising important questions about the extent to which attorneys discuss court-connected ADR options with their clients and whether there is room for improvement in this regard (Shestowsky, 2017, 2024). Without a clear understanding of their options and the relative suitability of each alternative to meet their needs, litigants cannot make informed decisions about how to proceed with their cases.

Preferences

In state courts—the court system that handles most civil disputes (Galanter, 2004) —judge or jury trials constitute the default procedures for filed cases, unless a litigant initiates or is directed by the court to pursue an alternative (Federal Rules of Civil Procedure Rule 38 n.d.). Consequently, to understand litigants' motivation to

[10] Litigants rated how favorably they viewed the court where their case was filed using a scale from 1 = *extremely negative* to 9 = *extremely positive.*

[11] We asked litigants to list every procedure that they had considered using "at some point" in their case. We then used chi-square analysis to assess the dependence between whether litigants responded "yes" or "no" to whether they considered using arbitration and whether they did or did not identify their court's arbitration program (i.e., we compared those who answered "yes" to whether their court offered arbitration with those who answered either "no" or "don't know").

[12] Court-connected ADR often has unique benefits to parties. For example, at the time of the study, the Utah court allowed impecunious parties to request a pro bono mediator; in the California court, judges had the discretion to order "no fee mediation." Moreover, some courts have rules in conjunction with their programs that encourage ADR to take place early, before litigants expend significant resources on discovery or become psychologically committed to having a trial (Shestowsky, 2017). Neutrals also tend to be reviewed by the court for quality control purposes and are expected to follow ethical guidelines imposed by the courts, providing quality control in an otherwise unregulated field (Shestowsky, 2017). Courts also oversee non-binding arbitration, imposing penalties for bad faith or rejection of awards, ensuring parties take the process seriously. Moreover, the potential for lawyers to face disciplinary action for failing to engage in court-sponsored arbitration in good faith can shape how they engage in that procedure.

use ADR in situations where ADR use is voluntary, we must consider their perspective on how ADR compares with the default options of trial and trial-adjacent procedures.

Since the 1970s, studies situated within the procedural justice literature have attempted to elucidate why people prefer some legal procedures to others, including the factors associated with people preferring ADR to trial. A small but intriguing group of these studies has analyzed the ex post preferences of disputants who directly experienced both mediation and trial.[13] Though limited, the results suggest that disputants who experience both of these procedures tend to prefer mediation. This trend has been observed among small claims litigants who proceeded to trial after failing to reach a settlement in mediation (Wissler, 2004), as well as in other contexts (Roehl et al., 1992; Wissler, 1995), although there have been exceptions, with one study finding no discernible differences in preferences between the two procedures (Hermann et al., 1993). A second small body of research consists of field studies that assess how litigants evaluate specific procedures before or after experiencing them for their dispute (see Shestowsky, 2020). A third—and much larger—group of studies consist of laboratory experiments wherein college students evaluate procedures for hypothetical disputes (see Shestowsky, 2023).

In the 2002 symposium volume of the *Journal of Dispute Resolution*, leading dispute resolution scholars debated the conclusions that could be drawn from the prevailing research (Bingham, 2002; Hensler, 2002). Lisa Amsler (formerly Lisa Bingham), for example, argued that the then-existing research suggested that litigants preferred mediation. Deborah Hensler, by contrast, contended that there was a lack of clear empirical evidence supporting the idea that litigants favor mediation over trial and similar forms of adjudication. In my initial effort to reconcile these conflicting viewpoints, I examined the methodologies used in the studies that substantiated each position and identified several notable trends. First, studies indicating a preference for adjudication typically assessed ex ante (i.e., pre-experience) preferences regarding cases that were to be resolved in the future. Second, research suggesting a preference for mediation predominantly evaluated ex post (i.e., post-experience) perceptions (Shestowsky, 2004, 2008).

These observations resonate with the "two psychologies of conflict resolution" thesis coined by Tyler et al. (1999), which posits that people use different criteria to evaluate procedures before versus after experiencing them and, as a result, they might have different procedural preferences at different points in time. In a series of studies on this topic, Tyler and his colleagues examined how participants assessed procedures for resolving hypothetical conflicts (capturing ex ante perceptions) and compared these with how the same participants evaluated the procedures they employed in resolving real-life conflicts (assessing ex post evaluations). Their research revealed that ex ante preferences were better explained by how much they believed the procedures would help them obtain favorable outcomes, reflecting a

[13] These parties experienced either both procedures for the same case (e.g., a trial following a mediation impasse) or across different disputes.

self-interest motive. By contrast, their ex post assessments were generally better explained by how much procedures ministered to them respectfully and fairly (Tyler et al., 1999). Thus, evaluation standards differed depending on whether individuals made their assessments ex ante or ex post. Reflecting on these results, they stated: "These findings help to explain the puzzling literature on the psychology of mediation. By demonstrating that preference and evaluation are not based on the same psychological model, [our work] may provide an explanation for the difficulty of getting people to participate in mediation programs, in spite of the high approval ratings of those who do participate" (Tyler et al., 1999, p. 116). Some have labeled this challenge the "paradox of the hesitant but satisfied mediation participant" (McEwen & Milburn, 1993, p. 23; see also Nolan-Haley, 2009; Watkins, 2010).

In a longitudinal study, my team and I directly examined the potential for different temporal perspectives, not only for mediation but also for other legal procedures (Shestowsky, 2020). We asked participants to provide attraction ratings ("initial attraction") for eight legal procedures shortly after their cases were filed in court (i.e., in the ex ante survey), which are listed and described in Table 4. Then, at the end of their cases, they identified the procedure that resolved their case and re-evaluated it, this time using fairness and satisfaction metrics.[14] To compare their ex ante and ex post perceptions, we divided participants into two categories based on the procedure type—a "settlement" category including procedures premised on the parties controlling the outcome (i.e., negotiation, mediation, nonbinding arbitration, and judicial settlement conferences) and an "adjudication" category including procedures in which a third party imposes an outcome (i.e., judge trials, jury trials, motion/hearings, and binding arbitration).[15] The settlement category included litigants whose cases resolved via negotiation, mediation, nonbinding arbitration, or other ADR procedures (e.g., judicial settlement conferences). The adjudication category included those who resolved their cases via judge or jury trial, a motion, or hearing (i.e., judge deciding without trial) or binding arbitration.[16]

The line graphs in Figs. 1 and 2 illustrate the significant interaction effects between the procedure type and initial attraction that emerged from our regression analyses for satisfaction and fairness, respectively. Although litigants assessed the procedures based on distinct metrics at two separate time points—specifically, attractiveness in the ex ante phase and satisfaction and fairness in the ex post phase—the ex ante attractiveness ratings predicted ex post satisfaction and fairness metrics for adjudication but not for settlement procedures. Those who were more eager to "have their day in court" were generally happier when they received that

[14] The ex ante survey administered shortly after litigants' cases were filed asked them to rate the attractiveness of each procedure for their case (1 = *not attractive at all*; 9 = *extremely attractive*). In the ex post survey, they rated fairness and satisfaction using parallel scales from 1 to 9.

[15] This categorization largely aligns with the traditional distinction between ADR and adjudication, with one exception: binding arbitration, which is technically an ADR procedure, was included in the adjudication category since it did not conceptually fit in the settlement group.

[16] Among those who resolved their cases through adjudication, 83.5% did so through motions or hearings.

Table 4 Legal procedure descriptions for cases filed in court

Legal procedure	Description
Attorneys negotiate w/ out clients	The lawyers negotiate with each other on behalf of their clients, in order to settle their client's case. The negotiations may be done in person (face-to-face), but are more often done by phone, fax, or email. The clients are never present at any of the negotiation discussions. The outcome could be based on the law, or it could be based on some other rules or principles that the clients and/or their lawyers find relevant or important. If the lawyers agree on an outcome that their clients find acceptable, that is the outcome for the case.
Attorneys negotiate w/ clients present	The lawyers negotiate with each other on behalf of their clients, in order to settle their clients' case. The negotiations may be done in person (face-to-face) with lawyers and clients present, or by phone, with lawyers and clients on the phone at the same time. The clients are present and may participate in the negotiation discussions. The outcome could be based on the law, or it could be based on some other rules or principles that the clients and/or their lawyers find relevant or important. If the clients agree on an outcome that they both find acceptable, that is the outcome for the case
Mediation	A mediator (a neutral third person) facilitates the discussion between opposing lawyers and clients to help them settle the case. The mediator has no power to decide the outcome. Instead, the mediator helps the lawyers and clients communicate their different perspectives, discuss their needs and interests, and explore ways to resolve the case in a way that is acceptable to both clients. The outcome could be based on the law, or it could be based on some other rules or principles that the clients and/or their lawyers find relevant or important. If the clients agree on an outcome that they both find acceptable, that is the outcome for the case.
Judge decides w/out trial	Sometimes a judge can decide a case early on, so that a trial is never required. This is because the judge has determined there is no question about the facts, and the case can be decided on the basis of law alone. The lawyers submit documents to the court and may make a presentation to the judge at a hearing. Clients rarely attend and, if they do, they do not speak during the hearing. The judge later announces the outcome in writing, and explains why they decided as they did. This outcome is based on legal rules or principles. A party who is dissatisfied with the outcome can appeal it to a higher court, which will require additional time and proceedings.
Jury trial	A jury hears the lawyers' arguments and witnesses' answers to the lawyers' questions and reviews physical evidence. Often, the clients testify. The plaintiff's (party making the claim) lawyer presents his/her case first and then the defendant's lawyer presents his/her case. The judge instructs the jurors about the law they must apply to the evidence they have seen and heard. After the evidence has been presented, the jurors decide the outcome in private and then announce it in court, without explaining why they decided as they did. This outcome is based on legal rules or principles. A party who is dissatisfied with the outcome can appeal it to a higher court, which will require additional time and proceedings

(continued)

Table 4 (continued)

Legal procedure	Description
Judge trial	A judge hears the lawyers' arguments and witnesses' answers to the lawyers' questions and reviews physical evidence. Often, the clients testify. The plaintiff's (party making the claim) lawyer presents his/her case first and then the defendant's lawyer presents his/her case. After the evidence has been presented, the judge decides the outcome in private and announces it in writing, and explains why they decided as they did. This outcome is based on legal rules or principles. A party who is dissatisfied with the outcome can appeal it to a higher court, which will require additional time and proceedings
Binding arbitration	The clients and lawyers select an arbitrator (or group of arbitrators). Arbitrators are neutral third parties who are not actual judges, but who will have the authority to decide the outcome of the case. The clients will also decide among themselves what the rules for presenting evidence to the arbitrator will be. These rules are generally less formal than the rules used at trial. The lawyers, their clients, and client's witnesses present evidence. Often, the clients testify. After the evidence has been presented, the arbitrator(s) decide(s) the outcome of the case. This outcome is typically based on legal rules or principles, but it could be based on other rules or principles that the clients agree in advance should be used to decide the outcome, such as industry standards. Arbitrators typically report the outcome in writing, without explaining why they decided as they did. Because this type of arbitration is "binding," it is extremely difficult to appeal their decisions.
Nonbinding arbitration	The clients and lawyers select an arbitrator (or group of arbitrators). Arbitrators are neutral third parties who are not actual judges, but who will have the authority to decide the outcome of the case. The clients will also decide among themselves what the rules for presenting evidence to the arbitrator will be. These rules are generally less formal than the rules used at trial. The lawyers, their clients, and client's witnesses present evidence. Often, the clients testify. After the evidence has been presented, the arbitrator(s) decide(s) the outcome of the case. This outcome is typically based on legal rules or principles, but it could be based on other rules or principles that the clients agree in advance should be used to decide the outcome, such as industry standards. Arbitrators typically report the outcome in writing, without explaining the reasons why they decided as they did. Afterwards, because this type of arbitration is "nonbinding," either of the clients may reject the outcome and go to trial.

Note. Adapted from "The Psychology of Procedural Preference: How Litigants Evaluate Legal Procedures Ex Ante" by D. Shestowsky, 2014, *Iowa Law Review 99*(637), p. 701–03. Adapted with permission

opportunity, and conversely, those with less initial interest in having that experience were generally less pleased when they received it. In contrast, initial expectations for settlement did not predict post-experience evaluations, which were overall quite positive. This finding raises questions about what information and expectations litigants have regarding ADR procedures in the ex ante phase and whether they use different post-experience criteria to evaluate these procedures compared to adjudicative ones. An older longitudinal study produced similar findings that raised comparable questions (Shestowsky & Brett, 2008).

Figures 1 and 2 also show that litigants' post-experience evaluations of settlement procedures typically surpassed the midpoint for both satisfaction and fairness, even among those who initially expressed lower levels of enthusiasm for their settlement procedure. These findings document the fact that some individuals engage in settlement procedures that initially hold little appeal for them, even in the absence of court mandates requiring the use of such procedures. They also align with previous observations that disputants often view mediation favorably ex post even when they exhibit reluctance toward mediation ex ante (Tyler et al., 1999; Welsh, 2004). They demonstrate the applicability of this phenomenon to a broader range of settlement procedures: among those who reached a settlement, 59.9% utilized negotiation, 21.9% employed mediation, 7.0% used nonbinding arbitration, and 8% participated in judicial settlement conferences.

Ultimately, the "two psychologies" framework (Tyler et al., 1999), together with the results of longitudinal research on litigants' procedural preferences (Shestowsky & Brett, 2008; Shestowsky, 2014, 2020), converge to underscore a pivotal insight regarding litigants' preferences: understanding what drives individuals to engage in

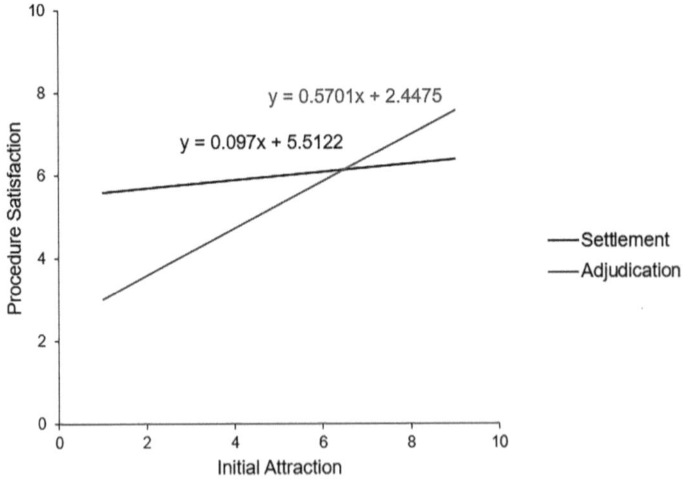

Fig. 1 Relation between initial attraction and ex post satisfaction as a function of procedure type. *Note.* $F(3, 160) = 6.67$, $p < 0.001$. Adapted from "Great Expectations? Comparing Litigants' Attitudes Before and After Using Legal Procedure" by D. Shestowsky, 2020, *Law and Human Behavior 44*(3), p. 185–6. Adapted with permission

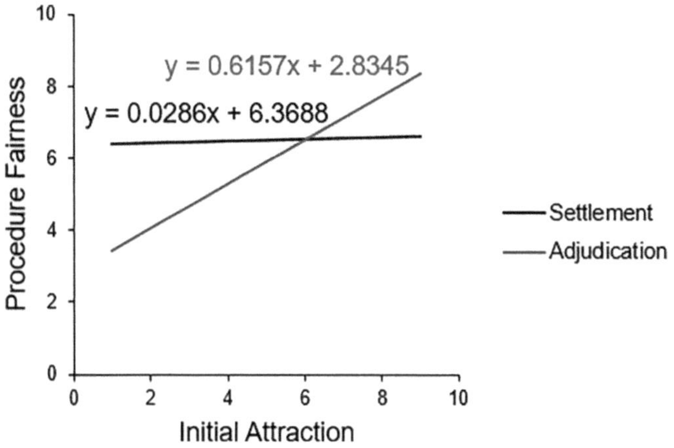

Fig. 2 Relation between initial attraction and ex post fairness as a function of procedure type. *Note.* $F(3, 156) = 8.85$, $p < 0.001$. Adapted from "Great Expectations? Comparing Litigants' Attitudes Before and After Using Legal Procedure" by D. Shestowsky, 2020, *Law and Human Behavior 44*(3), p. 185–6. Adapted with permission

ADR necessitates a concentrated analysis of their *ex ante* (as opposed to ex post) perspectives. Unfortunately, just as there are few studies exploring litigants' awareness or knowledge of ADR, there is also a notable dearth of projects examining their ex ante attitudes towards procedures.

Ex Ante Preferences for Procedures

While the research on ex ante procedural preferences is limited, the existing work offers valuable initial insights. One relevant study surveyed parties who had EEOC disputes pending before the Illinois Human Rights Commission ("EEOC study") (Stallworth & Stroh, 1996) after an initial investigation into their disputes (but not necessarily at the outset of their cases). The parties were asked to rate their interest in utilizing arbitration and mediation using scales that ranged from "very interested" to "not very interested." The findings revealed a significantly greater interest in using mediation.[17] The study also found that disputants were more inclined to submit their cases to ADR the more they perceived the current (non-ADR) process being used to handle their case as unfair, and the less time their case had already spent in the current process. However, perceptions of the ideal duration of the process did not predict their level of interest in using ADR.[18]

[17] Stallworth & Stroh at 36 (Table 2 reports the results of a statistical analysis concluding that interest in mediation was significantly stronger than interest in binding arbitration).

[18] The researchers also noted that a major obstacle to ADR use had to do with brokering or matching interest in ADR across the disputants within a given dispute. They reported that "in some 200 cases, one party expressed a significant willingness to use ADR and the other side would not

Another valuable avenue for understanding litigants' ex ante perceptions is through post-experience studies that inquire whether litigants would opt for the same procedure again in the future. While researchers commonly employ these questions to assess ex post satisfaction (i.e., how much disputants liked the procedure they utilized), at a glance, they also appear useful for estimating ex ante interest in ADR for future cases. These studies consistently reveal that individuals who use mediation tend to be willing to use it again (Clarke & Gordon, 1997; Jones & Bodtker, 1998; Wissler, 1997), with one studying explicitly comparing those who resolved their cases through mediation and trial and concluding that those who mediated were significantly more inclined to say they would use the same procedure in the future (Wissler, 1995).

A longitudinal study conducted by my research team (Shestowsky, 2016) is another relevant project. Our methods differed from that of the EEOC study (Stallworth & Stroh, 1996) along several dimensions: we recruited state court litigants, examined attitudes shortly after cases were filed, included litigants with a broader range of case types and from a greater number of jurisdictions. We also assessed attitudes toward a broader range of procedures: (1) attorneys negotiate without clients, (2) attorneys negotiate with clients present, (3) mediation, (4) judge decides without trial (e.g., motions/hearings), (5) jury trial, (6) judge trial, (7) binding arbitration, and (8) nonbinding arbitration. Table 4 provides the procedure descriptions that were provided to the litigants.

The mean attractiveness ratings for the procedures they evaluated are depicted in Fig. 3. By conducting HLM analyses, we discovered a three-way tie for litigants' favorite procedure: attorneys negotiate with clients present, mediation, and judge trial. Specifically, the mean attractiveness ratings for mediation, negotiation involving parties and their lawyers, and judge trial were statistically equivocal, and all three received significantly higher ratings than each of the other examined procedures. Thus, even under the umbrella of "ADR," some options were preferred to others. And, just like in the EEOC study, parties showed greater interest in mediation compared to binding arbitration. One implication is that litigants may be motivated to use ADR because they find some forms of it—namely negotiations that include the parties along with their lawyers, and mediation—*as* appealing as judge trials and significantly *more* appealing than jury trials.

The findings from studies on ex ante attitudes (Stallworth & Stroh, 1996; Shestowsky, 2016) appear to be in tension with those from laboratory experiments, suggesting that litigants initially favor adjudication over mediation (see Shestowsky, 2023). The reason for this disparity between laboratory and field studies remains unclear. The disparity may be attributable to methodological differences (i.e., laboratory studies generally involve evaluating hypothetical disputes) or due to historical factors (i.e., most field studies originated during a period when ADR was quite new to the court system) (Shestowsky, 2023). Whatever the reasons for this

agree" (p. 36). This observation highlights the point that typical cases are inherently dyadic in nature; if one party wants to use ADR, their ability to do so may hinge on the consent of the other party.

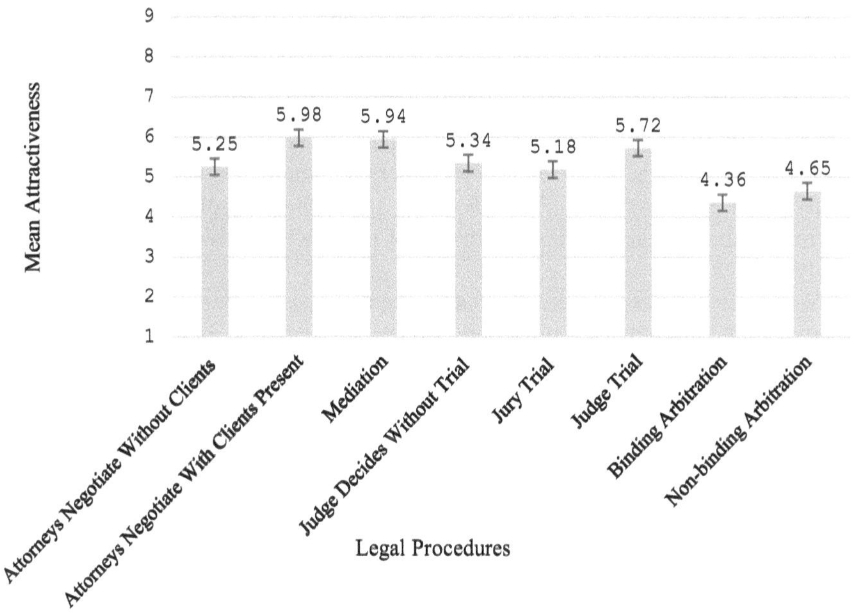

Fig. 3 Procedure attractiveness. *Note.* Adapted from "The Psychology of Procedural Preference: How Litigants Evaluate Legal Procedures Ex Ante" by D. Shestowsky, 2014, *Iowa Law Review* 99(637), p. 665. Adapted with permission

incongruity, it prompts reflection on the observed reluctance of disputants to engage in mediation. Why would disputants resist using mediation when it is generally appealing to those who use it? In our research, even though mediation emerged as a favorite procedure ex ante, fewer than one-third of litigants completing the ex post survey reported that they had even considered mediation[19] (Shestowsky, 2017). Negotiation emerged as the most frequently considered option, with 71.9% of litigants indicating it was contemplated for their case.[20] We also found that more cases in our sample resolved through negotiation (42%) than through any other procedure. One possible explanation, then, is that cases resolved through negotiation at an early stage, obviating the need to contemplate more complex procedures that entailed neutral third-party involvement.

[19] Litigants were asked, in free-response form, to list all the procedures that were contemplated for their case ("Before you started thinking about what procedure was best for your case, you or your lawyer probably thought about all the possible ways that could resolve your case. What are all the procedures you or your lawyer considered?") (Shestowsky, 2017). Research assistants noted each procedure that the litigants listed using the following categories: arbitration, mediation, negotiation, trial, hearing or motion, judicial settlement conference, dropping the case, or "other." For each option, we created a dichotomous variable for which litigants received a "1" if they had considered that procedure or a "0" if they had not.

[20] The two forms of arbitration had the lowest attractiveness ratings and the lowest contemplation levels.

Nonetheless, the findings indicating that litigants initially prefer certain ADR procedures over trial raise the question of what factors drive their interest in different procedures. Given that we worked with a reasonably large data set and surveyed litigants about numerous demographic, relational, and attitudinal issues, we were able to use multiple regression analysis to determine the factors that predicted their attraction to legal procedures, conducting a separate regression analysis for each procedure. Table 5, which presents the results for binding arbitration as an example, catalogues the list of predictor variables included in each analysis.[21]

When all the factors were evaluated simultaneously, the model significantly predicted attraction to each procedure, except for mediation and nonbinding arbitration. Several findings from the analyses of the six procedures for which the model reached significance are particularly noteworthy. First, different variables emerged as significant predictors for different procedures, suggesting that determining preferences for ADR procedures is not a one-size-fits-all endeavor. Second, numerous factors traditionally presumed to shape procedural preferences (and often studied in laboratory studies) seldom predicted attraction or failed to do so altogether. For instance, gender was associated with attraction to only two procedures: jury trial and binding arbitration. Age group was significantly related only to attraction to negotiations that involved clients and attorneys (i.e., those in older age groups liked this option less than younger ones, and vice versa). Litigant ethnicity did not predict attraction to any of the procedures. Court location was a significant predictor only for the jury trial (i.e., disputants with cases in California were less attracted to the jury trial than those with cases filed in Oregon). Role in the case was significant only for binding arbitration (i.e., litigants acting as both a plaintiff and defendant liked binding arbitration more than those acting only as plaintiffs). Notably, the frequently examined plaintiff-versus-defendant comparison revealed no significant differences in attraction to any of the procedures. Opposing party-type predicted attraction to the jury trial and binding arbitration only (i.e., compared to litigants who opposed individuals, those opposing groups or organizations liked the jury trial more, and those opposing companies liked binding arbitration more).

As concluded in the article reporting these results: "Even though previous studies found certain factors to be predictive when evaluated individually, the overall

[21] The results for binding arbitration, presented in Table 5, serves as an example. Litigants found this procedure more appealing when they were acting as both a plaintiff and defendant in their case (i.e., people involved with counterclaims) (compared to those acting as a plaintiff only), those who were repeat-litigants (versus first-time litigants) and who opposed a company (versus an individual). Gender also played a significant role—compared to men, women showing less interest in binding arbitration. Our analyses were exploratory in nature and investigated main effects only; future research should examine whether interactions between factors explain additional variability in attractiveness ratings.

Table 5 Factors predicting the attractiveness of binding arbitration

Predictor	B	SE	t	p	β
(intercept)	4.304	1.035	4.158	0.000	–
Sex: Female**	−1.525	0.338	−4.510	0.000	−0.304
Ethnicity: Nonwhite	0.733	0.462	1.587	0.114	0.101
Age group	−0.025	0.114	−0.218	0.829	−0.014
Party: Company	0.319	0.410	0.777	0.438	0.060
Party: Group/org.	0.220	0.569	0.387	0.699	0.025
Opp. Party: Company**	0.920	0.343	2.679	0.008	0.181
Opp. Party: Group/org	0.494	0.633	0.781	0.436	0.051
Relation. Before filing: Yes	−0.522	0.354	−1.474	0.142	−0.107
Importance of Fut. Relation.	0.084	0.133	0.632	0.528	0.041
Case type: Contract	−0.233	0.552	−0.422	0.673	−0.043
Case type: Employment	1.001	0.832	1.202	0.230	0.080
Case type: Property	−0.207	0.506	−0.408	0.684	−0.029
Case type: Other†	0.867	0.502	1.729	0.085	0.131
Case type: 2 or more	0.181	0.505	0.359	0.720	0.024
Insurance comp. Interest: Yes	0.217	0.415	0.524	0.601	0.044
P. Or D. Before*	0.703	0.331	2.121	0.035	0.143
Estimated trial win	−0.001	0.007	−0.159	0.874	−0.011
State: CA	0.005	0.479	0.011	0.991	0.001
State: UT	0.146	0.345	0.424	0.672	0.029
Role: Defendant	−0.207	0.361	−0.573	0.567	−0.041
Role: Both*	2.317	1.109	2.090	0.038	0.132
Impression of the court	−0.018	0.093	−0.197	0.844	−0.012

** $p < 0.01$ * $p < 0.05$ † $p < 0.10$
Note. Adapted from "The Psychology of Procedural Preference: How Litigants Evaluate Legal Procedures Ex Ante" by D. Shestowsky, 2014, *Iowa Law Review 99*(637), p. 710. Adapted with permission

pattern suggests that when a multitude of factors are considered simultaneously, relatively few may actually be associated with attraction for procedures" (Shestowsky, 2014, p. 687). This takeaway is likely to surprise lawyers and court personnel who have strong views regarding the factors that motivate interest in ADR and which procedure is likely to appeal to "a certain kind of litigant" or "someone with a certain kind of case" (Shestowsky, 2014, p. 687). Thus, this work serves as an illustration of how important it is for lawyers and court personnel to rely on empirical research to anticipate litigants' perspectives on ADR when they educate and counsel them on their options or design ADR programs. Additionally, it can help lawyers anticipate potential resistance from opposing parties with certain characteristics or attitudes when proposing specific procedures. An essential takeaway is for legal practitioners to examine the factors driving interest in each procedure individually, acknowledging that these determinants often vary between ADR procedures.

Role of Self-Interest and Control

Having addressed the fundamentals of disputants' procedural preferences concerning ADR, I will introduce an additional layer of analysis: the influence of contextual factors on these preferences. The prevailing literature indicates that two factors—self-interest and control—exert particularly meaningful effects on disputants' procedural preferences.

The "two psychologies" framework established by Tyler and his colleagues (Tyler et al., 1999) suggests that, at the outset of litigation, individuals prefer procedures that might advance their self-interest, particularly with respect to material outcomes. Accordingly, one might hypothesize that litigants who are more confident in their likelihood of prevailing at trial would display a stronger attraction to adjudicative procedures. This hypothesis was tested in one of my longitudinal studies (Shestowsky, 2016). In an ex ante survey, litigants provided a 0–100% estimate of their chances of winning their case at trial. This variable was subsequently incorporated into multiple regression analyses aimed at predicting initial attraction to each examined procedure, as discussed *supra*. As anticipated, we found a significant positive relationship between litigants' confidence ratings and their level of attraction to the three court-connected procedures that necessarily entail a third party deciding the outcome under the law: jury trials, judge trials, and judicial decisions without trial (e.g., motions or hearings). This pattern aligns with the "two psychologies" framework: the greater the confidence litigants had in winning at trial, the more they favored procedures that might facilitate achieving the outcomes they believe they deserve, reflecting a self-interested approach. Notably, the evaluations may also have been influenced by egocentric bias[22]—24% believed they had a 100% chance of winning; 57% believed they had at least a 90% chance.[23]

In addition to self-interest, control has been a recurring theme in ex ante preference research (Peirce et al., 1993; Shestowsky & Brett, 2008). When *ex ante* attitudes toward procedures for *legal* disputes are studied in the laboratory, control tends to emerge as a dominant basis for explaining litigants' preferences (Shestowsky, 2016, p. 800; Lind & Tyler, 1988, pg. 830–32; *see also* Conlon et al., 1989,

---

[22] In one example of a laboratory study demonstrating this bias in the litigation context, participants were assigned to the role of plaintiff or defendant and asked to estimate what a judge would award based on the same information. They then negotiated the resolution of the case. Regardless of their role in the case, participants believed that a judge would more likely rule in their favor, suggesting that, on average, judgments of how much they would get from a judge if negotiations failed were inflated relative to what objective assessments would suggest (Loewenstein et al., 1993).

[23] We were unable to directly determine whether these confidence statistics reflected egocentric bias versus us having a sample of litigants with particularly strong legal cases. However, a follow-up analysis pointed toward the former explanation as more likely. Specifically, when we examined the outcomes of litigants who resolved their cases through adjudication by comparing the proportions of winners and losers based on court dispositions, the difference in proportions between the "winning" group (56.8%, $n = 42$) and the "losing" group (43.2%, $n = 32$) was not statistically significant ($z = 1.66$, $p = 0.10$). This result suggests that the group was not skewed in regard to case strength.

p. 1087).[24] This observation found support in two longitudinal field studies (Shestowsky, 2016; Shestowsky & Brett, 2008). In both studies, litigants evaluated 14 unlabeled procedure characteristics or "feature options" falling in three categories: (1) who could determine the outcome of the dispute; (2) how the process would evolve; and (3) the substantive rules or norms that would be used (e.g., would the law apply or could parties determine the rules or principles that should be used to decide the outcome?). The options were inspired by previous laboratory research in the procedural justice arena but modified and expanded to reflect options available to contemporary litigants. A summary of these characteristics appears in Table 6. Litigants rated how attractive each characteristic was for their case, using scales from 1 to 9 (1 = *not at all attractive*; 9 = *extremely attractive*).

In both studies, factor analysis was used to distill patterns in ratings, and both studies reached the same conclusion. Although, theoretically, litigants could have categorized or compared the characteristics along many dimensions, two factors clearly emerged as best explaining their ratings, and both related to control: attraction to litigant control and attraction to third-party control.

When we delved deeper in one study (Shestowsky, 2016) by creating separate means for ratings that fell under each factor (Table 7 catalogues the items included in these means) and comparing them, we found that litigants significantly preferred third-party control to litigant control ex ante. We also found that, paradoxically, they also evaluated procedures that theoretically granted parties significant control—such as negotiation involving clients and lawyers, and mediation—as highly appealing ex ante. To explore these puzzling results, we investigated the relation between their mean ratings for attraction to third-party control and their attraction ratings for the three procedures that were their overall favorites (i.e., mediation, attorneys negotiate with clients present, and judge trial) and found a significant positive correlation for each procedure. Since negotiation involves no third parties and mediators lack authority over case outcomes, this pattern may reflect a misinterpretation of the nature of these procedures. This interpretation of the mediation correlation aligns with findings from analyses of mediation center intake call transcripts, which suggest that callers often misunderstand mediation and frequently decline mediation services after learning that mediators are impartial (Stokoe, 2013). Such outcomes underscore the complexities underlying litigants' procedural preferences and suggest that these preferences may be shaped, at least in part, by misunderstandings.

In summary, procedural preference research offers insights into the role that preferences play in motivating litigant interest in ADR. It suggests that several ADR procedures, notably mediation and negotiation involving lawyers and clients, stand as strong competitors against traditional adjudication. But procedures vary in the factors that predict how attractive litigants find them ex ante, and several factors that

[24] Although procedural justice studies have generated other theories to explain why disputants evaluate procedures as they do, they generally stem from research on ex post attitudes or contexts other than legal disputes, such as interpersonal conflicts that fail to rise to the level of legal claims, including intra-organizational conflicts (Shestowsky & Brett, 2008).

Table 6 Procedure characteristics evaluated by participants

	Characteristic name	Characteristic definition
1	Third party decides	A neutral third **person** will decide the outcome of the case.
2	Group decides	A neutral **group of people** will decide the outcome of the case.
3	Parties veto third-party suggestion	A neutral third **person** will suggest how the case should be resolved, and the other party and I can either agree to accept that suggestion as the outcome, or either of us can reject it.
4	Parties decide using third-party help but no suggestion	A neutral third **person** will help me and the other party decide the outcome of the case ourselves, without making suggestions as to how the case should be resolved.
5	Parties decide lawyers can advise	The other party and I will decide what the outcome of the case will be ourselves, **without** the advice of a neutral third person, but, if we want to, we can get advice and suggestions from our own lawyer before we decide which outcome to ultimately choose.
6	Parties present to third party	Both the other party and I will attend the procedure and each of us will present evidence favorable to our own position to a neutral third person.
7	Lawyers to third party no parties	The other party and I will each have our own lawyer. Our lawyer will present evidence favorable to our own position to a neutral third person. **Neither** the other party **nor** I will attend the procedure.
8	Lawyers to third party with parties	The other party and I will each have our own lawyer. Our lawyer will present evidence favorable to our own position to a neutral third person. **Both** the other party **and** I **will** attend the procedure along with our lawyers.
9	Parties speak to third party when directed	The other party and I will be able to speak during the procedure **only** when a neutral third person or our lawyers direct us to do so.
10	Speak freely to each other	Both the other party and I will be able to speak freely to each other during the procedure whenever we like, and as informally as we like.
11	Speak freely to each other and third party	Both the other party and I will be able to speak freely to each other during the procedure whenever we like, and as informally as we like and speak to the neutral third person as freely and informally as we like as well.
12	Court rules	The outcome will be decided using the same rules or principles that apply in a court of law.
13	Rules by parties	The other party and I will decide what rules or principles should be used to decide the outcome.
14	Third-party rules	A neutral third person will decide what rules or principles should be used to decide the outcome.

Note. Adapted from "How Litigants Evaluate the characteristics of Legal Procedures: A Multi-Court Empirical Study" by D. Shestowsky, 2016, *UC Davis Law Review 49*(793), p. 839–41(footnotes). Adapted with permission

have theoretical support through individual laboratory studies do not deliver the same results when combined and analyzed in the real-world context. The literature also suggests that third-party control and self-interest, which initially emerged as significant factors in laboratory studies, play key roles in early stages of litigation: litigants evaluate procedure characteristics using a control framework and tend to prefer third-party control. These findings suggest that effective client-centered

Table 7 Standardized factor loadings from higher-order confirmatory factor analysis

Factors	B	S.E.	Z	P
Factor 1—Parties control process and rules				
Speak freely to each other	0.91	0.02	54.76	<0.01
Speak freely to each other and third party	0.95	0.02	59.37	<0.01
Rules by parties	0.53	0.04	13.75	<0.01
Factor 2—Parties decide with advice or help				
Parties veto third-party suggestion	0.53	0.05	11.71	<0.01
Parties decide using third-party help but no suggestion	0.82	0.04	19.64	<0.01
Parties decide lawyers can advise	0.60	0.04	13.59	<0.01
Factor 3—Process managed by others				
Lawyers to third party with parties	0.89	0.07	12.32	<0.01
Parties speak to third party when directed	0.62	0.06	10.82	<0.01
Factor 4—Third-party process focus and decision control				
Third-party decides	0.65	0.05	12.82	<0.01
Group decides	0.58	0.05	10.96	<0.01
Parties present to third party	0.62	0.05	11.84	<0.01
Litigant control (highest order)				
Factor 1—Parties control process and rules	0.73	0.04	20.65	<0.01
Factor 2—Parties decide with advice or help	0.73	0.04	20.65	<0.01
Third-party control (highest order)				
Factor 3—Process managed by others	0.68	0.05	12.98	<0.01
Factor 4—Third-party process focus and decision control	0.68	0.05	12.98	<0.01

Note. Adapted from "How Litigants Evaluate the characteristics of Legal Procedures: A Multi-Court Empirical Study" by D. Shestowsky, 2016, *UC Davis Law Review 49*(793), p. 839–41(footnotes). Adapted with permission

counseling might involve contrasting procedures in terms of the control they offer to parties versus third parties. Additionally, research points to the possibility that litigants' initial attraction to mediation may stem from a misunderstanding about the nature of control in this procedure, underscoring the importance of effective litigant education. The observation that settlement procedures are often perceived more favorably ex post, even by litigants who were initially less inclined toward them, raises important questions about litigants' initial understanding of settlement options, the sources informing their attitudes, and why initial attraction ratings tend to more accurately predict ex post assessments for adjudicative procedures than for settlement options.

Decision Criteria: The Gap between Preference and Use

The foregoing findings lead to an important question regarding the connection between preferences and choice: when multiple procedures align with a litigant's preferences for a given dispute, what criteria guide their decisions regarding which procedure to use?[25] Intriguingly, despite evidence suggesting that litigants misunderstand ADR procedures (Shestowsky, 2016; Stokoe, 2013), they capably recognize that their procedural preferences alone will not determine the procedures they will ultimately use. The outcomes of one of my longitudinal field studies (Shestowsky, 2014) underscore this point effectively. Litigants were presented with the same list of procedures they had previously rated for attractiveness, but this time, they were asked to assess these procedures in terms of "how likely [they thought they] were to use them at some point for their case" (1 = *not at all likely*; 9 = *extremely likely*). We then conducted paired t-tests to evaluate differences between attractiveness ratings and anticipated use ratings for each procedure individually.

The results, depicted graphically in Fig. 4, revealed two key findings. First, for every procedure—except for "attorney negotiation without clients"—the attractiveness of the procedure significantly differed from its expected use. The exception for "attorney negotiation without clients" is logical, as it is the only procedure we examined that does not require the participation or consent of any party other than the litigant's own representative (i.e., their attorney). This unique characteristic likely enables litigants to utilize this procedure precisely to the extent they prefer it. The second finding was that, for each procedure (except for "attorney negotiation without clients"), the observed difference followed the same pattern: litigants consistently rated procedures as more attractive than they expected to use them. This consistent trend suggests that litigants recognize that factors beyond their personal preferences will influence the procedures they ultimately utilize.

To determine what these factors might be, litigants were asked the following question at the start of their case (i.e., in the "ex ante" survey): "How will you decide which procedure(s) to try? That is, what factors will you consider or weigh when deciding which procedure(s) to use?" This question was posed with the understanding that some litigants would utilize ADR, others would opt for adjudication, and some might employ both methods. By soliciting responses prospectively, we aimed to mitigate the potential influence of hindsight bias (Fischhoff, 1975). Several law students coded the responses to this open-ended question. The factors and their frequencies appear in Table 8.

[25] Peirce and his colleagues (1993) conducted laboratory studies on the relation between preference and choice. In one study, participants were randomly assigned to the role of either complainant or respondent in a landlord-tenant dispute. They subsequently reviewed the facts of the case, rated their attraction to various procedures, and rank-ordered these procedures based on their attractiveness. To accomplish this task, participants evaluated unlabeled descriptions of each procedure; for instance, they read a brief description of mediation without being informed that it was "mediation." They were also led to believe that they would engage in whatever procedure they indicated as their first choice, with a law professor available to serve as a third party. The researchers operationalized "choice" by rank-ordering the attraction ratings: the procedure that participants indicted as their first choice was assumed to reflect the procedure they would choose. Ultimately, they found that while some procedures were popular, their popularity did not translate into being chosen to resolve their case. For example, mediation and negotiation were tied for having the highest mean attraction ratings, but negotiation was their clear first "choice."

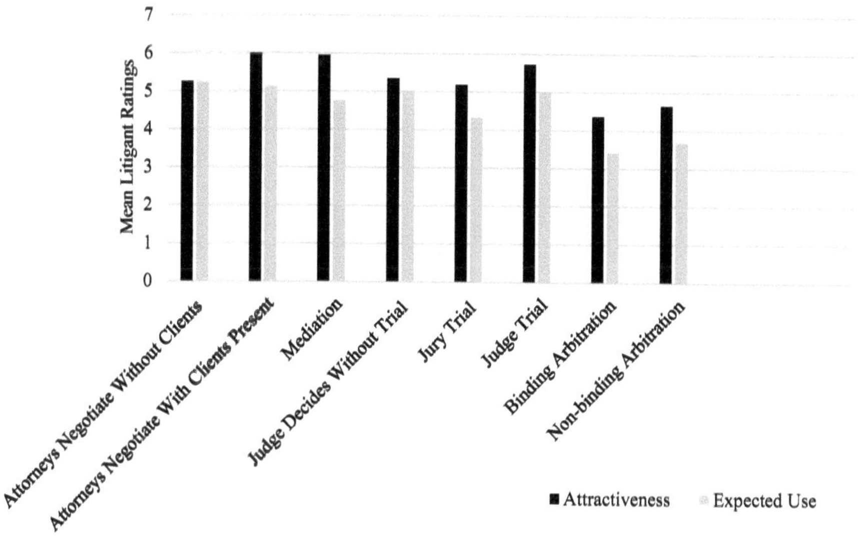

Fig. 4 Attractiveness vs. expected use. *Note.* Comparison of mean litigant attraction to, and expected use of, legal procedures. Error bars are SEs of the ratings. Litigants rated their attraction to, and expected use, of each procedure using 9-point Likert scales. Adapted from "The Psychology of Procedural Preference: How Litigants Evaluate Legal Procedures Ex Ante" by D. Shestowsky, 2014, *Iowa Law Review 99*(637), p. 669. Adapted with permission

The most notable pattern that emerged concerned the role they envisioned their attorneys would play—over one-quarter (25.3%) reported that they expected their lawyer to influence their decisions (Shestowsky, 2018). Representative examples include: "I would rely on counsel"; "based on discussions [with my] attorney and his advice"; "I will ask my attorney which to choose."[26] The next most common responses reflected an interest in saving cost and time and desire to use the law.[27] An overt desire to choose based on self-interest rounded out the top five, akin to what the "two psychologies" framework would anticipate. Prototypical responses included, "my ability to win," and "whichever procedure I feel that would benefit me—the victim." Even a desire to use the law could be interpreted as falling under "self-serving," particularly when viewed alongside the data we gathered that suggested that most litigants thought they had an excellent chance of winning their case in court[28] (i.e., an institution that is obligated to follow the law) (Shestowsky, 2014).

[26] Importantly, these data were collected at the start of litigation but not necessarily before they discussed their case with an attorney.

[27] Some participants (7.5%) mentioned both cost and time. A chi-square test assessing the dependence between whether time was listed (yes vs. no) and whether cost was listed (yes vs. no) revealed that if one of these factors was listed, the other was significantly more likely to be listed, $\chi^2(1) = 82.90, p < 0.001$.

[28] Twenty-four percent believed they had a 100% chance of winning; 57% believed they had at least a 90% chance.

Table 8 Factors litigants plan to consider

Factor	N	%
Lawyers advise or decide	62	25.3
Minimize economic cost	46	18.8
Minimize time	34	13.9
Use law	32	13.1
Self-serving	31	12.7
Assess other party	18	7.3
Fairness	16	6.5
Strength of case	13	5.3
Representation	13	5.3
Decision based on evidence	12	4.9
Neutrality	12	4.9
Case at hand	11	4.5
Opposing party preferences	10	4.1
Tell story	10	4.1
Allows party participants	9	3.7
Complexity of case	8	3.3
Wants settlement	8	3.3
Info on decision-maker	8	3.3
Minimize contact	6	2.4
Value of case	6	2.4
Wants bindingness	6	2.4
Inputs from others	5	2.0
Wants appealability	4	1.6
Informality	4	1.6
Other	76	31.0

Note. Reported percentage based on n = 245 because participants those who gave a single nonresponsive answer by indicating any of the following were excluded: The question was not applicable (n = 3), they did not understand the question (n = 1), they did not know what factors they would consider (n = 13), they have no choice/say (n = 12), or they already had a procedure in mind (n = 31)."Other" includes any response for which n < 4. Adapted from "Inside the mind of the client: An analysis of litigants' decision criteria for choosing procedures" by D. Shestowsky, 2018, *Conflict Resolution Quarterly* *36*(69), p.77. Adapted with permission

Although some litigants mentioned factors that were related to procedural justice, such as voice (i.e., "a desire to tell their story"), the percentage of litigants suggesting these factors would affect their procedural choices was small, just as the "two psychologies" framework would predict.[29]

When we interviewed litigants at the conclusion of their cases (i.e., the "ex post" survey), we revisited this issue by asking them why they used the procedures they ultimately used (Shestowsky, 2018). Several factors mentioned in the ex ante survey re-emerged as reasons for choosing the procedures that ultimately resolved their cases as well as for the procedures they used prior to that procedure (e.g., using negotiation, then mediation). Results are reported in Table 9. Once again, the predominant response underscored a reliance on attorneys, with 20.2% of litigants indicating that their lawyer influenced the selection of their final procedure and 27.1% stating the same for earlier procedures.[30] While some litigants described engaging in extensive discussions with their attorneys, others simply deferred to their legal counsel, stating reasons such as "the lawyer just handled it for me" or "my attorney decided." This finding aligns with earlier work on domestic relations cases suggesting that, compared to disputants who refused to mediate, a higher percentage of disputants who accepted opportunities to mediate reported that their lawyers were enthusiastic about mediation (Pearson et al., 1982).

The next most-cited factors on the list were time and cost, which mirrored the appearance of these factors in the top three criteria from the ex ante list. The prevalence of cost is notable given that empirical evaluations of parties' post-experience ratings of fairness and satisfaction tend to show little relationship to the financial cost associated with resolving disputes, and the research on time to resolution is mixed (Shestowsky, 2023). Additionally, selecting a procedure based on its potential to yield a favorable outcome ranked among the top five ex post criteria, reflecting the intention to make self-serving decisions regarding procedural choices that was observed in the ex ante survey.

The longitudinal design of our methodology enabled us to investigate the temporal consistency of the top five decision criteria (Shestowsky, 2018). We accomplished this task through chi-square analyses that tested the dependence between participants listing a criterion ex ante and subsequently indicating (ex post) that it was used to determine the procedures they experienced. Several intriguing results emerged from this analysis.

[29] Litigants appear to not realize that the other party might influence which procedures they use, which suggests that they may not appreciate the need to negotiate the use of some of these procedures by the other party or recognize that the other party can essentially force them into using trial by refusing to settle.

[30] We did not investigate litigants' views regarding why their lawyers made those procedure recommendations. This topic would be a valuable focus for future research, complementing existing studies that have examined why lawyers advocate for arbitration and mediation. In other words, it remains unclear whether the reasons lawyers report in surveys for recommending certain procedures align with the explanations they provide to their clients or are fully understood by those clients. Ideally, research filling this gap in the literature would be conducted on lawyer-client dyads to capture both perspectives on the same cases.

Table 9 Reasons for using procedure, reported ex post

	Procedure that ended case		Earlier procedure(s)	
Factor	N	%	N	%
Encouraged by own lawyer	40	20.2	54	27.1
Time efficiency	31	15.7	23	11.6
Cost effective	30	15.2	18	9.0
Likely to provide favorable outcome	22	11.1	17	8.5
Encouraged by outside party	20	10.1	18	9
Desire to avoid court	17	8.6	15	7.5
Opposing party's failure to participate	13	6.6	7	3.5
Seemed like only remaining option	11	5.6	5	2.5
Logical next step	10	5.0	9	4.5
Required by contract or norm	–	–	8	4.0
Seemed relatively easy	10	5.1	6	3.0
Seemed like only reasonable option	7	3.5	–	–
Fairness	6	3.0	–	–
Required by court	6	3.0	5	2.5
Encouraged by court	5	2.5	–	–
Felt trial was unnecessary	5	2.5	–	–
Desire for third party involvement	4	2.0	–	–
Does not know	6	3.0	1	0.5
Unclear response	20	10.1	29	14.6
Other	6	3.0	9	4.5

Note. For the question regarding the procedure that ended the case, N = 198. For the question regarding earlier procedures, N = 199. Adapted from "Inside the mind of the client: An analysis of litigants' decision criteria for choosing procedures" by D. Shestowsky, 2018, *Conflict Resolution Quarterly 36*(69), p.79. Adapted with permission

First, individuals who expressed an intention to rely on their attorney's judgment in deciding which procedure to utilize were significantly more likely to report that they ultimately relied on their attorneys for decision-making (Shestowsky, 2018). In fact, they were 2.35 times more likely to report using a procedure because of their lawyer's input. This analysis, conducted only on those who had legal representation, suggests the powerful role lawyers play in determining ADR usage. Similarly, participants who initially stated that cost would be a determining factor in their decisions were 2.22 times more likely to report having made decisions based on cost. Thus, for many, access to free or inexpensive mediation and arbitration services might motivate ADR use, provided they are aware of these options. In contrast, litigants initially listing time or the pursuit of self-serving options[31] as selection criteria were no more likely to report having chosen procedures for these reasons than those who did not list these criteria initially. And yet comparable percentages of litigants

[31] For the analysis, we compared references falling in the self-serving (ex ante) category with those included in the likely to provide favorable outcome (ex post) category.

listed these as criteria at both timepoints. Thus, the pursuit of self-serving outcomes and time savings appear to be more flexible goals that change over the trajectory of disputes. Future research should examine whether lawyers influence these shifts in priorities, and if so, how.

The principal conclusion from this line of litigant survey research is evident: for represented litigants, lawyers play a significant role in shaping decisions about what procedures they use. And this conclusion aligns with earlier research that surveyed lawyers. Wissler, for example, found that attorney education in, and experience with, ADR significantly predicted their likelihood of advising clients to utilize it (Wissler, 2002a). In her work, the variable that best distinguished lawyers who recommended ADR and those who did not was whether the attorney had previously used ADR in their capacity as counsel (Wissler, 2002a). The second most influential factor was whether the attorney had served as a neutral, followed by whether they had participated in continuing education ("CLE") courses on dispute resolution. Experience with ADR procedures was a more influential predictor than taking courses in ADR. As Wissler has argued, one way to increase attorneys' willingness to recommend ADR to clients is to mandate their exposure to it (Wissler, 2002b).

In a separate survey investigation by Wissler, litigators reported that they discussed the potential use of voluntary ADR in approximately 78% of their filed civil cases (Wissler, 2004). Taken together, the extent of judicial encouragement of ADR, attorney's knowledge and view of ADR, and attorney discussions with clients and opposing counsel explained 50% of the variation in the frequency of ADR use, further suggesting the influence that lawyers have in shaping ADR use (Wissler, 2004). While judicial encouragement was the strongest examined predictor of ADR discussions and ADR use (Wissler, 2004), judicial encouragement and attorneys' knowledge and views of ADR mainly exerted their influence on ADR usage indirectly, through their impact on how much attorneys discussed ADR with clients and opposing counsel, which in turn strongly related to ADR utilization (Wissler, 2004). These findings suggest that court rules that encourage or require attorneys to discuss ADR with their clients and opposing counsel hold potential for motivating voluntary ADR use (Wissler, 2004; Shestowsky, 2017; McAdoo & Hinshaw, 2002; Wissler & Dauber, 2005).

More recently, as procedures have transitioned to online formats, such as text and video, researchers have begun to examine how lawyers and disputants perceive these different modalities (Eisenberg et al., 2023; Shack & Shestowsky, 2024; Wolfs et al., 2024). Consistent with the field research indicating that lawyers influence their clients' choices among procedures, laboratory research has shown that participants' interest in different modalities for mediation are significantly altered by the recommendations of their (hypothetical) attorneys (Wolfs et al., 2024). This work on mediation lays the foundation for additional studies that compare litigants' interest in, and reaction to, different formats for a wider range of ADR procedures.

In summary, survey studies of both lawyers and litigants highlight the crucial role that lawyers play in encouraging litigants to consider using ADR and in determining its utilization. At the start of their cases, litigants primarily anticipate relying on their attorney's guidance to decide which procedures to employ. Litigants are unlikely to initiate discussions about ADR on their own (McAdoo & Hinshaw, 2002), and, on their part, attorneys are more likely to initiate ADR discussions if they have prior experience with ADR or believe judges encourage its use (Wissler, 2004). Consequently, many represented litigants' exposure to ADR will largely be contingent upon their lawyers' familiarity with these procedures and their awareness of the court's interest in promoting ADR.

Research also suggests that some litigants will choose procedures that seem self-serving, highlighting the importance of directing them to procedures that will best serve their needs and ensuring they understand how they could meet those needs. Litigants also strive to choose procedures that minimize time or financial investment (Shestowsky, 2018), which underscores the importance of informing litigants of free or low-cost court ADR opportunities.[32] For unrepresented litigants, courts and legal aid organizations can play a pivotal role in ensuring informed decision-making regarding their options. For represented litigants, lawyers play a crucial role in guiding their procedural choices.

Overall, the interaction between litigants and their attorneys is critical in shaping the utilization of ADR, emphasizing the need for attorneys to be well-versed in these procedures so that they can effectively counsel their clients. When attorneys lack sufficient knowledge of ADR, are unable to effectively communicate options to their clients, fail to accurately understand their clients' goals and whether those goals are best served by ADR procedures, or lack the requisite skills to represent clients in the procedures they use, a litigant's reliance on legal counsel may ultimately prove detrimental to their pursuit of civil justice. Unfortunately, lawyers do often misunderstand their clients' interests, goals, and priorities. Empirical analyses comparing lawyers and litigants suggest they often operate in parallel worlds, and that the interests and values that clients bring to litigation deviate from what lawyers believe those interests and values are or should be (O'Barr & Conley, 1988; Relis, 2007; Relis, 2009; Sarat & Felstiner, 1997). Research on lawyer–client dyads specifically designed to explore how they discuss and evaluate ADR options is long overdue (Shestowsky, 2023).

Conclusion

Research indicates that the civil trial is approaching extinction, with the rise of ADR contributing to its decline. However, the complete elimination of the civil trial is neither inevitable nor desirable. Decisions to pursue adjudication are often rational and justified. For instance, adjudication through trial is ideal when litigants' interests are best served by publicly airing their grievances or establishing legal precedents that will guide future similar cases. When litigants opt for adjudication

[32] Relatedly, the absence of third-party costs associated with negotiation may explain its high prevalence (Shestowsky, 2020).

because it aligns optimally with their objectives, it is reassuring to note that research demonstrates a positive association between an initial interest in adjudication and subsequent satisfaction with this method of dispute resolution.

Conversely, the goals and needs of many litigants may be more appropriately addressed through ADR, whether due to the diversity of outcome possibilities it offers, its process-related advantages, or a combination of both. Consequently, a resistance or refusal to engage in ADR can result in some litigants having suboptimal experiences within the civil justice system. Delayed decisions regarding the utilization of ADR can lead to wasted time and financial resources, which many litigants aim to avoid when selecting procedures (Shestowsky, 2018). Moreover, access to alternatives to trial may encourage individuals to pursue legal claims they might otherwise abandon, thereby enhancing access to justice. These realities underscore the importance of understanding the factors that predict ADR use and the barriers to its utilization.

A comprehensive review of the relevant psychological literature suggests that three factors play a key role in motivating ADR use: laypeople's awareness of ADR options, litigants' preferences for procedures, and the selection criteria employed by litigants when choosing procedures. Field research on litigants has documented a relationship between the awareness of ADR options and procedure consideration for some procedures (Shestowsky, 2017), an association between preferences and expected use (Shestowsky, 2014), and the selection criteria that litigants use to decide among procedures (Shestowsky, 2018).

With respect to knowledge, it is misguided to assume that laypeople know what ADR is or that they are aware of all their ADR options, even when courts make procedures readily available (Shestowsky, 2017). The latter is a concern even for represented litigants (Shestowsky, 2017). Public education campaigns aimed at increasing general knowledge about ADR might ease the road to ADR use. These initiatives could be undertaken as a public service by national organizations, such as the American Bar Association, state-wide bodies, or providers of ADR services. Furthermore, courts should adopt a proactive role in educating their constituents about ADR through their websites and public outreach efforts (Shestowsky, 2017). These endeavors should educate them on what different procedures entail, including differences in how parties or third parties control the process, outcomes, and rules that shape the outcome. They should also emphasize that litigants tend to evaluate settlement procedures favorably ex post, even when they do not find them very appealing ex ante (Shestowsky, 2020). Importantly, these education efforts should be specifically tailored for laypeople who may have limited understanding of the legal system, ensuring that the language used is appropriately clear and accessible to this audience. Ideally, these initiatives would also empower laypeople to initiate conversations about ADR with their lawyers and foster an understanding of their right to influence the procedures used to handle their dispute, subject to any contractual or other constraints.

Providing litigants with information that highlights the generally positive evaluations of ADR procedures from past participants can be instrumental in piquing their interest. Data reflecting the satisfaction levels of participants from specific programs being promoted to them could be particularly compelling. Furthermore, it is essential to inform litigants that their interest in adjudication—rather than ADR—often correlates with their case strength perceptions (Shestowsky, 2014), which are frequently infected by egocentric bias and therefore may be inflated and unwarranted. Attorneys would serve their clients well by having discussions with clients, early in litigation, that include a candid assessment of the strengths and weaknesses of their case, under the applicable law (Lande, 2022). While mitigating egocentric bias presents a challenge, research suggests that requiring individuals to explicitly articulate the weaknesses in their cases can serve as an effective strategy (Babcock & Loewenstein, 1997). This approach encourages individuals to confront the potential flaws in their legal positions, thereby fostering a more balanced consideration of options that include settlement alternatives.

Courts should undertake their responsibility to educate both unrepresented and represented litigants by providing informational pamphlets, establishing helpdesk or hotline services, and sponsoring informational meetings about ADR options (Shestowsky, 2017). Having judges conduct these informational meetings may be particularly influential (Wissler, 2004). To minimize the high financial costs associated with the litigation discovery process (Hannaford-Agor, 2013), and to avoid escalation of commitment biases (Brockner et al., 1979), it is important that these communications take place early in the dispute trajectory, before litigants and their attorneys become too committed to a particular pathway for the case. Courts can also require lawyers to counsel their clients on ADR options (Shestowsky, 2017) and clearly articulate judicial endorsement of ADR in cases where it is deemed appropriate.

Regarding litigant preferences, it is essential that courts offer ADR procedures that appeal to the people whose needs they are meant to serve: the litigants. Some courts already strive to improve the appeal of their ADR offerings by surveying litigants who have used their program to determine how to improve it from the litigant perspective. They should also survey litigants who did not utilize their programs to understand their reasoning (Shestowsky, 2017). If litigants were aware of their programs but chose not to use them, courts should explore ways to make ADR options more appealing and address any institutional or systemic barriers revealed by their survey data (Shestowsky, 2017). Courts might discover that litigants were not aware of the programs for which they were eligible (Shestowsky, 2017). In such instances, obtaining feedback to improve the dissemination of information about ADR options would be critically important. Furthermore, courts should survey lawyers to assess how they are describing ADR options to their clients and to gather their feedback on court ADR programs. This information could help illuminate potential impediments to litigants' understanding of, or enthusiasm for, ADR generally and court ADR programs specifically. Surveying both lawyers and litigants is critical given the role that lawyers play in motivating procedure selection (Shestowsky, 2018).

The preceding synthesis of the literature raises pressing questions about what attorneys communicate about ADR to their clients and how they communicate that information. Specifically, what extent and type of education do attorneys provide regarding ADR (when they provide it)? What efforts do they make to mitigate clients' egocentric biases prior to the discussion and consideration of procedures? Do they propose specific reference points or decision criteria for choosing amongst options? Furthermore, to what extent do attorneys impose their own procedural preferences onto their clients? Is their influence largely inadvertent, the result of deliberate persuasion strategies, or due to their clients' deference to them as authoritative figures? Despite the routine nature of decision-making regarding procedural choices in litigation and the presumably common lawyer–client discussions about these choices (Shestowsky, 2024), there is a conspicuous lack of research on these critical issues. What *is* clear is that investigations into these issues should be conducted using a dyadic approach, studying lawyer–client pairs. It would involve assessing what lawyers communicate to their clients, why they convey it, and how they convey it. And it would involve determining what clients understand from these communications, how this understanding impacts their decision-making, and why.

This line of research could significantly aid lawyers in cultivating a more nuanced, research-informed approach to client counseling. The existing body of research provides a useful starting point. For example, lawyers could orient clients early in their case to the expected relational and fair treatment advantages of settlement procedures. This strategy might help clients appreciate how disputants often prioritize relational and fair treatment criteria when evaluating procedures ex post, which could, in turn, increase their initial interest in ADR. By emphasizing how ADR procedures tend to be associated with favorable ex post evaluations, litigants may be better equipped to anticipate their satisfaction with ADR, thereby reducing the discrepancies in their perceptions of settlement procedures when considered ex ante versus ex post.

However, when litigants are disinterested in the anticipated ex post relational or fair treatment benefits associated with settlement procedures, directing them to ADR procedures designed to save time and money may garner their interest. But utilizing ADR does not necessarily guarantee savings in time or money. Much depends on the design of the court's ADR program and the attorney's approach to case management, particularly concerning the prioritization of early settlements (Lande, 2008, 2022) and the curtailment of expenses associated with the discovery process prior to employing ADR (Hannaford-Agor, 2013). Moreover, it is crucial for attorneys to establish and meet realistic expectations for their clients regarding these issues—subjective perceptions of cost and time spent on cases tend to hold greater ex post significance for litigants than absolute objective values of these metrics (Lind et al., 1989; Wissler, 1995; Shestowsky, 2023). Arguments that ADR can help them achieve self-serving outcomes are also likely to resonate with litigants. On this issue too, much will hinge on their lawyers. Attorneys can help to ensure that their client's outcome objectives are not influenced by unrealistic egocentric views of their case and direct them to procedures that are suited to best achieve those objectives. Importantly, lawyers need to possess the requisite skills for achieving these objectives within the contemplated procedure.

The National Conference of Bar Examiner's announcement that dispute resolution will be tested on the new bar exam set to debut in 2026 is an optimistic development in terms of ensuring that future generations of lawyers possess those skills. It heralds a promising shift toward ensuring that legal education better reflects contemporary legal practice where ADR plays a central role. Furthermore, it amplifies the urgency for psychological research that can inform practices related to litigant education and client counseling regarding dispute resolution, as well as the design of ADR procedures that not only engage litigants' interest ex ante but also ensure their satisfaction ex post. By capitalizing on this current momentum created by this change in licensure requirements, stakeholders can proactively influence the future landscape of legal education and transform the experiences of future litigants within the civil justice system.

References

American Bar Association. (n.d.). *Alphabetical list of jurisdictions adopting model rules.* American Bar Association. https://www.americanbar.org/groups/professional_responsibility/publications/model_rules_of_professional_conduct/alpha_list_state_adopting_model_rules/

Babcock, L., & Loewenstein, G. (1997). Explaining bargaining impasse: The role of self-serving biases. *Journal of Economic Perspectives, 11*(1), 109–126. https://doi.org/10.1257/jep.11.1.109

Binder, D. A., Bergman, P. A., Tremblay, P. R., & Weinstein, I. S. (2019). *Lawyers as counselors, a client-centered approach* (4th ed.). West Academic Publishing.

Bingham, L. B. (2002). Why suppose? Let's find out: A public policy research program on dispute resolution. *Journal of Dispute Resolution, 2002*(1), 101–126. https://ssrn.com/abstract=1827263

Blankley, K. M., Votruba, A. M., Bartz, L. M., & Pytlik Zillig, L. M. (2022). Never assume what your clients know about mediation and arbitration. *Alternatives to the High Cost of Litigation, 40*(5), 81–85. https://doi.org/10.1002/alt.21946

Blankley, K. M., Votruba, A. M., Bartz, L. M., & Pytlik Zillig, L. M. (2021). ADR is not household term: Considering the ethical and practical consequences of the public's lack of understanding of mediation and arbitration. *Nebraska Law Review, 99*(4), 797–847. https://ssrn.com/abstract=3878988

Brockner, J., Shaw, M. C., & Rubin, J. Z. (1979). Factors affecting withdrawal from an escalating conflict: Quitting before it's too late. *Journal of Experimental Social Psychology, 15*(5), 492–503. https://doi.org/10.1016/0022-1031(79)90011-8

Clarke, S. H., & Gordon, E. E. (1997). Public sponsorship of private settling: Court-ordered civil case mediation. *Justice System Journal, 19*(3), 311–340. https://doi.org/10.1080/23277556.1997.10871266

Conlon, D. E., Lind, E. A., & Lissak, R. I. (1989). Nonlinear and nonmonotonic effects of outcome on procedural and distributive fairness judgments. *Journal of Applied Social Psychology, 19*(13), 1085–1099. https://doi.org/10.1111/j.1559-1816.1989.tb01241.x

Drahozal, C. R. (2001). Unfair arbitration clauses. *University of Illinois Law Review, 2001*(3), 695–790. https://ssrn.com/abstract=250167

Eisenberg, T., & Miller, G. P. (2007). The flight from arbitration: An empirical study of ex ante arbitration clauses in the contracts of publicly held companies. *DePaul Law Review, 56*(2), 335–374. https://via.library.depaul.edu/law-review/vol56/iss2/7

Eisenberg, D. T., Shestowsky, D., & Niccolini, R. R. (2023). What matters to employment attorneys when considering online or in-person mediation? *Alternatives to the High Cost of Litigation, 41*, 151–158. https://ssrn.com/abstract=4636514

Federal Arbitration Act, 9 U.S.C. §10 (1947).

Federal Rules of Civil Procedure Rule 38 (n.d.).

Fischhoff, B. (1975). Hindsight ≠ foresight: The effect of outcome knowledge on judgment under uncertainty. *Journal of Experimental Psychology: Human Perception and Performance, 1*(3), 288–299. https://doi.org/10.1037/0096-1523.1.3.288

Galanter, M. (2004). The vanishing trial: An examination of trials and related matters in federal and state courts. *Journal of Empirical Legal Studies, 1*(3), 459–570. https://doi.org/10.1111/j.1740-1461.2004.00014.x

Galanter, M., & Frozena, A. (2011). The continuing decline of civil trials in American courts. *Retrieved from.* https://www.poundinstitute.org/wp-content/uploads/2019/04/2011-Forum-Galanter-Frozena-Paper-1.pdf

Gilles, M. (2016). The day doctrine died: Private arbitration and the end of law. *University of Illinois Law Review, 2016*(2), 371–424. https://doi.org/10.2139/ssrn.2488575

Goldberg, S. B., Shaw, M. L., & Brett, J. M. (2009). What difference does a robe make? Comparing mediators with and without prior judicial experience. *Negotiation Journal, 25*(3), 277–305. https://doi.org/10.1111/j.1571-9979.2009.00227.x

Gundavaram, H. C. (2022, September 19). *Reimagining the bar exam to include dispute resolution: New ways to test competency.* https://www.americanbar.org/groups/dispute_resolution/publications/dispute_resolution_magazine/2022/september/reimagining-the-bar-exam-to-include-dispute-resolution/.

Hannaford-Agor, P. (2013). Measuring the cost of civil litigation: Findings from a survey of trial lawyers. *Voir Dire, 20*(1), 22–28.

Hensler, D. R. (2002). Suppose it's not true: Challenging mediation ideology. *Journal of Dispute Resolution, 2002*(1), 81–100. https://scholarship.law.missouri.edu/jdr/vol2002/iss1/5

Hensler, D. R. (2003). Our courts, ourselves: How the alternative dispute resolution movement is re-shaping our legal system. *Penn State Law Review, 108*(1), 165–198. https://ideas.dickinsonlaw.psu.edu/dlr/vol122/iss1/28

Hermann, M., LaFree, G., Rack, C., & West, M. B. (1993). *The metrocourt project final report.* Institute of Public Law, University of New Mexico.

Jones, T. S., & Bodtker, A. (1998). Satisfaction with custody mediation: Results from the York County custody mediation program. *Mediation Quarterly, 16*(2), 185–200. https://doi.org/10.1002/crq.3890160207

Katz, L. V. (1993). Compulsory alternative dispute resolution and voluntarism: Two-headed monster or two sides of the coin. *Journal of Dispute Resolution, 1993*(1), 1–55. https://scholarship.law.missouri.edu/jdr/vol1993/iss1/4

Kovach, K. K., & Love, L. P. (1996). Evaluative. *Mediation is an Oxymoron, 14*(3), 31–32. https://larc.cardozo.yu.edu/faculty-articles/280

Lande, J. (2022). Survey of early dispute resolution movements and possible next steps. *Alternatives to the High Cost of Litigation, 40*(4), 57–70.

Lande, J. (2008). The movement towards early case handling in courts and private dispute resolution. *Ohio State Journal on Dispute Resolution, 24*(1), 81–130.

Lind, E. A., MacCoun, R. J., Ebener, P. A., Felstiner, W. L., Hensler, D. R., Resnik, J., Tyler, T., & R. (1989). *The perception of justice: Tort litigant's views of trial, court-annexed arbitration, and judicial settlement conferences.* The Institute for Civil Justice.

Lind, E. A., & Tyler, T. R. (1988). *The social psychology of procedural justice.* Springer.

Loewenstein, G., Issacharoff, S., Camerer, C., & Babcock, L. (1993). Self-serving assessments of fairness and pretrial bargaining. *The Journal of Legal Studies, 22*(1), 135–159. https://www.jstor.org/stable/3085636

McAdoo, B. (2007). All rise, the court is in session: What judges say about court-connected mediation. *Ohio State Journal on Dispute Resolution, 22*(2), 377–442. https://ssrn.com/abstract=1910198

McAdoo, B., & Hinshaw, A. (2002). Challenge of institutionalizing alternative dispute resolution: Attorney perspectives on the effect of rule 17 on civil litigation in Missouri. *Missouri Law Review, 67*(3), 473–594. https://scholarship.law.missouri.edu/mlr/vol67/iss3/2

McAdoo, B., & Welsh, N. A. (1997). Does ADR really have a place on the lawyer's philosophical map? *Hamline Journal of Public Law & Policy, 18*, 376–393. https://scholarship.law.tamu.edu/facscholar/971

McEwen, C. A., & Milburn, T. W. (1993). Explaining a paradox of mediation. *Negotiation Journal, 9*, 23–36. https://doi.org/10.1111/j.1571-9979.1993.tb00687.x

Menkel-Meadow, C. (1995). Whose dispute is it anyway?: A philosophical and democratic defense of settlement (in some cases). *Georgetown Law Journal, 83*, 2663–2696. https://scholarship.law.georgetown.edu/facpub/1767

Nolan-Haley, J. (1996). Court mediation and the search for justice through law. *Washington University Law Quarterly, 74*(1), 47–102. https://openscholarship.wustl.edu/law_lawreview/vol74/iss1/3

Nolan-Haley, J. (2009). Mediation exceptionality. *Fordham Law Review, 78*(3), 1247–1264. https://ir.lawnet.fordham.edu/flr/vol78/iss3/7

O'Barr, W. M., & Conley, J. M. (1988). Lay expectations of the civil justice system. *Law & Society Review, 22*(1), 137–162. https://doi.org/10.2307/3053564

Pearson, J., Thoennes, N., & Vanderkooi, L. (1982). The decision to mediate: Profiles of individuals who accept and reject the opportunity to mediate contested child custody and visitation issues. *Journal of Divorce, 6*(1–2), 17–35. https://doi.org/10.1300/J279v06n01_02

Peirce, R. S., Pruitt, D. G., & Czaja, S. J. (1993). Complainant-respondent differences in procedural choice. *International Journal of Conflict Management, 4*(3), 199–222. https://doi.org/10.1108/eb022726

Priest, G. L., & Klein, B. (1984). The selection of disputes for litigation. *The Journal of Legal Studies, 13*(1), 1–55. https://doi.org/10.1086/467732

Quek, D. (2010). Mandatory mediation: An oxymoron examining the feasibility of implementing court-mandated mediation program. *Cardozo Journal of Conflict Resolution, 11*(2), 479–510. https://ssrn.com/abstract=2843509

Relis, T. (2007). "It's not about the money!": A theory on misconceptions of plaintiff's litigation aims. *University of Pittsburgh Law Review, 68*(3), 701–746. https://doi.org/10.5195/lawreview.2007.81

Relis, T. (2009). *Perceptions in litigation and mediation: Lawyers, defendants, plaintiffs, and gendered parties*. Cambridge University Press.

Riskin, L. L., Guthrie, C., Reuben, R. C., Robbennolt, J. K., Welsh, N. A., & Hinshaw, A. (2019). *Dispute resolution and lawyers, a contemporary approach* (6th ed.). West Academic Publishing.

Riskin, L. L., & Welsh, N. A. (2008). Is that all there is: The problem in court-oriented mediation. *George Mason Law Review, 15*(4), 863–932. https://scholarship.law.tamu.edu/facscholar/950

Roehl, J. A., Hersch, R., & Llaneras, E. (1992). *Civil case mediation and comprehensive justice centers: Process, quality of justice, and value to state courts, final report*. Institute for Social Analysis.

Sarat, A., & Felstiner, W. L. F. (1997). *Divorce lawyers and their clients: Power and meaning in the legal process*. Oxford University Press.

Shack, J., & Shestowsky D. (2024). *Implementing ODR family court: Insights from the first neutral program evaluation in the United States*. In P. Salem & K.B. Olson, The family dispute resolution handbook. Oxford University Press.

Shestowsky, D. (2004). Procedural preferences in alternative dispute resolution: Closer, modern look at an old idea. *Psychology, Public Policy, and Law, 10*(3), 211–249.

Shestowsky, D. (2008). Disputants' preferences for court-connected dispute resolution procedures: Why we should care and why we know so little. *Ohio State Journal on Dispute Resolution, 23*(3), 549–626. https://ssrn.com/abstract=4745608

Shestowsky, D. (2014). The psychology of procedural preference: How litigants evaluate legal procedures ex ante. *Iowa Law Review, 99*(2), 637–710. https://ssrn.com/abstract=2378622

Shestowsky, D. (2016). How litigants evaluate the characteristics of legal procedures: A multi-court empirical study. *U.C. Davis Law Review, 49*(3), 793–842. https://ssrn.com/abstract=2729893

Shestowsky, D. (2017). When ignorance is not bliss: An empirical study of litigant's awareness of court-sponsored alternative dispute resolution programs. *Harvard Negotiation Law Review, 22*(2), 189–240. https://ssrn.com/abstract=2945706

Shestowsky, D. (2018). Inside the mind of the client: An analysis of litigants' decision criteria for choosing procedures. *Conflict Resolution Quarterly, 36*(1), 69–91. https://doi.org/10.1002/crq.21228

Shestowsky, D. (2020). Great expectations? Comparing litigants' attitudes before and after using legal procedures. *Law and Human Behavior, 44*(3), 179 193. https://doi.org/10.1037/lhb0000370

Shestowsky, D. (2023). Civil litigants' evaluations of their legal experiences. *Annual Review of Law and Social Science, 19*, 19–36. https://doi.org/10.1146/annurev-lawsocsci-111022-082509

Shestowsky, D. (2024). Discussing procedure. *Ohio State Journal on Dispute Resolution, 39*(2), 325–356. https://kb.osu.edu/server/api/core/bitstreams/cc849862-ac3b-407c-b222-166159b19b79/content

Shestowsky, D., & Brett, J. (2008). Disputants' perceptions of dispute resolution procedures: A longitudinal empirical study. *Connecticut Law Review, 41*(1), 63–108. https://doi.org/10.2139/ssrn.1103585

Stallworth, L. E., & Stroh, L. K. (1996). Who is seeking to use ADR? Why do they choose to do so? *Dispute Resolution Journal, 51*, 30–38.

Sternlight, J. R. (1997). Rethinking the Constitutionality of the Supreme Court's Preference for Binding Arbitration: A Fresh Assessment of Jury Trial, Separation of Powers, and Due Process Concerns, 72 Tul. L. Rev. 1.

Sternlight, J. R. (2015). Disarming employees: How American employers are using mandatory arbitration to deprive workers of legal protection. *Brooklyn Law Review, 80*(4), 1309–1356. https://brooklynworks.brooklaw.edu/blr/vol80/iss4/3

Stipanowich, T. J. (2001). Contract and conflict management. *Wisconsin Law Review, 2001*(3), 831–918. https://ssrn.com/abstract=1377917

Stokoe, E. (2013). Overcoming barriers to mediation in intake call services: Research-based strategies for mediators. *Negotiation Journal, 29*(3), 289–314. https://doi.org/10.1111/nejo.12026

Tyler, T. R., Huo, Y. J., & Lind, E. A. (1999). The two psychologies of conflict resolution: Differing antecedents of pre-experience choices and post experience evaluations. *Group Processes & Intergroup Relations, 2*(2), 99–119. https://doi.org/10.1177/1368430299022001

United States Courts. (2023, March 31). *Table C-4: U.S. district courts–civil cases terminated, by nature of suit and action taken, during the 12-month period ending*. https://www.uscourts.gov/statistics/table/c-4/federal-judicial-caseload-statistics/2023/03/31.

Watkins, D. (2010). Nudge to mediate: How adjustments in choice architecture can lead to better dispute resolution decisions. *American Journal of Mediation, 4*, 19–38. https://ssrn.com/abstract=1472470

Welsh, N. A. (2001). Making Deals in Court-Connected Mediation: What's Justice Got to Do With It?, 79 Wash. U. L. Q. 787.

Welsh, N. A. (2004). Stepping back through the looking glass: Real conversations with real disputants about institutionalized mediation and its value. *Ohio State Journal on Dispute Resolution, 19*(2), 573–678. https://scholarship.law.tamu.edu/facscholar/947

Wissler, R. L. (1995). Mediation and adjudication in the small claims court: The effects of process and case characteristics. *Law & Society Review, 29*(2), 323–358. https://doi.org/10.2307/3054014

Wissler, R. L. (1997). The effects of mandatory mediation: Empirical research on the experience of small claims and common pleas courts. *Willamette Law Review, 33*(3), 565–604. https://ssrn.com/abstract=1724817

Wissler, R. L. (2002a). Court-connected mediation in general civil cases: What we know from empirical research. *Ohio State Journal on Dispute Resolution, 17*(3), 641–704. https://ssrn.com/abstract=1723292

Wissler, R. L. (2002b). When does familiarity breed content? A study of the role of different forms of ADR education and experience in attorneys' ADR recommendations. *Pepperdine Dispute Resolution Law Journal, 2*(2), 199–240. https://ssrn.com/abstract=1723345
Wissler, R. L. (2004). Barriers to attorneys' discussion and use of ADR. *Ohio State Journal on Dispute Resolution, 19*(2), 459–508. http://hdl.handle.net/1811/77172
Wissler, R. L., & Dauber, B. (2005). Leading horses to water: The impact of an ADR "confer and report" rule. *Justice System Journal, 26*(3), 253–271. https://ssrn.com/abstract=1724989
Wolfs, A. C. F., Shestowsky, D., & Goldfarb, D. (2024). Justice via chat? How litigants' preferences and attorneys' recommendations influence the choice to use online dispute resolution. *Psychology, Public Policy, and Law, 30*(3), 348–362. https://doi.org/10.1037/law0000424

Justice and Culture

Kees van den Bos

Justice and culture are fundamental features of human life. After all, cultural norms and values make up essential elements of who we are as humans, how we construe the world around us, feel about important issues, and shape our behaviors. Thus, culture affects legal judgment and human motivation, either in direct ways or as a context in which legal decision-making takes place, and we are inspired to take some course of action (e.g., Fiske et al., 1998; Hofstede, 2001; Markus & Kitayama, 1991; Morris & Peng, 1994).

Related to this, justice motivates people, and making just decisions inspires (or should inspire) legal judgment. Furthermore, justice is one of the most important social norms and values in people's culture (see, e.g., Folger, 1984; Folger & Cropanzano, 1998; Tyler & Smith, 1998). In most situations most people judge unjust treatment to be in violation with cultural norms and values and think of just treatment as being in correspondence with the norms and values of good behavior and conduct (Lind & Tyler, 1988; Tyler et al., 1997). In other words, unjust treatment violates people's cultural worldviews, whereas just treatment bolsters people's cultural worldviews (Van den Bos et al., 2005; Van den Bos & Miedema, 2000; see also Rosenblatt et al., 1989).

The relationship between justice and culture seems obvious yet it may be more unclear than we sometimes realize. For example, some justice scholars have argued that the meaning of justice is culturally determined, suggesting a very strong impact of culture on justice judgments and that justice judgments change radically across cultures (e.g., Kidder & Muller, 1991). Other justice researchers, however, point at empirical findings that suggest that procedural justice is defined in much the same

K. van den Bos (✉)
Department of Psychology, Utrecht University, Utrecht, The Netherlands

School of Law, Utrecht University, Utrecht, The Netherlands
e-mail: k.vandenbos@uu.nl

R. L. Wiener, D. J. Hansen (eds.), *Legal Judgment and the Motivation for Justice*, Nebraska Symposium on Motivation 71,
https://doi.org/10.1007/978-3-031-98812-7_9

way across widely different cultural contexts, implying that justice judgments could be largely invariant across cultures and that justice theories generalize across cultural contexts (e.g., Lind et al., 1997). Following these differential insights about the relationship between justice and culture, the current chapter focuses on this relationship. I also study justice and culture because it can be argued that issues of social justice could well be a growing concern both within culturally diverse societies (e.g., Tyler et al., 1997) and between different cultures and societies in our world (see also Tyler et al., 1998, 2000).

What I try to do in what follows in this chapter is to delineate conceptual reasons why justice and culture can impact each other. I then present findings that suggest that cultural differences in legal judgment are sometimes hidden in society and that differences between groups within a culture in fact influence the judgments of trust in law. These findings indicate that behavioral research on justice judgments has been relying heavily on not only participants but also researchers from Western, Educated, Industrialized, Rich, and Democratic (WEIRD) backgrounds (Henrich et al., 2010a). I end the chapter by discussing how experimental methods can be used to study cross-cultural effects on justice judgments in controlled ways.

Justice Is Where Individuals Meet Their Culture

Ever since the pioneering work by Lind and Tyler (1988) on the group-value model on perceived procedural justice, we know that a key reason why perceived justice is such a motivating force for many people is because whether your culture (or subculture) is treating you in just or unjust manners symbolizes how the culture (or subculture) is viewing your worth as a member of your community, working organization, and society. In other words, justice is where individuals meet their culture: When important people, organizations, and institutions in your culture are treating you in fundamentally just ways, this signals that you matter in your culture, that you are credited with standing, and that your culture is respecting you as an important member of the culture. In contrast, when you are treated in unjust manners, this conveys that you do not matter that much in your culture, that important constituents of your culture do not award you high-standing, and that you are not respected as someone who is valued in your culture.

The value-expressive function of fair and unfair and just and unjust treatment is one of the reasons why perceived procedural justice is so important to people: Fair and just treatment signal that you are valued by important people from your group, community, or society. And unfair and unjust treatment hurt so badly because they communicate that your group, community, or society does not care that much about you (Lind, 1995; Van den Bos, 2024).

This also implies that social identity concerns are an important aspect of justice motivations. For example, perceived procedural justice communicates something about your standing and social status within the group (Tyler, 1989; Tyler & Lind, 1992; van Prooijen et al., 2002). These effects are particularly strong when the just or unjust treatment is originating from groups to which you want to belong (Lind & Tyler, 1988). Furthermore, being excluded from groups also hurts when these groups are not very important to you or even when you do not like these groups at all. For instance, Gonsalkorale and Williams (2007) showed that liberal students felt ostracized when they were excluded from taking part in tossing a virtual ball back and forth in a cyber game by members of an extreme right-wing group that they despised. These kinds of findings reflect the social quality of us, human beings, and how much we value and need social connections with other people (Van den Bos, 2024).

The fair and just distribution of outcomes also can have this value-expressive function, but it is not always easy to know with confidence whether the distribution of outcomes was indeed fair and just, in part because information about other people's outcomes is lacking or ambiguous. This is why perceived procedural justice often impacts people's reactions so strongly: Information about just and unjust treatment tends to be accessible with relative ease (Van den Bos et al., 1997; but see also Van den Bos, 1999). The implication of this line of reasoning, when it holds up, is that just and unjust treatments by important members within your culture have important symbolic values, with unfair treatment and own personal experiences having the strongest effect on your judgments of trust and distrust and your other responses toward other people, organizations, and institutions in the culture (Van den Bos, 2024).

As Tyler and Lind (1992) argued convincingly, within their culture, people are often strongly oriented toward what authorities think of them and how they evaluate them. One reason for this is that authorities have power over people and can exclude them from important groups or grant them permission to become full-fledged members of those groups. Related to this, and in correspondence with the theories of symbolic interactionism (Blumer, 1969; Mead, 1934), the way institutions evaluate you conveys important symbolic information whether you are viewed as a valuable member of society. In turn, when you assess or suspect that your views are not taken seriously into consideration, this increases the chances of distrust in the social institutions at hand and the people representing those institutions (Van den Bos, 2023, 2024).

People tend to be oriented toward information that conveys that they can trust or should distrust a certain person in society, such as an individual person representing a particular societal institution. In contrast, processing information about what happens in society in abstract ways tends to facilitate the formation of distrusting attitudes. This fits with the idea of the current chapter that justice is a fundamentally cultural process because whether your culture treats you in fair and just ways reflects how the culture thinks of you. In this process, being evaluated in negative ways and experiencing concrete instances of unfair and unjust treatment may have special significance and increase the chances of societal discontent and unwarranted distrust to develop and flourish (Van den Bos, 2024).

Hidden Social–Cultural Differences in WEIRD Psychology and Law

Henrich and colleagues argue convincingly that research in the behavioral sciences, including studies on psychology and law, rely heavily on research participants with Western, Educated, Industrialized, Rich, and Democratic (WEIRD) backgrounds (Henrich, 2020; Henrich et al., 2010a, 2010b). Indeed, a 2008 survey of the top psychology journals found that 96% of participants were, in fact, WEIRD participants (Arnett, 2008). The fact that the vast majority of studies use WEIRD participants presents a challenge to the understanding of human psychology and behavior (Henrich et al., 2010a).

In a recent paper, my colleagues and I explored some of the possible implications of these observations for studies on legal judgment and human motivation (Van den Bos et al., 2023). In particular, building and extending on notions of WEIRD Psychology and Law, we wondered whether one reason why cultural effects on justice and legal judgments are not always found (Lind et al., 1997) may have to do with the social–cultural distance between those who conduct and those who participate in the research on psychology and law. We examined these issues by conducting field experiments on trust in law. Let us examine these studies and its underlying reasoning in some detail. To this end, I rely in what follows on the original report of these findings (see Van den Bos et al., 2023). I also refer the reader to that report for more details on the studies than I discuss here.

We began our project with the observation that the issue of trust in law serves a prominent role in many interview studies, surveys, and other research projects. These studies on trust in law typically begin with researchers introducing themselves with their affiliation. For example, when a questionnaire is used to measure people's trust in law, the introduction page mentions the organization responsible for the research. We were especially interested in research done by university researchers on trust in law, which are frequently conducted by researchers affiliated with law schools. Thus, these studies often begin by researchers introducing themselves as coming from university law schools, interested in how people trust judges. We proposed that the results of interviewers introducing themselves in this manner may have systematic effects on how respondents with lower educational backgrounds may respond to trust questionnaires.

We further noted that ordinary citizens often perceive interviewers from law schools as being from another social category in which ordinary citizens who hold no positions of power, are not represented, and do not participate. We also argued that studies on trust in law typically do not systematically incorporate let alone vary systematically the affiliation of the interviewer in the research designs of the studies involved. We proposed, therefore, to vary experimentally whether interviewers in our studies on trust in law were from university law schools or were not from institutions affiliated with university law schools. Our primary aim was to explore whether the way in which trust researchers present themselves to research participants influences the degree of trust in law reported, especially among lower educated participants who view judges and law schools as socially and culturally different from themselves, occupying positions in society generally to be considered higher in terms of status and education.

In the three studies that we presented, we interviewed participants about their trust in judges. We conducted all three experiments in indoor shopping malls and train stations in the Netherlands. These are places that are visited by people from different social demographic backgrounds. We interviewed by means of paper-and-pencil questionnaires that participants completed on their own in anonymous ways. In all studies, interviewers used standard, pre-scripted communication in their interaction with participants. Sampling procedures were the same across interviewer conditions, and various measures were taken to minimize possible experimenter demands in our studies.

In some conditions of our field experiments, the interviewers introduced themselves to the participants as coming from a university Law School. We contrasted this with conditions in which the same interviewers presented themselves as coming from a Regional Community College. Regional community colleges in the Netherlands offer lower secondary education, which more closely aligns with the education level of the lower educated participants in our studies. In all three studies, we tested whether university Law School interviewers versus the Regional Community College interviewers would lead to different levels of reported trust in law among participants with lower, intermediate, and higher educational levels.

As predicted, we found that when the trust survey was presented as coming from university Law Schools, participants with lower educational levels reported higher degrees of trust in judges compared to when the interviewer was presented as coming from Regional Community Colleges. Interestingly, lower educated participants returned their envelopes to the Regional Community College interviewer with statements indicating that judges do not know what lives they and the interviewer are living. We did not hear any of these reactions when the interviewer presented himself or herself as coming from a university Law School.

As we mentioned in a previous study (Van den Bos et al., 2023), follow-up research is needed to test for the robustness of these effects. Future studies also are important to delineate and distinguish between the various reasons why these effects are there. For now, I interpret these findings as tentative evidence that the social–cultural distance between researchers and participants in scientific research on law and psychology can play an important role. If this assumption has merit, then future studies could examine its possible implications.

For example, future research could examine whether the different trust ratings that lower educated respondents give can be explained by outgroup (law school interviewers) versus ingroup effects (community college interviewers). Perhaps lower educated respondents feel socially closer to the latter than to the former interviewer. And perhaps higher respondents may have learned to "speak up" and indicate their trust responses, irrespective of who is interviewing them.

Future research might also want to study whether social status—related to the hierarchical rank ordering in society (Schooler, 1994; Waters & Waters, 2015)—can account for these interviewer effects. For example, participants with lower status may respond with higher trust ratings to interviewers affiliated with higher status organizations (such as Law Schools) than when interviewed by interviewers from lower status organizations (such as Regional Community Colleges oriented toward vocational training). And perhaps these effects are especially prevalent when people are interviewed on high status issues such as the legal system.

I also think there is a possibility that these findings can be linked to polarization between groups of higher versus lower educated people across our globe. These groups have divergent social–cultural orientations and increasingly tend to live in separate social environments (Bovens et al., 2014; Kriesi et al., 2008, 2012; Stubager, 2010). Moreover, the rise of populist political movements—whose actions typically involve targeting and systematically discrediting the judiciary as part and parcel of the "elite" (Council of Europe, 2017; Müller, 2016)—makes the issue of obtaining a precise understanding of how lower educated citizens trust judges and the judiciary even more urgent.

Speculation aside, I think it is fair to conclude that we need to examine the possible effects of culture (including but not limited to the social–cultural distance) on legal judgment and motivation for justice both within and between different countries. The current section presented reviewed experimental works on testing effects between different subcultures pertaining to education within a culture. The next section discusses how we can examine effects with experimental control between cultures.

Studying Cross-Cultural Differences with Experimental Control

An important concern when studying cross-cultural differences on justice and legal judgment and human motivation is to obtain findings with sufficient levels of internal validity. As Van den Bos et al. (2013) note, often cross-cultural research examines people from two or more countries and assumes that the participants differ along certain psychological dimensions, which, in turn, elicit differences in the dependent variables of cognition, affect, or behavior. If the research findings suggest that the participants in the different countries react differently, and that these reactions are in accordance with the psychological dimensions presumed to differ across cultures, it is still necessary to provide evidence that the culturally varying reactions can be attributed to the hypothesized psychological dimensions.

Sometimes researchers try to provide such evidence by measuring the relevant psychological dimensions (Brockner, 2003) and then conducting tests of mediation to see whether the cultural differences were attributable to the psychological dimensions. However, measuring the hypothesized mediating psychological dimensions may be difficult (see, e.g., Spencer et al., 2005). For example, measuring psychological dimensions in cross-cultural research typically involves self-reports, which may be problematic because of people's unwillingness or inability to disclose their true beliefs (e.g., Nisbett & Ross, 1980). Furthermore, a well-known issue in cross-cultural studies is that measures of the same construct may not mean the same thing to people from different cultures (Hui & Triandis, 1985). Thus, there may be important problems associated with measuring the psychological dimensions presumed to account for cross-cultural differences. Furthermore, even when it is possible to measure reliably the hypothesized psychological mediators of the effects of culture, the ensuing statistical analyses can at best provide only correlational evidence which limits the empirical strength of the study in question (Van den Bos et al., 2013).

In short, in our 2013 paper, we argued that there is a need in cross-cultural research to not only provide evidence of why people from different cultures show different reactions but also to do so in ways that entail a high degree of internal validity. Therefore, we suggested that it is important to complement extant cross-cultural inquiries with studies that provide experimental control over the psychological dimensions hypothesized to account for differences between cultures. We further proposed that for purposes of internal validity, it is better to use an experimental approach in which participants are randomly assigned to conditions differing along the dimension hypothesized to account for the results. Indeed, one of the main virtues of such an approach is that it is likely to hold constant all factors other than the construct being manipulated. As a result, differences that emerge on the dependent variable are likely to have been causally influenced by the manipulated construct (Van den Bos et al., 2013).

We noted that in cross-cultural research it is typically not possible to randomly assign participants to different cultures. However, it is possible to randomly assign people from different cultures to either an experimental condition in which values and beliefs are made salient that are directly contrary to the default ones in a given culture or to a control condition without manipulated salience in which people are likely to default to the values and beliefs that are predominant to their culture. If differences emerge on the dependent variable when this methodology is used, it is quite likely that they were caused by the construct inherent to the experimental manipulation (Van den Bos et al., 2013).

Van den Bos et al. (2013) further argued that if the values in the experimental conditions are counter to what is default in the culture that is studied, then making countercultural beliefs salient should lead to reliably different effects on participants' reactions to subsequent events, compared to participants' reactions in control conditions in which no explicit values have been made salient. Thus, we put forward an experimental research method to study cross-cultural differences that involves (1) studying participants from cultures that differ in ways that theory suggests will produce meaningful effects on important human reactions (see, e.g., Heine, 2010; Hofstede, 2001; Hui & Triandis, 1985; Leung, 2005; Markus & Kitayama, 1991) and (2) incorporating the concept of a countercultural psychological state in a controlled experimental design (Van den Bos et al., 2013).

In our 2013 article, we illustrated the method of studying cross-cultural differences with experimental control by examining how participants from India (a high-power distance culture) and the Netherlands (a low-power distance culture) react to being allowed or denied an opportunity to voice their opinions. We argued that one way to evaluate the influence of the assumed cultural differences in power distance is to assign participants to conditions that elicit "countercultural" psychological states, that is, conditions that make low-power distance salient in India and high-power distance in the Netherlands.

Specifically, following the definition of power distance by Hofstede (2001), low-power distance was made salient among our Indian participants by asking them to describe a situation out of their own life in which there was a small distance between them and a person who formally had power over them. High-power distance was made salient among our Dutch participants by asking them to describe a situation out of their own life in which there was a large distance between them and a person who formally had power over them. (For more information about the exact experimental procedures used, please see Van den Bos et al., 2013.)

We argued that to the extent that the results in the countercultural (experimental) conditions meaningfully differ from those observed in the control conditions in which no values are emphasized explicitly, we gain insights into the psychological dimensions that account for cross-cultural differences in people's reactions (Van den Bos et al., 2013). The findings we obtained in this way indeed suggest that the random assignment of participants to countercultural conditions provides cross-cultural researchers with a powerful tool to examine the causal impact of meaningful psychological dimensions that are presumed to differ across cultures. The results further reveal that when high-power distance was emphasized either because of national culture or situational cues, participants showed less strong reactions to the voice versus no-voice manipulation than when low-power distance was emphasized as a result of either national culture or situational cues. (Implications and limitations of this countercultural–experimental approach for the study of cross-cultural differences as well as the psychology of voice and power distance are discussed in the 2013 article.)

In another paper, Van den Bos et al. (2010) used a similar approach to examine the hypothesis that in masculine cultures that emphasize competitive achievement (Hofstede, 2001), those with higher performance capabilities will feel empowered to have input into decisions and hence will desire opportunities to voice their opinions about decisions to be made. In contrast, in more feminine cultures that value the importance of nurturing people with lower capability (Hofstede, 2001), those with lower capabilities will feel valued as important group members, thus will feel worthy of receiving voice, and hence will appreciate actually voice-receiving opportunities. We provided evidence for these predictions in two studies, one conducted in the United States (a more masculine culture) and one in the Netherlands (a more feminine culture). Evidence also came from experimental conditions in both studies, in which we made salient participants' "countercultural" norms and values, that is, nurturing the less capable in the United States and competitive achievement in the Netherlands (Van den Bos et al., 2010). (For more information about the exact experimental procedures used, see Van den Bos et al., 2010.)

Specifically, our findings suggest that when competitive achievement was emphasized, either because of national culture or because of a situational cue inducing participants to do so, responses of participants who believed they were highly capable of providing meaningful input were significantly affected by whether they got versus were denied opportunities to voice their opinions about tasks to be completed. Responses were not statistically different among those with lower capabilities who got versus were denied voice. In contrast, when as a result of national culture or situational cues emphasis was put on nurturing those with lower capability, voice versus no-voice effects were significant among participants who had lower capabilities and were not significant among those with higher capabilities. (For a detailed report of the findings obtained, see Van den Bos et al., 2010.)

Finally, Van den Bos et al. (2015) used the same method of both cross-cultural comparisons and comparisons obtained by experimental manipulation to examine how cultural and contextual factors influence responses to personal and group-relative deprivation. Two studies were conducted, one in an individualistic country (The Netherlands) and one in a collectivistic country (Singapore; Hofstede, 2001). The influence of the assumed cultural differences in individualism–collectivism was examined by assigning participants to "countercultural" conditions that make collectivistic mindsets salient in the Netherlands and individualistic mindsets in Singapore.

Specifically, in the countercultural condition, Dutch participants were asked to think about their friends and family and indicate what they have in common with their family and friends. In the countercultural condition of the experiment conducted in Singapore, participants were asked to think about their own distinctiveness and how they are a unique being. (For more information about the exact experimental procedures used, see Van den Bos et al., 2015.)

Results showed that cross-cultural differences have reliable effects on responses to relative deprivation and gratification. Furthermore, findings in the countercultural (experimental) conditions meaningfully differed from those observed in the control conditions in which participants were exposed to neutral stimulus materials. This suggests again that countercultural experiments can be used to study cross-cultural and contextual differences with high levels of internal validity (Van den Bos et al., 2015).

Specifically, people in an individualistic mindset, either because this is embedded in their national culture or because they were reminded of their personal uniqueness, responded in more negative terms when they were deprived as an individual person than when they were deprived as a group member and responded in more positive terms when they were advantaged as a person than as a group member. These findings suggest that individualistic or self-interested types of reactions are likely when individualistic mindsets are salient as a result of cultural background or experimental manipulation.

Furthermore, our 2015 studies also show that when people adhere to collectivistic mindsets, either because of national culture or because they are experimentally reminded of their similarities with family and friends, they responded more negatively to being deprived than to being advantaged, irrespective of whether this manipulation affected them as individuals or as group members. One way to interpret these findings is to conclude that in our collectivistic mindset conditions (derived by experimental manipulation or national background), we observed reactions that are indicative of a more inclusive view of the self in which both personal and group treatments matter to participants. (For a detailed report of the findings, see Van den Bos et al., 2015.)

Conclusions

There are good reasons to assume that one of the core reasons why justice is so motivating for people is because when you and your group are treated in fair and just ways, this conveys that your culture perceives you to be an important person who is valued in the culture to which you belong. When you and your group are treated in blatantly unfair and unjust manners, however, this is an indication that you are not a full-fledged member of society, are not really valued in your culture, and perhaps even are not considered to belong to that culture (Lind & Tyler, 1988; Tyler & Lind, 1992). In other words, fair and unfair treatment are important symbols of how culture views you (Van den Bos, 2024). Authorities (including judges, police officers, law professors, and others affiliated with the legal system; Tyler, 2006) hold powerful and valued positions within your culture. Therefore, how they treat you plays a special role in this process of symbolic interactionism (Blumer, 1969; Mead, 1934).

Thus, justice judgments seem to entail a fundamentally cultural process (Tyler et al., 1997, 1998, 2000; Van den Bos & Miedema, 2000; see also Bal & Van den Bos, 2019, 2021, 2022; Lerner, 1977, 1980, 1981). It may be difficult, however, to get a good grip on effects of culture on justice judgments. This may have to be, in part, with null effects in quantitative research methodology (Lind et al., 1997; Van den Bos, 2020) and an overreliance on WEIRD participants and researchers (Arnett, 2008; Henrich et al., 2010a, 2010b; Van den Bos et al., 2023). To help overcoming some of these issues, I discussed two examples of recent lines of work that my colleagues and I did to get a better empirical handle on justice and culture.

One line of work relied on experimentally varying how interviewers or research projects are presented to research participants (Van den Bos et al., 2023). Experiments conducted within that line of research hinted at discovering lower levels of trust in law among participants with lower education when they were taking part in research conducted from a regional community college instead of a law school (or psychology department at a university).

How to interpret these pioneering findings is an issue that needs to be resolved in future research studies, and I would be strongly in favor of these studies being conducted. For now, it is my assumption that social identification with a high or low societal status plays an important role. We should not forget that people who are affiliated with the legal system, including researchers who work at law schools, are part of the status quo and hold high status in society. This may partly explain why participants with lower status in terms of educational background responded with higher trust ratings to interviewers affiliated with higher status organizations (such as law schools) than when interviewed by interviewers from lower status organizations (such as regional community colleges oriented toward vocational training) on topics such as trust in law that these participants might perceive as high-status topics. Future studies are needed to sort out these and other topics that play a role in justice judgments and trust assessments in different groups within society and our culture (Van den Bos et al., 2023).

Another line of work used experimental manipulation to complement cross-cultural comparisons. Experiments within this line of research compared responses of research respondents from cultures that differ on cultural dimensions such as individualism–collectivism (Van den Bos et al., 2015), masculinity–femininity (Van den Bos et al., 2010), and power distance (Van den Bos et al., 2013). In experimental conditions, we made countercultural norms salient that were counter to the assumed culture (thus, collectivistic norms in individualistic cultures, individualistic norms in collectivistic cultures, and so on). In the control conditions, norms were not made salient, and we assumed that respondents would react to their default cultural norms in those conditions. Reactions in the experimental conditions helped us to make sense of the assumed cultural dimensions. That is, we reasoned that when the assumed cultural dimensions indeed play a role, then making salient norms that are on the opposite of the assumed dimension should be especially likely to impact respondents' judgments. This is indeed what we found (Van den Bos et al., 2010, 2013, 2015).

I do not want to imply that the method of manipulating countercultural psychological states in cross-cultural research is the only important methodological tool that can be used to examine the causal impact of a wide array of cultural influences on justice and legal judgments and human motivation. I am also not suggesting that these experimental manipulations will always have strong effects on human motivation and people's reactions. After all, while for reasons of internal validity the experimental method has important advantages, effects of experimental manipulations are sometimes notoriously weak, thus unable to overcome the default cultural norms. Furthermore, many cultures differ on multiple dimensions, and focusing on one dimension only may result in a conceptually narrow and empirically feeble basis of cross-cultural comparisons in the legal domain, especially when studying human motivation (Van den Bos et al., 2013). Furthermore, future research with different stimulus materials and different samples from different cultures is needed to check the robustness and the discriminant validity of the countercultural experiments used in our three papers on this issue (Van den Bos et al., 2010, 2013, 2015). Thus, I am stating explicitly that future research on countercultural experiments is needed. I hope that the approach reviewed here, together with other studies (e.g., Bechtoldt et al., 2010; Oyserman, 2011; Oyserman & Lee, 2007), will stimulate cross-cultural research on justice and legal judgments and human motivation (Van den Bos et al., 2013).

In closing, I want to stipulate that part of what makes the study of justice and culture so exciting is (1) these issues probably matter a lot in the legal domain and in human motivation, and (2) they can be hard to study (which I think is a fun and not an annoying aspect for academic researchers). Furthermore, justice and culture are associated with a huge variety of human responses, within legal judgment and human motivation as well as beyond those domains of inquiry. In this chapter, I focused on only some issues.

What I like about the combined study of psychology and law is that it allows for various empirical research methods, including observational studies, qualitative interviews, surveys that use both qualitative and quantitative answering options, and laboratory and field experiments (Van den Bos, 2020). Furthermore, psychology and law scholars aim to integrate empirical work with in-depth and creative conceptual reasoning that makes use of different scientific disciplines and relies on input from the various domains of society. Thus, I hope that by conducting various kinds of empirical studies and combining this with a careful conceptual thought, we are getting more and more of a grip on the important issue of justice and culture and how this motivates people and impacts legal judgment.

References

Arnett, J. J. (2008). The neglected 95%: Why American Psychology needs to become less American. *American Psychologist, 63*, 602–614.

Bal, M., & van den Bos, K. (2019). Worldview defense, prejudice, and derogating others. In *Oxford research encyclopedia of psychology*. Oxford University Press. https://doi.org/10.1093/acrefore/9780190236557.013.266

Bal, M., & van den Bos, K. (2021). Coping with an unjust world. In F. Maggino (Ed.), *Encyclopedia of quality of life and well-being research* (2nd ed., pp. 1–7). Springer.

Bal, M., & van den Bos, K. (2022). Social justice and the justification of social inequalities. In M. A. Yerkes & M. Bal (Eds.), *Solidarity and social justice in contemporary societies: An interdisciplinary approach to understanding inequalities* (pp. 41–51). Palgrave.

Bechtoldt, M. N., De Dreu, C. K. W., Nijstad, B. A., & Choi, H. S. (2010). Motivated information processing, social tuning, and group creativity. *Journal of Personality and Social Psychology, 99*, 622–637. https://doi.org/10.1037/0003-066X.63.7.602

Blumer, H. (1969). *Symbolic interactionism: Perspective and method.* Prentice-Hall.

Bovens, M., Dekker, P., & Tiemeijer, W. (Eds.). (2014). *Gescheiden werelden? Een verkenning van sociaal-culturele tegenstellingen in Nederland*, Sociaal en Cultureel Planbureau/Wetenschappelijke Raad voor het Regeringsbeleid.

Brockner, J. (2003). Unpacking country effects: On the need to operationalize the psychological determinants of cross-national differences. In R. M. Kramer & B. M. Staw (Eds.), *Research in organizational behavior* (Vol. 25, pp. 335–369). JAI Press.

Council of Europe. (2017). State of democracy, human rights and the rule of law: Populism—How strong are Europe's checks and balances? In *Fourth annual report of the Secretary General of the Council of Europe*. Retrieved from https://edoc.coe.int/en/an-overview/7345-pdf-state-of-democracy-human-rights-and-the-rule-of-law.html.

Fiske, A. P., Kitayama, S., Markus, H. R., & Nisbett, R. E. (1998). The cultural matrix of social psychology. In D. T. Gilbert, S. T. Fiske, & G. Lindzey (Eds.), *The handbook of social psychology* (Vol. 2, 4th ed., pp. 915–981). McGraw-Hill.

Folger, R. (Ed.). (1984). *The sense of injustice: Social psychological perspectives*. Plenum.

Folger, R., & Cropanzano, R. (1998). *Organizational justice and human resource management*. Sage.

Gonsalkorale, K., & Williams, K. D. (2007). The KKK won't let me play: Ostracism even by a despised outgroup hurts. *European Journal of Social Psychology, 37*(6), 1176–1186. https://doi.org/10.1002/ejsp.392

Heine, S. J. (2010). Cultural psychology. In S. T. Fiske, D. T. Gilbert, & G. Lindzey (Eds.), *Handbook of social psychology* (Vol. 2, 5th ed., pp. 1423–1464). Wiley.
Henrich, J. (2020). *The WEIRDest people in the world: How the West became psychologically peculiar and particularly prosperous*. Macmillan.
Henrich, J., Heine, S. J., & Norenzayan, A. (2010a). The weirdest people in the world? *Behavioral and Brain Sciences, 33*, 61–83. https://doi.org/10.1017/S0140525X0999152X
Henrich, J., Heine, S. J., & Norenzayan, A. (2010b). Most people are not WEIRD. *Nature, 466*, 29. https://doi.org/10.1038/466029a
Hofstede, G. (2001). *Culture's consequences: Comparing values, behaviors, institutions, and organizations across nations* (2nd ed.). Sage.
Hui, C. H., & Triandis, H. C. (1985). Measurement in cross-cultural psychology: A review and comparison of strategies. *Journal of Cross-Cultural Psychology, 16*, 131–152. https://doi-org.libproxy.unl.edu/10.1177/0022002185016002001
Kidder, L. H., & Muller, S. (1991). What is "fair" in Japan? In R. Vermunt & H. Steensma (Eds.), *Social and psychological origins of justice: Societal and psychological consequences of justice and injustice* (Vol. 2, pp. 139–154). Plenum.
Kriesi, H. E., Grande, E., Dolezal, M., Helbling, M., Höglinger, D., Hutter, S., & Wüest, B. (2012). *Political conflict in Western Europe*. Cambridge University Press.
Kriesi, H., Grande, E., Lachat, R., Dolezal, M., Bornschier, S., & Frey, T. (2008). *West European politics in the age of globalization*. Cambridge University Press.
Lerner, M. J. (1977). The justice motive: Some hypotheses as to its origins and forms. *Journal of Personality, 45*(1), 1–52. https://doi.org/10.1111/j.1467-6494.1977.tb00591.x
Lerner, M. J. (1980). *The belief in a just world: A fundamental delusion*. Plenum.
Lerner, M. J. (1981). The justice motive in human relations: Some thoughts on what we know and need to know about justice. In M. J. Lerner & S. C. Lerner (Eds.), *The justice motive in social behavior: Adapting to times of scarcity and change* (pp. 11–38). Plenum.
Leung, K. (2005). How generalizable are justice effects across cultures? In J. Greenberg & J. A. Colquitt (Eds.), *Handbook of organizational justice: Fundamental questions about fairness in the workplace* (pp. 555–586). Erlbaum.
Lind, E. A. (1995). *Social conflict and social justice: Lessons from the social psychology of justice judgments*. Inaugural address, Leiden University.
Lind, E. A., & Tyler, T. R. (1988). *The social psychology of procedural justice*. Plenum.
Lind, E. A., Tyler, T. R., & Huo, Y. J. (1997). Procedural context and culture: Variation in the antecedents of procedural justice judgments. *Journal of Personality and Social Psychology, 73*(4), 767–780. https://doi.org/10.1037/0022-3514.73.4.767
Markus, H. R., & Kitayama, S. (1991). Culture and the self: Implications for cognition, emotion, and motivation. *Psychological Review, 98*, 224–253. https://doi.org/10.1037/0033-295X.98.2.224
Mead, G. H. (1934). *Mind, self, and society: From the standpoint of a social behaviorist*. University of Chicago Press.
Morris, M. W., & Peng, K. (1994). Culture and cause: American and Chinese attributions for social and physical events. *Journal of Personality and Social Psychology, 67*(6), 949–971. https://doi.org/10.1037/0022-3514.67.6.949
Müller, J. (2016). *What is populism?* University of Pennsylvania Press.
Nisbett, R. E., & Ross, L. (1980). *Human inference: Strategies and shortcomings of social judgment*. Prentice-Hall.
Oyserman, D. (2011). Culture as situated cognition: Cultural mindsets, cultural fluency, and meaning making. In W. Stroebe & M. Hewstone (Eds.), *European review of social psychology* (Vol. 22, pp. 164–214). Psychology Press.
Oyserman, D., & Lee, S. W. S. (2007). Priming "culture": Culture as situated cognition. In S. Kitayama & D. Cohen (Eds.), *Handbook of cultural psychology* (pp. 255–279). Guilford Press.
Rosenblatt, A., Greenberg, J., Solomon, S., Pyszczynski, T., & Lyon, D. (1989). Evidence for terror management theory: I. The effects of mortality salience on reactions to those who violate or

uphold cultural values. *Journal of Personality and Social Psychology, 57*(4), 681–690. https://doi.org/10.1037/0022-3514.57.4.681

Schooler, C. (1994). A working conceptualization of social structure: Mertonian roots and psychological and sociocultural relationships. *Social Psychology Quarterly, 57*(3), 262–273. https://doi.org/10.2307/2786880

Spencer, S. J., Fein, S., Strahan, E. J., & Zanna, M. P. (2005). The role of motivation in the unconscious: How our motives control the activation of our thoughts and shape our actions. In J. P. Forgas, K. D. Williams, & S. M. Laham (Eds.), *Social motivation: Conscious and unconscious processes* (pp. 113–129). Cambridge University Press.

Stubager, R. (2010). The development of the education cleavage: Denmark as a critical case. *West European Politics, 3*, 505–533.

Tyler, T. R. (1989). The psychology of procedural justice: A test of the group-value model. *Journal of Personality and Social Psychology, 57*, 830–838. https://doi.org/10.1037/0022-3514.57.5.830

Tyler, T. R. (2006). *Why people obey the law*. Princeton University Press.

Tyler, T. R., Boeckmann, R. J., Smith, H. J., & Huo, Y. J. (1997). *Social justice in a diverse society*. Westview.

Tyler, T. R., & Lind, E. A. (1992). A relational model of authority in groups. In M. P. Zanna (Ed.), *Advances in experimental social psychology* (Vol. 25, pp. 115–191). Academic Press.

Tyler, T. R., Lind, E. A., & Huo, Y. J. (2000). Cultural values and authority relations: The psychology of conflict resolution across cultures. *Psychology, Public Policy, and Law, 6*, 1138–1163. https://doi.org/10.1037/1076-8971.6.4.1138

Tyler, T. R., Lind, E. A., Ohbuchi, K.-I., Sugawara, I., & Huo, Y. J. (1998). Conflict with outsiders: Disputing within and across cultural boundaries. *Personality and Social Psychology Bulletin, 24*, 137–146. https://doi-org.libproxy.unl.edu/10.1177/0146167298242003

Tyler, T. R., & Smith, H. J. (1998). Social justice and social movements. In D. T. Gilbert, S. T. Fiske, & G. Lindzey (Eds.), *The handbook of social psychology* (Vol. 2, 4th ed., pp. 595–629). McGraw-Hill.

van den Bos, K. (1999). What are we talking about when we talk about no-voice procedures? On the psychology of the fair outcome effect. *Journal of Experimental Social Psychology, 35*, 560–577. https://doi.org/10.1006/jesp.1999.1393

van den Bos, K. (2020). *Empirical legal research: A primer*. Edward Elgar.

van den Bos, K. (2023). Trust in social institutions: The role of informational and personal uncertainty. In J. P. Forgas, W. D. Crano, & K. Fiedler (Eds.), *The psychology of insecurity: Seeking certainty where none can be found* (pp. 287–306). Routledge.

van den Bos, K. (2024). *The fair process effect: Overcoming distrust, polarization, and conspiracy thinking*. Cambridge University Press.

van den Bos, K., Brockner, J., Stein, J. H., Steiner, D. D., Van Yperen, N. W., & Dekker, D. M. (2010). The psychology of voice and performance capabilities in masculine and feminine cultures and contexts. *Journal of Personality and Social Psychology, 99*(4), 638–648. https://doi.org/10.1037/a0019310

van den Bos, K., Brockner, J., Van den Oudenalder, M., Kamble, S. V., & Nasabi, A. (2013). Delineating a method to study cross-cultural differences with experimental control: The voice effect and countercultural contexts regarding power distance. *Journal of Experimental Social Psychology, 49*, 624–634. https://doi.org/10.1016/j.jesp.2013.02.005

van den Bos, K., Hulst, L., Robijn, M., Romijn, S., & Wever, T. (2023). Field experiments examining trust in law: Interviewer effects on participants with lower educational backgrounds. *Utrecht Law Review, 19(1)*, 1–19.

van den Bos, K., Lind, E. A., Vermunt, R., & Wilke, H. A. M. (1997). How do I judge my outcome when I do not know the outcome of others? The psychology of the fair process effect. *Journal of Personality and Social Psychology, 72*(5), 1034–1046. https://doi.org/10.1037/0022-3514.72.5.1034

van den Bos, K., & Miedema, J. (2000). Toward understanding why fairness matters: The influence of mortality salience on reactions to procedural fairness. *Journal of Personality and Social Psychology, 79*(3), 355–366. https://doi.org/10.1037/0022-3514.79.3.355
van den Bos, K., Poortvliet, P. M., Maas, M., Miedema, J., & van den Ham, E.-J. (2005). An enquiry concerning the principles of cultural norms and values: The impact of uncertainty and mortality salience on reactions to violations and bolstering of cultural worldviews. *Journal of Experimental Social Psychology, 41*(2), 91–113. https://doi.org/10.1016/j.jesp.2004.06.001
van den Bos, K., van Veldhuizen, T. S., & Au, A. K. C. (2015). Counter cross-cultural priming and relative deprivation: The role of individualism–collectivism. *Social Justice Research, 28*(1), 52–75. https://doi.org/10.1007/s11211-014-0230-6
van Prooijen, J.-W., van den Bos, K., & Wilke, H. A. M. (2002). Procedural justice and status: Status salience as antecedent of procedural fairness effects. *Journal of Personality and Social Psychology, 83*(6), 1353–1361. https://doi.org/10.1037/0022-3514.83.6.1353
Waters, T., & Waters, D. (2015). The distribution of power within the Gemeinschaft: Classes, Stände, parties. In T. Waters & D. Waters (Eds.), *Weber's rationalism and modern society: New translations on politics, bureaucracy and social stratification*. Palgrave Macmillan.

Legal Judgment and the Motivation for Justice: What Have We Learned?

Richard L. Wiener, Kitra Monnier, Daniella Cluver, and David J. Hansen

Motivation for (in) Justice

So, what then can we conclude about the role of the motivation for justice in the psychology of legal decision-making? The review presented here focused on the subjective perception of what people perceive as fair in a variety of ways including judgments about distributive, procedural, retributive, and restorative justice. Furthermore, the disruption of equity in any of these types of justice sometimes, but not always, leads to negative moral emotions and the motivation to right the wrong—but again, not always. The "not always" part is, to a large extent, the result of people's fundamental belief that the world is fair and just. Therefore, people who engage in unjust actions or who observe others behave in an unjust manner will sometimes morally disengage to protect their own self-esteem from the cognitive dissonance that results from believing the world is just but being cognizant of times when it is not. Furthermore, people hold dearly the illusion that the world is a just place, in part, because it allows them to engage in a long-term socially prescribed behavior with the belief that in the end the outcome will be fair.

Threats to the just world fallacy are met with rational and irrational strategies to bolster the illusion, and those strategies can influence legal decision-making in both positive (altruist) and negative ways (victim derogation and blaming). There are moderators like empathy that help determine which of the substitutable rational and irrational strategies are likely to manifest at any given time. One moderator is the similarity of the victim to the perceiver and whether the perceiver sees the victim as

R. L. Wiener (✉) · D. J. Hansen
Department of Psychology, University of Nebraska-Lincoln, Lincoln, NE, USA
e-mail: rwiener2@unl.edu

K. Monnier · D. Cluver
University of Nebraska-Lincoln, Lincoln, NE, USA

R. L. Wiener, D. J. Hansen (eds.), *Legal Judgment and the Motivation for Justice*, Nebraska Symposium on Motivation 71,
https://doi.org/10.1007/978-3-031-98812-7_10

an in-group member. If the victim is an in-group member, this ironically may lead to derogation and blaming, in part, in order to protect the self from similar negative outcomes. The logic here is, "It happened to him or her because he or she is a bad person, it won't happen to me because I'm not a bad person like he or she is." Furthermore, victim blaming or derogation can occur at an experiential (associative) or rational (deliberative) level of processing, the former through heuristics, and implicit attitudes that define the victim as deserving, and the latter through recognizing threat to the just world illusion. At the same time, people's belief in the just world illusion shows individual differences with predictable outcomes. Those who believe that the world is just for themselves tend to have a stronger sense of psychological well-being, show more positive emotion, and are generally more satisfied with their lives, while those who believe that the world is just for everyone are less sensitive to discrimination against others and more likely to support the political status quo. Finally, belief in a just world is not the same as social justification ideology but instead supports the psychological well-being of those who adhere to it, regardless of the status level that they occupy in society. In short, the motivations for justice and injustice are complex phenomena, shaped by a variety of psychological processes that have significant implications for legal decision-making.

Motivation and Legal Decision-Making

The chapters in this volume of the Nebraska Symposium are examples of how these motivations play out in the context of legal decision-making. The authors discuss legal decision-making in civil and criminal law, in political systems, in the U.S. and in Western democracies more generally. They approach the issue sometimes from very practical perspectives and at other times from highly theoretical orientations. The chapters do not directly discuss the motivation for justice; instead, they all assume that people are motivated to seek justice or injustice and consider how that plays out in the legal system.

First, in chapter, "Toward a Community Model in the Motivations for Justice and Legal Judgment," Christian Bijoux takes as his starting point the deep-rooted trauma resulting from the systemic racial bias that people of color have historically faced and continue to face in the United States. The author challenges the just world fallacy by describing in detail the historically traumatic experience of Black, Latino, and American Indian people in the United States resulting in systemic racism that is a direct threat to the illusion of fairness that a substantial majority of U.S. citizens hold to be true. Bijoux argues that the source of systematic racism was literally "centuries of dehumanization and racially subjugated conditions" (pg. ___) and most importantly has currently shaped the collective consciousness of Black Americans and other American people of color. In an effort to protect the just world illusion that White Americans (and many Black Americans) share, many have adopted the irrational approach of degrading and blaming the victims of the trauma for their own condition. At the same time, a second irrational effort to bolster the justice fallacy has led many to convince themselves that racism has receded and, in fact, has nearly disappeared in U.S. culture despite the existence of empirical data that shows how extensive racial disparity still is in may institutions, the juvenile and criminal justice system being two examples. The author argues that the White majority needs to recognize that the world of America is not just for all but more importantly that Black Americans need to establish their own social and political organization at the community level to move the society closer to a justice system that is fair and impartial for all.

In chapter, "Police Discretion as a Vulnerability Factor for Disparate Treatment," Jack Glaser examines police officers' discretion, emphasizing its impact in cases that involve people of color. Glaser points out that the vagueness in the legal definitions of "reasonable suspicion" and "probable cause" opens wide the opportunity for law enforcers to rely on their own views of when it is just to pursue a suspect, make a stop, and conduct a search. As a result, officers' own biases can play a strong role in determining where to patrol, who to stop, whether to search, and whether to use force. The implications for distributive, procedural and retributive justice from the perspective of the officers, and perhaps more importantly, from the standpoint of the community members that they serve are substantial. While some of these biases may be deliberative and intentional, such as conducting a pretextual motor vehicle stop (i.e., a broken tail light) in order to get a better view of what is inside the car in the hopes of finding evidence of a more serious violation, others are undoubtedly the result of unconscious biases, automatically activated against people of color. As Glaser points out, it is impossible for police to enforce all laws, all the time so that officers must decide under conditions of uncertainty, which violations enacted by which suspects are worthy of investigation. Most importantly from the perspective of the motivational concerns pursued in this symposium, under this wide array of acceptable discretionary judgments, biases born out of stereotypical links between people of color and crime can be justified by the view that the world is ultimately a just place. To the extent that officers operate from the perspective that the world is just for all (BJWG), they are likely to be less sensitive to discriminatory conduct, which allows them to defend any biases because in the end, bad things only happen to bad people.

Glaser reviews research that shows that the conscious motivation to control prejudice, after it has been activated, offers one of the best antidotes to the abuse of bias in judgment under certainty, but this motivation is very unlikely to be mustered by those who believe the world is ultimately a just place. Glaser concludes that activating motivation to control bias and providing strategies to do so on an ongoing basis is much less successful as a tool to provide equitable treatment for people of color, than is instituting structural changes that make decision-making more formal. Thus, given that like the rest of us, police officers are susceptible to the just world illusion and the irrational strategies we use to uphold it, providing officers tools for structured decision-making such as checklists with criteria for when to make a stop or flowcharts that guide their discretion may be the best short-term fix for the disparate treatment of people of color in the investigatory phase of the criminal justice system.

In chapter, "Zeal, Motivation, and the Adversarial Bias," Dan Simon turns our attention to the defining feature of the U.S. litigation process as it is currently practiced in the federal and state courts, namely the clashing of adversaries. Simon argues that the adversarial process produces attorney bias and ultimately a state of "zeal" that colors all judgments about the case, ultimately creating an irrepressible motivation to win. Simon sets out to show that adversarial zeal is a product of cognition, that is what lawyers actually come to think about their cases, and not simple motivation to win. When lawyers take on the role of advocating for a client, they form a cognitive bond which alters, among other inferences, the way in which they perceive the strength of evidence, evaluate the rulings of judges, and predict verdicts, sentences, and damage awards. Simon argues that these effects are the result of coherence-based reasoning in which positively linked associations, as well as negatively linked associations, activate as units. However, after reviewing some more recent research, he points out that that coherence-based reasoning can itself be motivated. For example, a manipulation of prospering cheaters in a dishonest student scenario triggered a series of associative judgments that favored the university accusing the alleged cheater. The spreading activation also influenced a number of associated inferences including interpretations of the evidence, harsher punishments, and angrier affect toward the accused (Simon et al., 2015). Simon goes on to explain how emotional and motivational links influence the connectionist models that produce legal judgments and inferences and, in the end, concludes that motivated reasoning triggered by taking on an adversarial role can drive a connectionist network that favors one side of conflict or the other.

The attorney zeal that results from taking on an adversarial role can have a negative impact on both distributive and procedural justice for the litigants and the observing public who may question if the ratio of outputs to inputs that they observe for the litigants is equal and if both sides had an equal opportunity to tell their side of the story. Furthermore, the foundation of the adversarial system and adversarial zeal as described by Simon is likely related to a belief in the just world fallacy. It is likely that because attorneys and judges adhere to the belief that the world is fair and that justice will ultimately prevail in the end that opposing attorneys are comfortable with zealously pursuing a win in the case, regardless of the strength or weakness of the allowable facts. Indeed, to avoid the discomfort that accompanies the knowledge that their side may be responsible for at least some wrongdoing, lawyers very likely make use of some of the strategies of moral disengagement identified in chapter, "Toward a Community Model in the Motivations for Justice and Legal Judgment". Simon focuses on the negative side effects of the adversarial system, including lawyers being blinded to the weaknesses in their cases and as a result failing to advise clients accordingly, lawyers acting more like combatants on the battlefield than officers of the court seeking out justice, and attorneys proffering expert witnesses that adhere to the attorney's view of the case and testify accordingly. He concludes that the cost of adversarial zeal may be to compromise the very search for justice that the system sets out to find.

Similar to chapter, "Zeal, Motivation, and the Adversarial Bias," in chapter, "Sentencing for Multiple Offenses: When Seeking Justice Is Too Cruel and Cognitively Demanding," Dhami and Bechan wrestle with the balance between the roles of cognitive complexity and motivation in the sentencing of offenders who have committed simultaneous crimes. Examples of simultaneous or multiple-offense acts include an offender assaulting a store worker while stealing money from the store or committing burglaries at two different homes in a single day. Once the court finds an offender guilty of one or more criminal acts, it has the retributive justice responsibility to impose a penalty, but the process should be equitable to satisfy the demands of distributive justice. Furthermore, the process should proceed in a fair and dignified manner, consistent with the requirements of procedural justice. The task is cognitively challenging for single-offense offenders but is even more difficult when the decision-maker faces a defendant who has committed multiple offenses simultaneously, which is frequently the case. The sentencer's task is to consider multiple factors including offense seriousness, criminal history, aggravating circumstances, mitigating circumstances, victim impact statements, and expert testimony and come up with a just penalty among the many available options in a fair and balanced manner. The authors argue that the demands of the task are cognitively undoable for people without the use of decision guidelines, especially for multiple-offense cases.

The guideline that was in force in England and Wales between 2012 and 2023, "totality of multiple offenses" requires the sentencer to base the sentence on all the offending behavior, making sure that it is proportionate to the harm suffered after taking into consideration the defendant's personal mitigation factors. Dhami (2022) compared the sentences between single and multiple-offense cases meted out by the Sentencing Council for England and Wales from Crown Courts from 2012 to 2023 during which the totality rule was in effect and found that the imposition of incarceration as opposed to other penalties (e.g., discharge, fines, and community service) were equally likely for the multiple- as compared to the single-offense offenders for six out of seven offenses.[1] Furthermore, the sentence lengths when custodial penalties were imposed were not different between the single and multiple offenses for any of the convicted charges except that multiple-offense defendants received longer sentences for robbery. Thus, the multiple-offense guideline appeared to produce lenient sentences that did little to take into consideration the additional crimes. The sentencers violated the equity rule that underlies distributive justice in that both types of offenders received about the same level of penalty severity (outputs), even though the input (criminal conduct) was greater for the multiple offenders than single offenders.

The research suggested that the reason for this imbalance was the increased weight assigned to mitigators with the multiple-offense rule, as required under the totality guideline. Bolstering the earlier work were data reported in the current chapter, which examined the number of appeals in multiple-offense cases prior to the totality guideline compared to that after it was put into place, which showed a reduction in appeals after the guideline. This suggests that the defendants were more satisfied with the outcomes after the guideline, presumedly because of the

[1] Multiple offense defendants charged with possession of a controlled substance with the intent to distribute were more likely to receive a custodial sentence than were their single offense counterparts.

leniency in sentencing observed under the guideline rules. Partially, as a result of the Dhami et al. (2020) findings, the Sentencing Council for England and Wales modified the guideline to include consideration of aggravators as well as mitigators to correct the imbalance in distributive justice outcomes. Dhami and Beacon conclude the chapter by emphasizing the importance of empirical research on the use of sentencing guidelines to help sentencers achieve the norms of distributive and procedural justice.

In chapter, "Does Ideology Undermine Procedure-Based Legitimacy?," Tyler directly takes on the issues of procedural justice and legitimacy as they relate to the problems of ideological polarization and authoritarianism in democratic systems. The chapter starts off with a discussion of the central role of "loser's consent" or the willingness of losers of elections in a democratic society to agree to follow the leadership of winners of elections even when they did not vote for the winner. Tyler argues that loser's consent depends upon the public's belief that the election was in alignment with the elements of procedural justice. In other words, if people believe that the procedures that the authorities used to implement the election were fair, that belief legitimizes the leadership of the winner even for the loser and their followers. The literature over the years has demonstrated that legitimacy is more important for compliance with rules, and in this case, acquiescence is to accept leadership than are rewards for obedience and punishments for disobedience. In order for pluralistic democratic societies to benefit from procedural justice-based legitimacy, there needs to be invariance when it comes to effectiveness of procedural justice. That is, people, regardless of their backgrounds, should believe that the process was fair and therefore the election outcome was legitimate, to the extent that they had voice in an unbiased or neutral election process, that the authorities that ran the election treated them with respect, and that they could trust those authorities as benevolent actors who were sincerely trying to serve the needs of the community.

Tyler identifies extreme ideology and acceptance of autocratic values as two fissure lines that could threaten democratic elections and fracture the invariance of beliefs. He goes on to review five data sets that measure the legitimacy of recent U.S. elections and that examine legitimacy in European and in global values in recent years. First, the results show that polarization in ideology (i.e., liberals becoming more liberal and conservatives becoming more conservative) has increased substantially in the last five decades. At the same time, as measured through both the support for obedience and willingness to follow laws without question, autocratic values have not increased and may have even decreased slightly in the same time period.

The studies of elections showed that the losing side in each election did respond with a lower judgment of legitimacy, especially those who held extreme ideologies to the left or right. Moreover, stronger authoritarian values were associated with lower ratings of legitimacy. Most importantly, while the election study results showed that those who found the elections to be procedurally fair also found them to be legitimate, this effect interacted with the extremity of the participant's ideological position. Procedurally just election results did lower the de-legitimization that election losers recorded, but procedural justice was less effective in doing so for people with extreme ideological positions, especially for extreme conservatives on the right. Similarly, individuals who held stronger authoritarian values weighed the fairness of elections less when evaluating legitimacy. Finally, while the data from the two value surveys supported the predictive effects of ideological extremity and authoritarianism on general judgments of procedural justice and political legitimacy, these effects were more complicated and less certain for extreme conservatives.

Tyler concludes that while there is a positive relationship between procedural justice and legitimacy, especially for elections, that relationship is not invariant. In fact, the predictive effect of procedural justice on legitimacy is weaker for those who hold extreme ideological positions and those who hold strong authoritarian values. Tyler opines that with continued increases in ideological extremism procedural justice as a legitimizing political force may become even more undermined, resulting in a continued threat to "loser consent" and the legitimacy of democratic rule. The chapter concludes with some recommendations for strengthening procedural justice-based authority under conditions of increasing ideological polarization and authoritarian values.

Finally, while chapter, "Does Ideology Undermine Procedure-Based Legitimacy?" does not consider the just world thesis, our analysis in the current chapter would hypothesize that the moderating roles of ideological polarization and authoritarian values are consistent with the just world illusion. People with extreme ideologies and strong authoritarian viewpoints likely hold stronger just world illusions that are not amenable to procedural justice repairs to protect against the just world threats of election losses. Instead, extremists derogate the system that produced the threat and conclude that it must be corrupt and illegitimate. In other words, bad things (election losses) only occur in bad (illegitimate) systems. On the other hand, people with more moderate ideological positions and people low in authoritarian values hold weaker just world illusions so that when faced with a just world threat, i.e., their candidate lost the election, they look to procedural justice to repair the broken illusion. Even though my candidate lost, the election was fair. If this were indeed the case, one way to buttress procedural justice-based authority might involve directly challenging the just world fallacy at least in the context of politics.

In chapter, "Motives for Civil Justice," Robbennolt turns the symposium's attention to the role of motivation for justice in civil law and addresses the reasons why people bring tort disputes to court and the ways in which these motivations are impeded. The injuries that claimants suffer may not only be threats to their physical and psychological well-being, they are also threats to the illusion that the world is a fair and just place. One way to repair the illusion of a just world is to seek restorative justice to make the world safe again. Ellard et al. (2016) would call this a rational approach to restoring the just world illusion. Robbennolt points out that the major way in which people seek restoration in tort is through financial compensation but that this is not the only reason why people go to court. Injured parties also seek information to learn why they were injured, and in some cases, the explanation is sufficient for them not to pursue the case. In the language of just world theory, the injured party seeks a reasonable explanation as a rational way to resolve the threat and reinstate the just world model.

Other motivations to bring suit include gaining an acknowledgment that an error occurred, reforming the system to prevent additional injuries, and holding the wrongdoer accountable. For example, in a medical malpractice case, litigation can produce acknowledgment that a physical injury was caused by a defective medical procedure and hold the physician and hospital accountable of the injury, which not only prevents future injures from occurring but also gives support to the view that bad things do not happen to good people without justification. Robbennolt states that claimants may seek voice, respect, trust, and a neutral decision-maker in court to obtain a procedurally just outcome. That is, they are in pursuit of procedural justice.

The chapter outlines several motivations that prevent injured parties from bringing claims including lack of resources and lack of confidence in the ability to win the case. Interestingly, the chapter also discusses the injured party accepting individual responsibility and the fear of plaintiff blaming as other motivations to refrain from pursuing a law suit. Not only are people afraid of being blamed by others and being seen as greedy, they may also perceive themselves in that way. Blaming oneself for the injury does allow the harmed party to irrationally maintain the just world belief that bad things only happen to bad people. To help us understand the complexity of litigation motivation, Robbennolt introduces the metaphor of a dispute tree, with its branches suggesting ways in which people may seek justice for their grievances. The tree has equifinality, meaning that there are many ways to accomplish the goal of restorative justice, and it has multifinality, meaning that anyone of its branches (i.e., responses to the injury) may satisfy multiple goals at the same time. The restorative goals are consistent with the just world hypothesis, namely to reinstate the injured person's view of the world as one in which justice will ultimately prevail.

In the civil law, money is the customary compensation for injuries suffered in tort because it can help make the plaintiff whole with regard to her or his economic loss, but Robbennolt relying on the tree analogy and the property of equifinality offers other forms of conflict resolution that may satisfy the injured party, as much or even more than a financial award. Referring to the property of multifinality, the author points out that financial compensation can satisfy several of the other goals of bringing the case to court including holding the wrongdoer accountable, acknowledging the wrongdoing, reforming the wrongdoer, and allowing the plaintiff to achieve both restorative and procedural justice. In this way, financial compensation can restore the belief that the world is ultimately a just place. However, there are other ways to obtain the noneconomic goals, especially achieving procedural justice and repairing a vision of a just world. Two of the most important of these is for the wrongdoer to apologize for the injury that she or he caused to the victim and/or to reach a settlement outside of the courtroom. Robbennolt points out that apologies that acknowledge the wrongdoing, identify the harm caused, communicate regret, and offer to compensate the victim achieve many of the goals of civil justice. Moreover, settlement agreements outside of court often include apologies as part of the negotiated compensation and then go on to include other forms of redress in addition to money (i.e., reforming an institution, offering community service, and admitting historical accountability) that meet the other goals of achieving restoration and procedural justice. Indeed, apologies and settlements can go a long way to repair the injured party's belief that the world is ultimately just and fair. The chapter ends with a discussion of how mixing and matching different remedies may be the best strategy for satisfying injured parties who are driven to court by a variety of motivations. Robbennolt calls for new research to determine what kinds of remedies will result in meeting which of the many restoration goals. We would add that including the restoration of a just world belief should be included as potential motivation and goal to study with regard to civil compensation.

In chapter, "Why Do People Use ADR?," Shestowsky explores in greater detail the motivation for participating in one of the many paths that Robbennolt considers in the dispute tree analog, namely, alternative dispute resolution (ADR). The chapter focuses on answering the question, "Why and when do people favor mediation and non-binding arbitration over litigation to resolve their civil disputes?". Shestowsky maintains that three factors are central to understanding what motivates the use of these services: (1) people's knowledge of ADR, (2) their procedural preferences, and (3) factors that determine how litigants make their procedural choices.

With regard to people's awareness of ADR procedures, survey studies show that people were not very familiar with mediation procedures and at best had little if any experience at all with any of these procedures with the exception of negotiation (Blankley et al., 2021). In fact, Shestowsky's own research (2017) found that a large majority of litigants who had completed their cases in three different courts in three different states believed wrongly that the courts did not make mediation or arbitration procedures available. Moreover, laypeople's understanding of all legal procedures deviated substantially from the way in which experts described them. The full literature review concluded that lawyers should not presume their clients are aware of the availability of ADR options, not even those clients have been involved in the civil justice system in the past. The major recommendation from this work is that there is ample room for attorneys to educate their clients about ADR options and that they ought to do so. In fact, one could even argue that clients whose attorneys fail to educate them about ADR options are not able to fully use their voices to control their own disputes and, in that sense, may fail to fully obtain the procedural and restorative justice they seek.

Shestowsky moves on to examine litigants' preferences for traditional court process or ADR when they have the choice by noting inconsistent results in studies conducted before the cases were resolved (ex ante) and those in which the cases were resolved before the studies were conducted (ex post). Indeed, there is an ongoing debate in the literature in which some concluded that litigants preferred mediation (Bingham, 2002), while others stated that there was a lack of empirical support for preferences one way or the other (Hensler, 2002). Shestowsky's own work (Shestowsky, 2020) suggests that people make choices using different psychological rules in the ex ante and ex post studies. In one ex ante study, Shestowsky (2014) had litigants forecast the attractiveness of several different case resolution methods just after the cases were filed and found that they mostly favored attorneys negotiating with the clients present, along with mediation. They favored least arbitration and jury trial. Making the issue even more difficult to parse is the finding that in mock jury laboratory experiments, participants mostly favor adjudication over mediation. These contradictory findings point out the importance of determining what factors predict litigants' preferences for different types of conflict resolution procedures. Shestowsky (2017) found that demographic factors (i.e., gender and age) predicted different preferences for different procedures as did region (i.e., California and Oregon) and political party. Shestowsky (2025) in the current chapter concludes that attorneys need to be aware of the complex nature of different factors that predict preferences for or against the use of ADR when they advise and educate their clients.

Our review of the work in the context of our motivation for justice analysis (Wiener et al., 2025, chapter 1) clearly points out the need for additional research to help attorneys understand what kinds of clients prefer what types of procedures in different types of cases. One factor that researchers have not examined that we think might be fruitful is the extent to which potential litigants adhere to a belief in a just world. We would anticipate that those who score high on the Belief in a Just World generally—for everyone (BJWG) perceive the world to be a fair place for everyone and therefore would expect a positive outcome in a jury trial because in the end justice prevails. These individuals likely would favor more traditional litigation procedures because they anticipate victory. At the same time, those who score high on Belief in a Just World for the self but not necessarily for others (BJWS) might show more flexibility in their choice of conflict resolution procedure and likely favor mediation and nonbinding arbitration. Additional research examining theoretical models of litigation preference could help untangle this complex literature.

Finally, there is evidence that participants rate both ADR and traditional procedures as more attractive than they anticipated that they would be (Shestowsky, 2014). Shestowsky (2018) set out to understand the gap between preferences and utilization by asking participants how they would decide which procedures to use. She found that the most frequently mentioned response both ex ante and again ex post was that the participants would rely on their attorneys' advice and counsel—pointing out further the need for lawyers to educate their clients about possible ADR conflict resolution procedures. Also important were economic cost, time efficiency, and self-serving bias (whatever process would favor one's own case); however, only the importance of economic cost was supported with ex post data. Wissler's (2002) study supports the gatekeeping role that attorneys play in determining who makes use of ADR techniques, which found that lawyers who were educated about ADR or had experience using it were more likely to advise their clients to use those procedures. Shestowsky ends the chapter with a number of recommendations for increasing litigants' knowledge about ADR and when it might be favored over litigation but identifies the most important factors to be educating lawyers about ADR procedures and encouraging them to discuss the options with their clients ex ante. Adopting that approach likely increases peoples' interest in pursuing ADR procedures in the interest of their efforts to seek procedural and restorative justice in an efficient and cost-effective manner.

In chapter "Justice and Culture," Van den Bos analyzes the relationship between culture and justice with what seems to be an accepted truism, that justice in all its forms depends upon the social norms that make up different cultures. He points out that just treatment results from people acting in correspondence with the norms and values favored in their own cultures. Therefore, while it seems natural that the meaning of justice is defined by the context of culture (Kidder & Muller, 1991), some scholars have argued that procedural justice, at least, is culturally invariant (Lind et al., 1997). Van den Bos takes a somewhat different perspective arguing that culture and justice are reciprocal, each one influencing the other, and he sets out to describe the interplay in more detail. He begins by citing Lind and Tyler (1988) who emphasized the value-expressive function of procedural justice such that people seek voice and respect from authorities because it confirms that they hold a place of high esteem in their community. Although distributive justice can also indicate one's social status within the culture, it is less useful for this purpose because knowledge about the distribution of outcomes for others is often unavailable or ambiguous. Therefore, it is often difficult to compare the ratios of outputs to inputs for oneself and others to estimate a cultural ranking. Much more informative is the way authorities and institutional leaders treat people because it provides symbolic confirmation or refutation of our value within the community. In other words, when we are treated in unfair ways (i.e., denied voice, respect, trust, and a neutral judge), we take that as evidence that we are not valued members of the community.

This analysis would lead one to expect to find differing cultural effects on the perceptions of justice, but as Van den Bos points out, the research to date does not always find those effects. He suggests that some of this work may be misleading because it frequently relies on "WEIRD" (Western, Educated, Industrialized, Rich, and Democratic) participants to study trust in justice and legal institutions. Another reason for concern is that this research involves typically high-status university interviewers interacting with lower status research participants. Van den Bos et al. (2023) tested out this latter explanation by varying the status of interviewers as higher (i.e., coming from a university law school) or lower (i.e., coming from a community college).

The researchers approached participants in shopping malls and train stations in the Netherlands and asked them to complete surveys about their trust in judges. They found that participants with lower status education levels reported higher degrees of trust in judges when higher status, as compared to lower status, interviewers presented the surveys. Van den Bos (2025) invoked in-group and out-group concepts to explain these results by speculating that lower status individuals may have felt less social distance from lower status researchers and were therefore able to offer their true feelings about the way they saw judges. The low-status individuals felt higher social distance with high-status interviewers and disguised their true feelings by offering higher ratings of trust, perhaps in part, to protect their views of the world as a just place, where high-status judges ought to be more trustworthy.

Van den Bos et al. (2023) acknowledges one problem in studying cultural distance as a factor in justice studies is that is difficult to manipulate cultural distance so that most studies simply assume that people from different cultures have different underlying psychological states. Sometimes, this work will use measured dimensions of those states as mediators and conduct path analyses to test the associations, but these correlational techniques are lacking in internal validity, making causal inferences about the relationship between culture and justice difficult. Instead, Van den Bos recommends manipulating the underlying psychological states that are presumed to be instrumental in a culture by making the opposite of that psychological state salient (i.e., the countercultural manipulation). For example, Van den Bos et al. (2015) studied social distance in a high-power distance country, India—where there is presumedly a large power differential between citizens and authorities—and the Netherlands where the power distance between citizens and authorities is smaller. The control conditions in neither country mentioned the underlying cultural values, but the experimental conditions in India asked participants to imagine the opposite of the assumed, namely to describe a situation when the power distance between themselves and a person with formal power was small. The countercultural condition in the Netherlands asked people to describe a situation when the power distance between themselves and a person with formal power was large. If the countercultural condition deviates sharply from the control condition on the outcome measure in each country, this provides some evidence for the causal relationship that is presumed to be associated with two dominant cultures. In this case, the effects of manipulating voice, one component of procedural justice, was more impactful on judgments of fairness under low-power conditions, whether as a function of the manipulated treatment conditions or as observed in the control conditions between the low- and high-power cultures. The results show variance in the effects of voice on procedural justice as a function of social distance, as measured and manipulated in India and the Netherlands.

Van den Bos et al. (2023) provides other examples of this methodology in the chapter and calls for additional work on the role of culture in the perceptions of justice using the countercultural approach as well as other approaches. The chapter concludes by returning to the idea that justice, at least procedural justice, may be more dependent upon cultural variation because of its value-expressive function and calls on more nuanced studies to take a deeper dive into the reciprocal relationship between culture and justice.

Conclusion

The chapters in this volume of the Nebraska Symposium set out to examine how motivations play out in the context of legal decision-making. The authors took some very different approaches, with some focusing on civil law and others focusing on criminal law. Some examined motivation inherent in legal processes, and others studied it from a political point of view. Some of the chapters took a practical perspective, while others concentrated on theoretical issues borrowed from psychology, philosophy, and law. The unifying theme in the chapters was to develop an understanding of how the psychology of motivation can sometimes lead to justice and at other times injustice. In the end, the 71st volume of the Nebraska Symposium on Motivation returned to the symposium's motivational roots to help examine legal decision-making from the perspective of not only how we seek justice but also to answer the question of why we seek justice.

References

Bingham, L. B. (2002). Why suppose? Let's find out: A public policy research program on dispute resolution. *Journal of Dispute Resolution, 2002*(1), 101–126. https://ssrn.com/abstract=1827263

Blankley, K. M., Votruba, A. M., Bartz, L. M., & Pytlik Zillig, L. M. (2021). ADR is not household term: Considering the ethical and practical consequences of the public's lack of understanding of mediation and arbitration. *Nebraska Law Review, 99*(4), 797–847. https://ssrn.com/abstract=3878988

Dhami, M. K. (2022). Sentencing multiple- versus single-offence cases: Does more crime mean less punishment? *British Journal of Criminology, 62*(1), 55–72. https://doi.org/10.1093/bjc/azab030

Dhami, M. K., Belton, I., Merrall, E. L. C., McGrath, A., & Bird, S. M. (2020). Criminal sentencing by preferred numbers. *Journal of Empirical Legal Studies, 17*(1), 139–163. https://doi.org/10.1111/jels.12246

Ellard, J., Harvey, A. J., & Callan, M. J. (2016). The justice motive: History, theory, and research. In C. Sabbagh & M. Schmitt (Eds.), *Handbook of social justice theory and research* (pp. 127–143). Springer. https://doi.org/10.1007/978-1-4939-3216-0_7

Hensler, D. R. (2002). Suppose it's not true: Challenging mediation ideology. *Journal of Dispute Resolution, 2002*(1), 81–100. https://scholarship.law.missouri.edu/jdr/vol2002/iss1/5

Kidder, L. H., & Muller, S. (1991). What is "fair" in Japan? In R. Vermunt & H. Steensma (Eds.), *Social justice in human relations. Critical issues in social justice* (Vol. 2, pp. 139–154). Springer. https://doi.org/10.1007/978-1-4899-2629-6_8

Lind, E. A., & Tyler, T. R. (1988). *The social psychology of procedural justice*. Plenum Press. https://doi.org/10.2307/2073346

Lind, E. A., Tyler, T. R., & Huo, Y. J. (1997). Procedural context and culture: Variation in the antecedents of procedural justice judgments. *Journal of Personality and Social Psychology, 73*, 767–780. https://doi-org.libproxy.unl.edu/10.1037/0022-3514.73.4.767

Shestowsky, D. (2014). The psychology of procedural preference: How litigants evaluate legal procedures ex ante. *Iowa Law Review, 99*(2), 637–710. https://ssrn.com/abstract=2378622

Shestowsky, D. (2017). When ignorance is not bliss: An empirical study of litigant's awareness of court-sponsored alternative dispute resolution programs. *Harvard Negotiation Law Review, 22*(2), 189–240. https://ssrn.com/abstract=2945706

Shestowsky, D. (2018). Inside the mind of the client: An analysis of litigants' decision criteria for choosing procedures. *Conflict Resolution Quarterly, 36*(1), 69–91. https://doi.org/10.1002/crq.21228

Shestowsky, D. (2020). Great expectations? Comparing litigants' attitudes before and after using legal procedures. *Law and Human Behavior, 44*(3), 179–193. https://doi.org/10.1037/lhb0000370

Shestowsky, D. (2025). Why do people use ADR? In R. L. Wiener & D. Hansen (Eds.), *Legal judgment and the motivation for justice*. Springer.

Simon, D., Stenstrom, D. M., & Read, S. J. (2015). The coherence effect: Blending cold and hot cognitions. *Journal of Personality and Social Psychology, 109*, 369–394. https://doi.org/10.1037/pspa0000029

Van den Bos, K. (2025). Justice and culture. In R. L. Wiener & D. Hansen (Eds.), *Legal judgment and the motivation for justice*. Springer.

Van den Bos, K., Hulst, L., Robijn, M., Romijn, S., & Wever, T. (2023). Field experiments examining trust in law: Interviewer effects on participants with lower educational backgrounds. *Utrecht Law Review, 19*(1), 1–19. https://doi.org/10.36633/ulr.817

Van den Bos, K., Van Veldhuizen, T. S., & Au, A. K. C. (2015). Counter cross-cultural priming and relative deprivation: The role of individualism-collectivism. *Social Justice Research, 28*, 52–75. https://doi-org.libproxy.unl.edu/10.1007/s11211-014-0230-6

Wiener, R. L., Cluver, D., Monnier, K., & Hansen, D. (2025). Chapter 1: Legal judgment and the motivation for justice. In R. L. Wiener & D. Hansen (Eds.), *Legal judgment and the motivation for justice*. Springer.

Wissler, R. L. (2002). When does familiarity breed content? A study of the role of different forms of ADR education and experience in attorneys' ADR recommendations. *Pepperdine Dispute Resolution Law Journal, 2*(2), 199–240. https://ssrn.com/abstract=1723345

Index

A
Abstract information, 185
Adversarial bias, 11, 41–55
Adversarial expert testimony, 54–55
Alternative dispute resolution (ADR), 12, 143–178, 207, 208
Apologies and justice motives, 130–132
Authorities, 185
Awareness and knowledge of ADR, 148–153

B
Balance and justice, 3–11
Battle model, 53–54

C
Challenges and opportunities, 21
Chapter review, 12, 208
Coherence-based reasoning, 41, 43, 47–49, 51, 52, 202
Community Development Model, 22–23
Contextualizing racial injustice, 19–21

D
Decisions to use ADR, 144
Discretion and disparity, 25–37
Discretion in policing, 27–28, 37
Dispute resolution preferences, 154

E
Experiments and cross-cultural differences, 188–192
Extremity and legitimacy, 98, 103, 104, 107, 110

G
Goal management, 126–127

I
Ideological extremity, 91, 92, 94, 95, 98, 100, 107, 108, 110, 112, 205
Individual and structural disparities, 28–30
Individualistic and collectivistic cultures, 193
Individual meets the group, 184
Information, 185
  symbolic, 185
Invariance and ideology, 91–93

J
Just world, 3–12, 24, 199–202, 205–208
Just world and legal decision making, 12, 199
Justice and culture, 12, 183–194
Justice and legal decision making, 11–12, 183

L
Legal Institutions, 17, 19, 21–22, 145, 209
Limiting discretion, 35
Loser's consent, 87, 88, 92–93, 204

R. L. Wiener, D. J. Hansen (eds.), *Legal Judgment and the Motivation for Justice*, Nebraska Symposium on Motivation 71,
https://doi.org/10.1007/978-3-031-98812-7

M
Masculine and feminine cultures, 190
Mixed remedies in civil claims, 123
Motivated coherence, 48–52
Motivation for justice, 1–12, 21, 22, 188, 199–211
Motivations for injustice, 18, 200, 211
Motivations to use ADR, 144
Motives to make civil claims, 123–125, 134

P
Proactive remedies to undermining legitimacy, 112

R
Racial disparities, 17–21, 26, 30, 33–35, 201
Research on multiple *vs*. singe offense sentencing, 64, 67–69, 72–74, 82, 83

S
Sentencing and cognitive complexity, 65–68
Sentencing with multiple offenses, 63–83
Social culture differences, 186–188
Social identity, 184
Social institutions, 185
Symbolic value, 185

T
Totality approach to multiple offenses, 69–71, 73, 203
Totality sentencing guidelines, 75–81
Types of justice, 2–3, 199

V
Value of money damages, 130

W
What is discretion, 30–31

MIX
Papier aus verantwortungsvollen Quellen
Paper from responsible sources
FSC® C105338

If you have any concerns about our products,
you can contact us on
ProductSafety@springernature.com

In case Publisher is established outside the EU,
the EU authorized representative is:
Springer Nature Customer Service Center GmbH
Europaplatz 3, 69115 Heidelberg, Germany

Printed by Libri Plureos GmbH
in Hamburg, Germany